Compliments of David Mandell, JD, MBA

Principal

mandell@ojmgroup.com

www.ojmgroup.com

877.656.4362

866.913.4911(fax)

Wealth Secrets
of the Affluent

Wealth Secrets of the Affluent

KEYS TO FORTUNE BUILDING AND ASSET PROTECTION

Christopher R. Jarvis
David B. Mandell

WILEY

John Wiley & Sons, Inc.

Published by John Wiley & Sons, Inc., Hoboken, New Jersey
Published simultaneously in Canada

For general information on our other products and services or for technical
support, please contact our Customer Care Department within the United States at
(800) 762-2974, outside the United States at (317) 572-3993 or fax (317) 572-4002.

Wiley also publishes its books in a variety of electronic formats. Some content that
appears in print may not be available in electronic books. For more information
about Wiley products, visit our web site at www.wiley.com.

Library of Congress Cataloging-in-Publication Data:

Jarvis, Christopher R., 1970-
    Wealth secrets of the affluent : keys to fortune building and asset protection /
Christopher R. Jarvis and David B. Mandell.
       p.   cm.
    Includes index.
    ISBN 978-0-470-13979-0 (cloth)
      1. Finance, Personal. 2. Estate planning. 3. Tax planning. 4. Assets
(Accounting) I. Mandell, David B. II. Title.
HG179.J325 2008
332.024—dc22

          2007040686

Printed in the United States of America

10 9 8 7 6 5 4 3 2 1

We dedicate this book to Danielle and Sheila,
for their love and support.

Contents

Acknowledgments

This book would not have come to fruition without the hard work of all of the people at our firm O'Dell Jarvis Mandell, LLC, including Jason O'Dell, Michael Lewellen, Danielle Jarvis, Kim Renners, Jill Kniffin, Christopher Stout, Lynn Lukey, and Sheila Benedictos. Not only did they assist us with the writing of the book but also picked up the slack with our clients while we met deadlines. This was invaluable.

We would also like to thank the people at Wiley who made this book a reality. Deb Englander and her staff helped translate our vision into a viable book. Kelly O'Connor did tremendous work to turn our very rough manuscript into a finished product. The good people in the production department made it pleasing to the eye. Thank you!

Finally, there are so many colleagues in our fields that we need to acknowledge for their teaching, help, and support in serving clients. We can only mention a few here. Attorneys Dennis Brislawn, Claudio De Vellis, Scott Einiger, Matthew Howard, Stan Miller, Jonathan Mintz, John Shram, the entire team at Strazzeri Mancini, Ken Vanway, Carl Waldman, Danny Wexler and numerous other WealthCounsel attorneys across the U.S. who have been instrumental in helping us help clients. This includes the many "Collaborative Firms" that O'Dell Jarvis Mandell works with throughout the U.S.

About the Authors

Christopher Jarvis is a financial services professional who specializes in working with business owners, physicians, and other professionals around the country. Chris has experience as an actuary, entrepreneur, and financial consultant. He has helped start insurance companies for Fortune 100 firms and has created financial plans for individuals across the country.

Mr. Jarvis has been quoted in the *Wall Street Journal* and the *Los Angeles Business Journal.* Chris has appeared on Bloomberg Television and been a guest on more than 100 radio programs. He has co-authored financial and legal texts for doctors, business owners, real estate investors, and financial planners. Mr. Jarvis has co-authored five books with Mr. Mandell, including *Wealth Protection MD: The Ultimate Financial Guide for 21st Century Physicians* and *Wealth Protection: Build and Preserve Your Financial Fortress.*

Chris has addressed more than 100 groups, including the International College of Surgeons, American Association of Neurological Surgeons, the Association of Chamber of Commerce Executives, Associated General Contractors, the UCLA Law School, the Learning Annex, The American Medical Women's Association, and The Anderson School (MBA program at UCLA). Chris' articles have been featured in more than 100 national publications.

Chris holds an honor's degree in applied mathematics from the University of Rhode Island. He earned a Master's of Business Administration from UCLA where he majored in finance and entrepreneurial studies. Chris was awarded the Los Angeles Chapter of the Young President's Organization's (YPO) Ken Kennedy Fellowship for his entrepreneurial achievement. Mr. Jarvis grew up in Providence, Rhode Island, and now lives in Austin, Texas, with his wife Danielle. He can be reached at (512) 531-9089 or via e-mail at jarvis@ojmgroup.com.

David Mandell is an attorney, author, and renowned authority in the fields of risk management, asset protection, and financial planning. He serves as an attorney in the Law Office of David B. Mandell, P.C. in New York and is a principal of the financial planning firm Jarvis & Mandell, LLC.

As a writer, Mr. Mandell has co-authored the book *Wealth Protection: Build & Preserve Your Financial Fortress* and is the author of *Financial Secrets to Franchising Success* with Mr. Jarvis.

Mr. Mandell has also written *The Doctor's Wealth Protection Guide* (endorsed by five state medical societies) and *Risk Management for the Practicing Physician*. His articles regularly appear in more than 30 leading national publications, including *The American Medical News, Inflight Magazine, Yachts International,* and *JCK Circular,* the largest jewelry industry magazine in the U.S. He has been interviewed as an expert in such national media as Bloomberg and FOX-TV.

Mr. Mandell holds a bachelor's degree from Harvard University, from which he graduated with honors. His law degree is from the University of California Los Angeles' School of Law, where he was awarded the American Jurisprudence Award for achievement in legal ethics. While at UCLA, Mr. Mandell also earned a Master's in Business Administration from the Anderson Graduate School of Management. He can be reached at mandell@ojmgroup.com or 877-656-4362.

Do You Know the Secrets of Building Wealth and Protecting Assets?

In the last 12 years, tens of thousands of successful Americans have read our articles and books, subscribed to our free e-newsletter at www.ojmgroup.com, or attended one of our seminars. In the last five years, more than 5,000 strangers, ranging from school teachers to families worth over $150 million, have contacted us specifically asking for help managing their financial situations.

In our efforts to try to help as many of these people as possible, we had to interact with many of the attorneys, accountants, and financial advisors who represented those strangers before they contacted us in order to learn more about the clients' specific circumstances. Independent of those aforementioned meetings, we have also been contacted by hundreds of financial planners, attorneys, and accountants to help them with their clients' complex financial situations. These thousands of interactions, which ranged from short calls and e-mail exchanges to decade-long business and personal relationships, are what motivated us to write this book.

Our experiences gave us a large enough sample size to make this book a statistically significant, almost scientific, study on wealth in America. We know what people do to earn a little wealth. We know what people have to do to accumulate significant wealth. We know how people have lost big fortunes with one single mistake. We know how some families have continued their accumulation of wealth while experiencing numerous financial catastrophes that would have wiped out hundreds of other less-savvy families. In short, our experiences with our diverse clients led us to uncover the many tricks of the trade that help people build and preserve wealth in any economic climate. These are the *Wealth Secrets of the Affluent.*

You may be wondering why we would call these financial tools that help people build their wealth and protect their assets "secrets." We consider them to be secrets because so few people actually learn these valuable lessons and fewer actually apply them in their financial planning. This isn't because these people are stupid or careless. This is because there are so many hurdles to overcome just to uncover the right advice. Then, there are even more hurdles to overcome to actually implement these *Wealth Secrets.*

Wealth Secrets of the Affluent is uniquely valuable in so many ways. First, it teaches the valuable lessons to building a fortune and protecting assets. These lessons are valuable for the very wealthy, for those who want to become wealthy, and for those professional advisors whose job it is to help their clients build and preserve wealth.

Second, *Wealth Secrets* not only explains the many pitfalls to building and protecting wealth, but it also offers strategies and techniques to avoid these challenges now and into the future. These lessons can be applied immediately so the reader can realize an immediate return on the time and financial investment made to read *Wealth Secrets.*

Third, *Wealth Secrets* offers practical advice on implementing these secrets. This advice includes hundreds of "Do's" and "Don'ts" that cannot be found in any other book. These secrets or tips can also be applied to the Super Affluent, the hard-working Average American who aspires to build wealth, and the professional advisor who wants to provide better service to valuable clients.

More specifically, *Wealth Secrets of the Affluent* offers all of this valuable information in 10 Keys. There are 10 Keys to Fortune Building and Asset Protection. Within each Key, there are a number of valuable lessons. Here is a list of what readers will learn from *Wealth Secrets*:

The First Key: Understanding and Embracing Affluence teaches us that the Affluent are very different from Average Americans in so many ways. Apart from the obvious financial differences of higher income and higher net worth, the Affluent have greater lawsuit risk, greater tax risk, and face myriad financial and legal challenges the Average American family will never have to encounter.

Though many aspects of life are much easier for people who have money, it is almost impossible for wealthy people to get appropriate financial and legal advice. Nearly every book, magazine, web site, radio and television program that is dedicated to personal finance is for the Average American family that earns between $35,000 and $75,000 per year. The messages that have been written or spoken millions of times may be so common that people just assume they are true—without actually doing the research to see if they are true.

This widely accepted financial advice may be appropriate for Average Americans but can be financially detrimental for people who are wealthy or for people who are trying to build wealth and protect their assets. This broad acceptance of conventional wisdom is the most devastating factor when it comes to financial planning for the Affluent or aspiring-to-be Affluent. However, once you become open-minded to new strategies for building and protecting wealth, you still have a long way to go.

The Second Key: Using Leverage to Achieve Affluence teaches the fundamental financial philosophy that is the key to all fortune-building: leverage. The only practical way to move from being an Average American to an Affluent American or from the ranks of the Affluent to the Super Affluent is to use leverage. Chapters on the importance of leverage are followed up by the specific advice on leveraging effort, education, assets, and people. Examples of billionaires and how they used leverage are offered. The Second Key offers advice on how to start using leverage right away to increase wealth and improve one's quality of life.

The Third Key: Build the Right Team of Advisors teaches how to practically benefit from the leverage of people. More specifically, the Third Key offers self-tests to help readers determine if they have outgrown their advisors' competencies, how to spot planning pitfalls, and how to avoid them. The Third Key explains expectations readers should have for advisors and offers advice on how to find and work with the right advisors—whether you are rich, super rich, or just trying to become rich. The wrong advisors are responsible for most of the financial mistakes of the Affluent. This is why this Key is so important for anyone who wants to build or protect wealth.

The Fourth Key: Protect Assets explains how the litigation fascination in this country threatens anyone with any level of wealth and offers practical solutions to help you keep what is yours. The Fourth Key offers a discussion of asset protection myths to be avoided and a sliding scale of asset protection to determine how well protected your assets are. For example, *Wealth Secrets* explains why *no* asset should ever be owned in your own name, jointly with a spouse, or in a general partnership.

The Fourth Key also discusses a number of strategies for helping protect wealth. These strategies include the use of state and federal exemptions, limited liability companies, family limited partnerships, trusts, offshore planning, and the use of debt shields. Specific advice is given to help clients protect a home, protect future income, protect a family inheritance from divorce, and protect a business from many risks through the use of a captive insurance company.

The Fifth Key: Always Consider Taxes addresses one of the two certainties in life: death and taxes. An explanation of all of the potential taxes Americans face is followed up with solutions to these tax problems. More specifically, the Fifth Key offers suggestions to maximize retirement plans, minimize family tax by borrowing lower tax rates, getting the government to fund part of your long-term care costs, leveraging charitable options without completely giving away assets, and tax efficiently paying for educational costs. More advanced discussions about avoiding the only 70 percent tax trap and utilizing the tax-efficient investment secrets of the

Affluent are offered. Lastly, a chapter on how to tell if your tax advisor is helping or hurting you is invaluable for readers who want to apply lessons to reduce unnecessary taxes for themselves.

The Sixth Key: Preserving Your Estate addresses the combination of both certainties in life: death and taxes. The Sixth Key specifically explains why the potential estate tax "repeal" is misleading and why Americans can't rely on the government's help for their financial planning and offers solutions that do work. Practically, the Sixth Key focuses on what Affluent Americans have done for decades to avoid unnecessary taxes, fees, and aggravation at death. More specifically, this Key explains how wills, trusts, family limited partnerships, and limited liability companies can be valuable estate planning tools. Readers will also learn why they should never own any assets jointly with anyone (even a spouse) or hold any assets in their own names. Solutions to the 70 percent tax trap and to rising medical costs decimating an inheritance are discussed as well. Lastly, charitable planning is discussed as a way to reduce income taxes, estate taxes, and provide valuable benefits to a family all at the same time.

The Seventh Key: Avoid Financial Disasters discusses the financial catastrophes that have devastated many families for ages. Rather than just scare the reader, *Wealth Secrets'* Seventh Key offers valuable advice to help families prepare for inevitable problems without sacrificing quality of life. More specifically, the Seventh Key teaches how to avoid financial losses from the death or disability of a breadwinner, death or disability of a business partner, or the costly need for a family member to receive long-term care. In addition, families are taught how to never run out of money in retirement by using strategies that minimize tax, minimize or eliminate investment risk, and bring ultimate peace of mind.

The Eighth Key: Invest Wisely may seem like an obvious lesson, like "buy low and sell high," but the information in this Key is far from obvious. Readers are taught the importance of not relying on the Nobel Prize-winning strategy most investment advisors use. The Eighth Key explains the risks of inflation and taxes and offers practical solutions to address both.

A very interesting chapter on "Why Affluent Investors Have Outgrown Mutual Funds" is followed up with a chapter on alternative investments—including hedge funds—that people who earn less than $200,000 per year never learn. The Eighth Key ties together the important lesson of leverage from the Second Key and applies it to the knowledge shared in this Key.

The Ninth Key: Use the Secret Investments of the Affluent may be the most counterintuitive and valuable section of the book. This Key offers a detailed discussion of the two secret asset classes that are so important to wealth building for the Savvy and Super Affluent. These investments are so important to fortune building and asset protection that they needed their own Key. We address how these two investments classes maximize leverage and efficiency for investors and explain why they should play a very significant role in any comprehensive plan . . . if the investor hopes to achieve any level of Affluence.

The Tenth Key: Plan for Success offers motivation and practical steps. An explanation of why so many Americans plan, but do not succeed, is offered. Then, readers are taught the 10 steps to implementing a successful financial plan that will ensure that they use the lessons learned in this book. This is a surefire guide to help readers achieve the levels of wealth accumulation and asset protection they desire.

By reading the introduction, you have taken the first step. You have shown interest in building your fortune or protecting your assets. The next step is to finish reading *Wealth Secrets of the Affluent*. When you are ready to make the commitment to put these lessons into practice and start enjoying your increased wealth and peace of mind, you will need to build a multidisciplinary team of advisors to leverage your time and money. Certainly, we would be flattered if you choose to include us on your team. We work with clients nationwide and would be interested in speaking with you about this possibility. You can learn how our firm helps people just like you by visiting our web site at www.ojmgroup.com or by calling us at (800) 554-7233.

If you feel like you have never been armed with the right information to help you become wealthy, if you feel like your wealth is always threatened, or if you feel like you never knew how to help Affluent Americans with their planning, you have what you need. *Wealth Secrets of the Affluent* can help you address any and all of these concerns. We encourage you to become a member of the Super Affluent and hope our book is the first step to helping people build a fortune or protect their assets.

Christopher R. Jarvis, MBA
David B. Mandell, JD, MBA
Principals & Co-founders, O'Dell Jarvis Mandell, LLC
www.ojmgroup.com
(800) 554-7233

THE FIRST KEY

UNDERSTANDING AND EMBRACING AFFLUENCE

This First Key will set the stage for the rest of *Wealth Secrets of the Affluent*. Rather than throw you right into the "secrets of the affluent" and their keys to success, we think it is essential that you first understand what affluence means, how the Affluent are different from the Average, and how they each think about wealth. This perspective will help you answer a few of these questions that may be lurking somewhere in your thoughts:

- Who are the Affluent and how would I recognize them or separate them from most Americans?
- Would I be considered Affluent? If so, why? If not, why not?
- Why do the Affluent need such wealth secrets and why haven't I heard of them before? (Perhaps you are skeptical about the existence of such strategies.)

In this initial Key, we will attempt to answer these important questions and provide additional comments we hope prove helpful. This foundation will put you in a better position to absorb the information that will help you build your fortune and protect your assets.

1

CHAPTER 1

Who Are the Affluent?

Given the focus of this book, it is important that we first answer the obvious question: who are the Affluent? For the purpose of this book, we will make distinctions between different types of Affluent Americans. The differences between the groups are based on what makes them affluent, how affluent they are, and how they achieved their level of affluence. In this book, you will regularly see the following Affluent categories.

Affluent Categories

1. The Working Affluent
2. Wealthy Families
3. The Savvy Affluent
4. The Super Affluent

In some instances, a person or family may be categorized as both Working Affluent and a member of a Wealthy Family. That same family may be considered Super Affluent and may or may not be considered part of a group we call the Savvy Affluent. Despite their ability to share members of multiple Affluent categories, these groups can have very significant differences in characteristics, concerns and goals. Whether you are a member of any of these Affluent categories, hope to become a member of the Affluent through lessons in this book, or plan to work with members of these groups as an advisor, you will find the philosophical and practical Keys in this book apply almost universally. Of course, as with any lesson, some of the specific chapters within each of the 10 parts of the book—the

10 Keys—may be more appropriate for one group than another and will be more or less valuable to different people within each group based on their personal circumstances.

The Working Affluent

For the purposes of *Wealth Secrets*, we define Working Affluent as families that earn more than $150,000 per year. The strategies and philosophies offered in this book have come from individuals and families that earn $500,000 to $5 million per year and can be applied to any household earning $150,000 or more. By definition, the Working Affluent earn considerably more than the Average American. This will be quantified later in this Key. As a result, the Working Affluent have different financial challenges that require special attention. Generally, these challenges include business planning, tax planning, asset protection, retirement planning, wealth accumulation, and investment and insurance concerns. These topics will be discussed in greater detail within the 10 Keys to Fortune Building and Asset Protection.

Wealthy Families

For the purpose of *Wealth Secrets*, we define Wealthy Families as those families with a current or potential net worth in excess of $2 million. Here, we are simply calculating net worth as the sum of total assets less the total of liabilities or debts. Many of the authors' experiences have been with families that have a net worth between $5 million and $50 million. Wealthy Families may have many similar concerns to those of the Working Affluent. In addition, Wealthy Families are also likely to have estate planning, charitable, and business succession concerns. These unique concerns will be discussed in detail in the Sixth Key. Conversely, the Working Affluent may have more significant asset protection and tax concerns arising from operating a high liability business or professional practice. These concepts are discussed in the Fourth and Fifth Keys, respectively.

You Can Be Both—Working Affluent and a Wealthy Family

We acknowledge that many people will fall into both categories—the Working Affluent and Affluent Families—but that is not always the case. This is why we cannot use only net worth or income as an indicator of affluence. For example, a first-year neurosurgeon may earn $400,000 per year (according to www.mdsalaries.blogspot.com) but may not pay off all of his educational debt and begin to save money for a number of years. We did not think it accurate to categorize this person as Average; rather we call this professional a member of the Working Affluent as a result of his high income. Similarly, a woman who sold her business for $5 million and quit working shouldn't be considered Average because she doesn't have a job or a regular income. She would be a member of a Wealthy Family because she has such a high net worth. Clearly, these two people have concerns that are very different from those of the Average American. You can also see how the neurosurgeon may have very different concerns from the young retiree. This is why it is an either-or scenario and why there are solutions in this book that are more appropriate for each group.

The Super Affluent

The examples of the neurosurgeon and entrepreneur described above help explain why a person or family is considered Affluent. The neurosurgeon is considered Affluent because of significant income. The entrepreneur is considered Affluent through a measure of accumulated assets. Yet, these two Affluent groups have different financial challenges and wealth concerns. As such, the category of affluence is not the only important financial planning factor. The amount of wealth someone has acquired also has an impact on the goals and strategies used to achieve financial success.

For this reason, we introduce another category: the Super Affluent. The Super Affluent can also achieve their Affluent distinction through earnings or accumulation of wealth, albeit at higher levels. We consider the Super Affluent to be members of the Working Affluent who earn more than $1 million per year or members of Wealthy Families who have accumulated a net worth in excess of $10 million. You will find that many of the strategies in this book come from people who are members of this category and members of the next category, the Savvy Affluent.

The Savvy Affluent

The Working Affluent, Wealthy Families, and the Super Affluent designations are based on the amount of income or net worth a person or family has. This category, the Savvy Affluent, is based on what people have done with their money. A member of the Super Affluent isn't necessarily someone you want to mimic (see: Hilton, Paris). Inheriting money or winning the lottery are not planning strategies we endorse. Luck should not be part of your long-term financial plan.

The lessons in this book were learned from people and advisors who made great decisions and leveraged every opportunity they had to achieve a greater level of financial success. For example, turning a $100 investment into a $300,000 per year business and turning a $1 million inheritance into a $50 million fortune are both wonderful success stories worthy of inspection. These stories are those of the Savvy Affluent.

The Savvy Affluent are people who have made the most of their situation by utilizing the lessons in this book to either:

1. Improve their financial situation from Average American to Affluent American.
2. Improve their financial situation from Affluent to Super Affluent.

Throughout the book, we will refer to the Savvy Affluent as the ones who have wisely applied the lessons discussed to achieve greater wealth and peace of mind. Many of the tips in this book have come directly from interactions with thousands of Savvy and Super Affluent Americans who have successfully grown from Average to Affluent and then from Affluent to Super Affluent. The purpose of this book is to teach you what the Savvy Affluent have done to increase their levels of wealth and explain how you may be able to benefit from similar strategies.

If you are interested in improving your financial situation by employing the same techniques that were previously used only by the Super Affluent, you have picked up the right book.

Important Note

The reason we talk about Average, Affluent, or Super Affluent Americans has nothing to do with inherent differences in Americans' approach to achieving financial success. Many of the philosophies in this book are universal and could be applied in any city, state, province, or country. In fact, many of these lessons have been passed down within Wealthy Families and empires for thousands of years.

However, many of the practical tips in the areas of asset protection and tax and estate planning are based on the laws of the United States that will apply to anyone living in this country. So, if you are not an American citizen but you live in the United States, this book should be very helpful. If you are not an American citizen and you live outside the United States, the strategies in this book should help you, too, but you should work with local advisors to make sure the practical lessons apply in your country.

Consider This

Now that you understand what makes someone Affluent and what the different categories of Affluence are, you are almost ready to begin your practical training and learn the secrets to fortune building and asset protection. But before we tell you the secret of the Affluent, first it is imperative you read the next segments on the Average American and the differences between this group and Affluent Americans. Then you can proceed to the Second Key: Leverage. These discussions will be the cornerstones of the important philosophies throughout this book.

2

Understanding the Average American

Before you can understand the wealth secrets of Affluent Americans and what they do to achieve and maintain their fortunes and protect their assets, you must first understand the demographics of the Average American. This is crucial because in order to learn how the Affluent act differently in their wealth planning decision-making, you have to compare their financial circumstances with the circumstances of the norm. It is only through these comparisons that you can truly appreciate the different wealth challenges that the Affluent face and how they effectively deal with these challenges. This comparison may also help you see how, in your own financial life, you may share characteristics of Affluent Americans, Average Americans, or, perhaps, some combination of the two.

In this chapter, we will examine the Average American in terms of income level, federal income taxes paid, source of income, retirement, asset protection, and estate planning.

Important Note

Throughout this book, we will use the term "Average Americans." We recognize that, to some, this term may seem to be demeaning or condescending or to infer a value judgment. We do not intend it that way. It is simply a demographic term to describe a particular group defined by income, tax rate, financial circumstances, and so on.

Average American Income

The first, and perhaps most important, defining characteristic of the Average American is income level. According to the U.S. Census Bureau's August 28, 2007, Current Population Survey (CPS), the Average American household earns $48,201. Additional census data shows that, as of 2005:

20 percent of American households* earned less than $25,616.

40 percent of American households earned less than $45,021.

60 percent of American households earned less than $68,304.

80 percent of American households earned less than $103,100.

Another way the Census Bureau analyzes income numbers for households in the United States is to break down the population into fifths and look at the average income within each grouping (or quintile). Consider the following:

Segment of the Population	Average Annual Income
The lowest earning fifth	$14,767
The second fifth	$35,137
The third fifth	$56,227
The fourth fifth	$84,095
The highest earning fifth	$176,292

If you consider that families of the Working Affluent typically earn well in excess of $100,000 annually (we defined the threshold to be $150,000 per year in Chapter 1), then you can see that at least 80 percent of Americans would not be considered Working Affluent. By our definition, between 10 percent and 20 percent of the households in the United States would actually be considered Working Affluent based on our criteria and their annual income.

The significance of the income analysis is fairly simple. Average Americans, as a rule, are earning just enough to pay the bills on a

---

*Households may include more than one or two earners.

regular basis. In many areas of the country, where expenses are relatively high, Average Americans may not even be earning enough income to cover the bills. Long-term uses of income, such as to fund retirement accounts, insurance premiums, and college savings accounts are often luxuries Average Americans cannot enjoy.

Federal Income Tax Rates

The second defining characteristic of the Average American is federal income tax rates. As you will see later in the book, Affluent Americans consider their taxes in nearly everything they do because their tax rates can be very high. Contrast that to the situation of Average Americans here.

If you combine the household demographics stated previously with the 2006 federal tax rate schedule below for married couples filing jointly, you can draw some interesting conclusions. (See Table 2.1.)

After examining Table 2.1, you can conclude that about 20 percent of the population will pay less than 10 percent of their income to the government in federal income taxes (since the average income for the lowest fifth of the population is less than $15,100).

Further, almost 40 percent more of the population will pay 10 percent to 15 percent of their income in federal income taxes. Another 20 percent of the population will pay less than 18 percent of their income (average income for the fourth quintile of the population is about $103,000). Only about 5 percent of the population will earn enough to be subject to the highest marginal federal income tax bracket of 35 percent.

Table 2.1   2006 Federal Income Tax Table—Married Couples Filing Jointly

If taxable income is over:	But not over:	The tax is:
$0	$15,100	10% of the amount over $0
$15,100	$61,300	$1,510 plus 15% of the amount over $15,100
$61,300	$123,700	$8,440 plus 25% of the amount over $61,300
$123,700	$188,450	$24,040 plus 28% of the amount over $123,700
$188,450	$336,550	$42,170 plus 33% of the amount over $188,450
$336,550	no limit	$91,043 plus 35% of the amount over $336,550

In other words, Average Americans pay relatively few dollars in income taxes as a percentage of their income. Due to the lower tax rates and the sources of income described next, income tax planning is not a significant concern for the Average American.

Average American Source of Income

The third defining characteristic of Average Americans is their source of income. The Average American is almost always an employee who works for someone else. These workers are paid as "W-2 employees" and may or may not have modest benefits packages. Taxes are typically withheld from the Average American's paycheck each payday and the after-tax proceeds are then distributed. Many call this the take home amount. While this system eliminates the headaches of calculating and preparing complex quarterly estimated tax payments and saving for these large payments, it also means there is little opportunity for significant tax planning.

The Average American rarely owns his own business. This means that the Average American does not have to manage the complexities of a growing or complicated business that may have multiple locations, many employees, and regulatory reporting requirements. This also means that the Average American's income will be determined by someone else. The owner of the company or the management team determines when and if there will be any raises or promotions for the employees. Employees can work hard, but the financial rewards for such efforts are at the discretion of someone else. Because the cost of living increases every year, modest raises may provide relatively modest increased spending and saving potential over a lifetime.

Millions of Americans have made the decision to buy or build a small business. There are countless motivations that drive someone to leave the world of the employed to start or run a business. There are pros and cons to working for someone else instead of running your own business. Let's consider some of the pros and cons of being an employee:

Pros	Cons
Simplified tax reporting	Little opportunity for tax planning
Fixed or predictable income	Little opportunity for significant increases in income

Pros	Cons
Benefits managed by employer	No control over benefits offered
Job stability	Job stability controlled by employer
Employer leverages your work	No direct benefit from leverage
Little lawsuit risk as compared to the employer	
No business succession risk	

There is no doubt that running a business is hard work. The business owner has a lot of responsibility. Owning a business is certainly not for everyone. In fact, most small businesses fail. The point we are trying to make is that there is a trade-off for letting someone else handle all of the responsibility and headaches of running a business. Employees have little say in planning for the business. This is neither good nor bad. It is just the nature of the situation. This is one of the ways that Average Americans who are employees differ from Affluent business owners.

Average American Retirement Planning

The fourth area of difference between the Average American and the Affluent American is in the area of retirement planning. For almost a century, a major goal of employment for Average Americans has been to work hard and save enough money to retire. Most Americans would rather be doing something other than working and many look forward to the financial freedom of retirement.

In terms of retirement planning, most Average Americans invest in some type of retirement plan offered through their place of employment, typically a 401(k) plan. Most Average Americans also have checking and savings accounts and possibly an IRA or small investment account. However, they do not have substantial or sufficient savings in such accounts. This is the result of a combination of factors such as:

- People are living longer and need income for more years (and more savings) in retirement.
- Employers are focused on quarterly earnings and are forced to cut back on employee benefits, including retirement funding.

- Reduced fringe benefits from employers cause increased spending by the employees' families.
- Average Americans are spending more on consumer purchases than on retirement plans simply because their incomes don't afford them the opportunity to do both.

When companies give less to their employees and employees have to spend more just to pay the bills, the employees simply do not have the discretionary funds to save enough for their desired level of retirement and cannot put enough money in these plans. Many Americans may still be relying on Social Security to provide a large portion of their retirement income. You need only read a week's worth of articles in the newspapers listed later in this chapter to get a clear understanding that relying on Social Security is not a wise planning decision. Yet, most Average Americans do not have many retirement alternatives.

Average American Asset Protection

Next to estate tax planning, this is the area of financial planning where the needs and concerns of Average Americans and Affluent Americans differ most. Asset protection—the practice of shielding wealth from potential lawsuits, creditors, or other claims—is plainly not of interest to Average Americans for two reasons:

1. They do not have significant assets to protect.
2. They do not face significant liability through their work or investments.

Later in this chapter, you will see that Affluent Americans' asset protection situations are polar opposite those of Average Americans. As a result, asset protection becomes a critical factor in Affluent American financial planning. In fact, this issue is so important that the authors have written four other books on this topic and have dedicated an entire part of this book to it—the Fourth Key.

Average American Estate Tax Planning

Lastly, lack of significant concern for estate planning is a defining characteristic of the Average American. Under today's laws, an individual's heirs will only be subject to federal estate taxes if that individual has an estate worth greater than $2 million. By utilizing one particular estate planning document (you will learn which one in the Sixth Key), a family with two living parents can use both exemptions and save the heirs from paying federal estate taxes on estates worth less than $4 million. It is true that, under current law, the exempt amount (for estate tax purposes) will drop to $1 million per person ($2 million per couple) in 2011. The estate tax phaseout schedule is offered below:

Calendar year	Exemption per person	Highest rate
2002	$1 million	50%
2003	1 million	49
2004	1.5 million	48
2005	1.5 million	47
2006	2 million	46
2007	2 million	45
2008	2 million	45
2009	3.5 million	45
2010	Repealed	0
2011	1 million	55

With pretax income below $150,000 per year, it is highly unlikely that Average American families will be able to pay their living expenses, raise children, pay educational costs for children, secure a retirement, handle the unforeseen financial burdens we all encounter during our lifetimes, and *still* have over $2 million left at the time of death to leave to children as an inheritance. As a result, estate tax planning (focused on reducing estate tax liabilities) is not likely to be a major concern of the Average American family.

Temporary Estate Tax Phaseout

The federal government's tax window closes over the next decade as the top estate tax rate drops and the amount each person can pass along free of federal estate taxes increases. The tax expires in 2010, though possibly for just one year.

Consider This

Average Americans do not have as many opportunities to enhance their financial situations as the Affluent do. Average Americans must spend most of what they earn on income taxes (albeit at a low rate) and on all of their living expenses. As an employee or an owner running a small business, Average Americans have neither the opportunity to use many tax saving vehicles nor the flexibility to create their own benefits programs. The Average American family has precious few retirement assets and minimal risk of losing assets to judgment creditors. Upon death, almost all American families can easily pass their family assets to children with little or no estate tax due. Average Americans spend the majority of their time trying to manage their financial affairs for the week, month, or year. Few have the time or luxury of preparing for long-term needs. Because the needs of Average Americans are so different from those of the Affluent and the Affluent make up such a small piece of the population, the popular press has focused on delivering information that applies to the Average American. The illustration of this point and the implication this has on the Affluent is offered in the next chapter.

CHAPTER 3

Unique Advice for the Affluent

Most people believe that there is more financial information available on television, in newspapers and magazines, and on web sites than one person could possibly review in a lifetime. They may be right!

Our Google search for "financial advice" on August 11, 2007, yielded 112 million results. A search for "investing" yielded 104 million results. We then narrowed our search to sites that had all of the following tags: "investing," "high income," and "financial planning." This narrowed the results down to 133,000.

Obviously, we agree with the statement that there is practically an infinite amount of places one can look for financial advice. However, who is this advice for? Consider this statement:

> Most financial information available in newspapers or magazines, on television or within web sites is inappropriate and often detrimental to successful financial planning for the Affluent.

How can there be so many places to find financial information and so few reliable sources for the Affluent? To answer this question, let's start by looking at a list of television stations, newspapers, magazines, and web sites. Which of these outlets would you consider to be for Affluent Americans and which would you consider to be directed at Average Americans?

Television:　　　Fox News, MSNBC

Newspapers:　　the *New York Times, USA Today,* the *Wall Street Journal*

Web sites:　　　FoxNews.com, CNN.com, CNNMoney.com, USAToday.com, WSJ.com, Forbes.com

Magazines:　　　*Smart Money, Money, BusinessWeek, Fortune, Fortune Small Business*

Table 3.1　Media Source and Type by Income Demographic I

Media	Type	Income Demographic
Fox News	television	$70,929 median HHI
MSNBC	television	$75,588 median HHI (adults 25–54)
The *New York Times*	newspaper	$67,137 median HHI
USA Today	newspaper	$76,929 median HHI, 34% HHI > $70k
The *Wall Street Journal*	newspaper	$253,100 average HHI, $2.5MM net worth
FoxNews.com	web site	$73,000 median HHI
CNN.com	web site	$76,419 median HHI
CNNMoney.com	web site	$83,431 median HHI, 37% HHI > $100k
USAToday.com	web site	$89,263 median HHI, 42% HHI > $70k
WSJ.com*	web site	$111,250 mean HHI, mean inv ass $276,373
Forbes.com*	web site	$146,263 mean HHI, 17.8% HHI > $150k
SmartMoney	magazine	$81,742 median HHI
Money	magazine	$85,336 median HHI
BusinessWeek	magazine	$93,811 median HHI, 18% HHI > $150k
Fortune Small Business	magazine	$119,986 median HHI
Fortune	magazine	$137,000 median HHI

*By using a mean and not a median to represent that "average" visitor, the numbers can be skewed as a result of visitors with very high incomes. The mean is a simple average. The median is the HHI associated with the middle person (after all respondents' data are ranked in order). As an example, if three people with HHIs of $50,000, $80,000, and $320,000, the mean HHI would be $150,000 but the median HHI would be $80,000. When analyzing HHI and net worth numbers, you will find that the mean is almost always much higher than the median. In the case of Forbes.com, for example, only 17.8% of visitors have HHI over $150k, yet the mean is $146,263. This means that the total combined household income of the 17.8% of its visitors is approximately equal to the total HHI of the other 82.2% of its readers. We are not saying that the average reader doesn't earn $146k, but we are pointing out that fewer than one in five of the visitors to the site actually earn $150,000. The savvy advertisers understand what this data really means, and the content must be focused at the majority of its visitors.

If you are like all of the colleagues and clients we asked informally, you would say that almost all of the aforementioned media would deliver information that would target wealthier Americans.

To actually compare these media against each other, we went to each of their media kits and compiled Table 3.1 for you to view. We cannot verify any of the data, but can verify that all of this information was taken from each firm's online media kit as of August 2007. We use the abbreviation HHI to represent household income.

While you might be surprised to see how the media outlets focused almost exclusively on nonAffluent audiences, take a moment to review the popular outlets in Table 3.2. These have an even less-affluent audience than those above.

The important point we are trying to illustrate by showing you Table 3.1 and Table 3.2 is that virtually all of the media listed, including the high-end magazines and web sites in Table 3.1, have an average audience household income of less than $100,000. Every single one mentioned in that list, except the *Wall Street Journal (WSJ)*, has an audience with an average household income of less than $150,000.

For the purpose of our next statement, we would like to exclude the *WSJ*. Though the *WSJ* focuses on business and financial markets, its primary goal is to report the news. It does not take a position of encouraging or promoting any particular products, strategies, or financial philosophies. Given this caveat, our conclusion from the aforementioned data is:

Table 3.2   Media Source and Type by Income Demographic II

Media	Type	Income Demographic
ESPN (NFL games)	television	$62,200 median HHI
The *Los Angeles Times*	newspaper	$55,698 median HHI
ESPN.com	web site	$77,000 average HHI
Oprah.com	web site	$80,000 median HHI
ESPN	magazine	$62,132 median HHI
People	magazine	$63,599 median HHI
Sports Illustrated	magazine	$63,643 median HHI
GQ	magazine	$67,141 median HHI
Newsweek	magazine	$70,995 median HHI

Even the highest level media outlets in the United States are not targeting and delivering appropriate content to an audience with an average income above $150,000.

Why is this information important to our discussion of Wealth Secrets of the Affluent? Let us explain what we learned in publishing our last book *Wealth Protection: Build & Preserve Your Financial Fortress* with John Wiley & Sons.

The Media Business: "Get the Eyeballs"

If you are in the media business, it doesn't matter if you are publishing magazines or web sites or producing for television or radio programs. The goal is always the same if there is advertising involved—provide content that will generate a large enough audience to generate ad revenue. You generate ad revenue by proving that you can deliver a significant audience and that you can accurately track the demographics of the audience. All of the sites, magazines, and newspapers mentioned earlier are in business to make money. If they don't generate content that maintains an audience large enough to support the necessary ad revenue, the company will go out of business. They must "get the eyeballs." The business model is that simple.

To generate a large audience, these outlets have to deliver content that appeals to a large audience. After writing our last book, we appeared on over 120 radio and television programs. Though the book *Wealth Protection* had interesting philosophical lessons and over 62 practical lessons on advanced financial, legal, and tax-saving techniques, almost every producer and interviewer wanted us to discuss topics in the book we thought were the most basic. One host told us that his goal was to keep as many people interested as possible. He didn't care if the information was fresh and exciting. He wanted to make sure that "Joe Lunch-Bucket" (his words) wouldn't be put off by the discussion. He told us that talking about ways to save $100,000 in taxes or ways to efficiently buy rental properties would alienate most listeners—which, in turn, would cause them to lose eyeballs (or ears in radio). He was not going to allow that to happen.

Until John Wiley asked us to write a book about Affluent Americans, we had had very little interest from the popular press in regard to the education we have regularly offered to high-income clients for the last 12 years.

Consider the following:

- Every information company is in business to make money.
- The money almost always comes from advertisers.
- Advertisers pay more if the audience is larger.
- An information source must continuously offer appropriate content to the masses to maintain and grow an audience and attract advertisers.
- Even the high-end distribution channels don't target consumers earning over $100,000.

If you consider these five statements you can clearly conclude that:

> It is almost *impossible* for Affluent Americans to find useful and appropriate financial information from popular newspapers, magazines, web sites, and television programs.

This is why most of the information contained in this book may seem foreign to many readers. The tips, tools, and strategies offered here are not the kinds of things that most information outlets would ever deliver because, quite frankly, there is no business reason for doing so. Roughly 10 percent to 20 percent of Americans will find the information in this book applicable and beneficial. If it is important to you to fit in and do what everyone else does, even if it is not the best course of action, this book is not for you.

CH**4**PTER

The Affluent Don't Want to Fit In

We hope that you now understand that there are significant differences between Average and Affluent Americans—at least in terms of basic demographic data. Later in the book, you will learn how Affluent Americans, especially the Savvy Affluent, think and act when faced with financial and legal issues. Their very different attitudes and methods of approaching wealth planning are integral to their success—these are their psychographic differences.

We also hope you have gained some insight as to why nearly every newspaper, financial web site, and financial magazine is forced to focus its content on a group of subscribers or readers that have a very different set of concerns from the Affluent. These media outlets want to provide commonsense advice to the general public (i.e., Average Americans); this fits their business model because there are a lot more Average American eyeballs than there are Affluent eyeballs.

It stands to reason, then, if financial common sense has been developed for (and should generally be used by) Average Americans, this commonsense advice will not apply to Affluent Americans. In fact, the only way the Affluent can achieve desired levels of wealth and have peace of mind is to follow advice that doesn't make *common* sense.

Going against common sense is not easy. There are many deeply rooted psychological factors that push someone to go with the crowd, rather than against it—even in the financial planning context. As an example, consider this proposition:

> It may be a bad financial idea for you to pay off your mortgage
> and own your home outright.

For many of you reading this now, that statement may be difficult, if not impossible, to believe. It is exactly the opposite of what your parents told you (and they are the smart people who taught you many life lessons). It is the polar opposite of what personal finance expert Suze Orman and hundreds of web site and magazine articles and television programs suggest. Further, it just may not feel right, because it goes against what all of your friends are doing. Keep those feelings and thoughts in mind when you read the other Keys in the book.

Why Ignoring "Common" Sense Is So Difficult

Most children and adolescents try desperately to fit in. As we get older, we try to find the right groups in college. In our first jobs, we want to toe the company line. All states have laws that govern our behavior. Most religions have commandments, rules, or other condoned and forbidden activities.

Most people avoid actions they fear their friends and relatives would criticize—or at the very least, they refrain from sharing details of their potentially unpopular activities with their family and friends. We are not implying that Americans are sheep. Rather, we are saying that society typically rewards those who are similar and creates more challenges for those who are not.

This is not a particularly astute observation. It is merely support for the significance of the number one challenge that must be overcome if you are to take advantage of the Secrets of the Affluent. To successfully take advantage of the Secrets of the Affluent, you not only have to admit to being different from Average Americans, but you also have to *embrace* the fact that you are different.

Embrace Affluence and Your Differences: The First Key Secret

If you want to successfully achieve or maintain affluence, you must be comfortable with your different circumstances and be comfortable doing things differently from your friends. If your only comfort comes from doing something and knowing that everyone else is doing it, too, then you are destined to achieve and maintain mediocrity. Affluent Americans became affluent by being different or by doing something different. If they did what everyone else did, they would be like 80 percent of Americans who earn less than $80,000 per year, and they wouldn't have achieved the wealth they now have.

Affluent families don't want to fit in. The Affluent understand that Average Americans work very hard to pay their bills while scratching to save for retirement and occasional vacations and precious luxury items. The most successful clients we have met have felt very fortunate to have achieved their wealth or high income positions. They acknowledge having worked very hard, but still credit luck for a portion of their success. Because of this, most Affluent Americans respect the Average Americans who work hard but who may not have had that little bit of luck necessary to become wealthy. Despite the similarities that they share with Average Americans, the Affluent understand that the two groups have very different financial challenges that require different types of advisors and strategies.

What the Affluent don't need are the financial and legal advisors and firms that cater to 150 million Average Americans. The Affluent don't need techniques, strategies, and products that are adequate for the needs of the many. The Affluent don't need free checking, higher money market rates, lower online trading costs, do-it-yourself legal documents, or the advisor with the lowest hourly rate. The Affluent don't want advisors to tell them how nice their shoes or purse are or how wonderfully decorated their home or office is. They know these things are nice—they bought them. The Affluent don't want to be surrounded with yes-men or women who agree with all of their suggestions. They want advisors to question them, challenge them, and help them consider all alternatives before taking action. The Affluent don't need or want their advisors to send calendars, fruit baskets, or sports tickets. The Affluent don't want advisors who can take them golfing or buy them lunch or dinner. By definition, the Affluent can buy all of those things if they so desire.

The Affluent understand that there are millions of attorneys, accountants, investment advisors, and financial planners who would all like their business. They know that many of these advisors and their firms regularly give away special perks to try to convince people to become new clients or to guilt them into staying with the firm. They don't expect to be bought with gifts. The Affluent understand that an advisor referred by a friend can be a good start, but an advisor referred by a friend who is in a different financial situation is likely a waste of time. There is an entire section on how Affluent Americans pick their advisory team in the Third Key. The Third Key is titled "Build the Right Team" and is a must-read for anyone who picked up this book.

The Affluent have family and friends just like Average Americans do. They want to spend their valuable and limited free time with their friends (and some family members—just like Average Americans). When they spend time with their advisors, they want to make the most of the time and focus on the important issues they are paying those advisors to help them manage. They want their advisors to generate a significant return on the fees they pay in value for their family or business.

Like Average Americans, the Affluent can't help but talk business and finance with their friends. A common characteristic of successful Affluent Americans is that they don't need to brag about their planning or convince their friends to work with the same advisors to generate peace of mind. The Affluent cherish the novelty of being different. Practically, the Affluent put more effort into choosing their team than they do in criticizing the solutions and strategies their team recommends and implements. The Affluent do not ask their friends or other unqualified outsiders for approval of their planning. This would be like asking your barber for his advice on how your doctor planned to do your colonoscopy or triple bypass. This isn't to say that the Affluent don't review and challenge the suggestions and bring in other experts for second opinions. This is a significant and very important part of building and maintaining wealth (the Tenth Key).

Average Americans look for bits of cheap advice on web sites, in magazines and newspapers, and on television or radio. The Average American relies on mutual fund recommendations that come in a $5 magazine or on a free web site that might reach millions of different people per day. The Savvy Affluent never give a second thought to any financial or legal suggestion that isn't offered by someone who is intimately familiar with their situation and goals. Wealthy Americans don't *want* to spend the time and money for customized planning—they *must* spend the time and money on a specially trained and experienced team of advisors to customize a plan that will help them most efficiently and effectively reach their specific, personal goals.

Consider This

Whether you are an Average American trying to pay the bills and save for retirement or an Affluent American trying to save what you've earned from taxes, lawsuits, or a divorce, you have important challenges in your financial life. As we hope you have gleaned from our discussion above, there is an abundance of financial information and advice to be found. However, if you are Affluent or want to learn the lessons of the Affluent, the *Wealth Secrets of the Affluent* is for you. Much of the information presented in the 10 Keys may represent financial lessons and advice you literally cannot get anywhere else. The topic of the Second Key—Leverage—is the key to maximizing your income and wealth and protecting your assets. That is a great place to start.

THE SECOND KEY

USE LEVERAGE TO ACHIEVE AFFLUENCE

In the previous part of the book, you learned the First Key to fortune building and asset protection—understanding and embracing Affluence. You learned how it is important for wealthy and high-income earners to acknowledge their different characteristics and embrace their unique challenges. Many of you may have hoped that this book would tell you the secret of *how* the Affluent became Affluent in the first place so you could use that information to help you achieve higher levels of financial success and asset protection for you and your family. The Second Key, Leverage, may be that secret you could use.

Leverage is the most common characteristic of our Affluent clients, and it is universal among every single Super Affluent client we have encountered. If your goal is to increase and maintain wealth, you must fully understand the information presented in the Second Key so you can apply these lessons later.

In this Key, we will provide a basic definition and description of leverage and discuss how to increase leverage and overcome limitations to increasing leverage. Then, we will show you how the Savvy Affluent have applied these lessons to assets, credit, and people so that they could increase their wealth, build their fortunes, and protect their assets.

CHAPTER 5

The Basics of Leverage

If you go to the online Miriam-Webster dictionary and type the word "leverage," you will be given three definitions:

1. the action of a lever or the mechanical advantage gained by it
2. POWER, EFFECTIVENESS
3. the use of credit to enhance one's speculative capacity

With all due apologies to engineers and physicists reading this book, we will offer very simplified interpretations of the definitions of leverage stated above. The first definition states that leverage increases the amount of force exerted. To exemplify this concept, think of leverage as the act of wedging a stick between two heavy rocks that you could not move with just your hands. In order to efficiently move the rocks, you need to push down on the stick that you wedged between the rocks. In doing so, the rock can be moved. Leverage—the wedging of a stick—allows you to move a rock you would otherwise not be able to move.

The second definition of leverage simply states that the act of leverage allows people to be more efficient, effective, and powerful. This can be interpreted to mean that leverage allows people to get more done in less time. It can also be interpreted to mean that leverage allows people to get a job done with less effort. In either case, leverage enables people to be more effective.

The third definition of leverage applies to credit and loans. In this definition, leverage allows people to buy things they don't necessarily have the money to buy in an effort to increase their financial capacity. To illustrate this definition, think of a home loan—that is, the $500,000 home that is purchased by a family with only $100,000 of its own money. Leverage is the ability to enjoy the use of or participate in the upside potential of an investment you otherwise could not afford.

Quite simply, leverage is what allows you to do more with less. Less effort. Less money. Less time. If you are looking for a shortcut to financial success, leverage is the closest thing to it.

The Importance of Leverage

The Savvy Affluent know that leverage is an important tool to increase their wealth. Without leverage, people would have to do everything themselves, including running their own businesses, earning money, handling financial affairs, paying for everything with only their own money, micromanaging everything at work and at home, and still find time to eat and sleep.

If you feel like this is your life, then you are not using leverage. Leverage makes your life easier. Leverage frees you up to do the things that are most important, most profitable, or most enjoyable to you. Leverage is what allows you to achieve greater levels of financial success. No matter what your financial goals, by mastering the art of leverage and incorporating it into your planning, you will reach these goals faster. As we mentioned earlier, leverage is how the Affluent increase the power and effectiveness of their financial planning. You can do the same.

Leverage Limitations

A little leverage is good. A lot of leverage is better. Who wouldn't want to get more done with less effort or less money? The Affluent who understand leverage have tried to maximize its potential and use for thousands of years.

It may seem like the amount of leverage one can attain is endless, but there are restrictions on how much leverage you can achieve. This restriction can be referred to as capacity. Consider the following:

- You can only exert so much force.
- You only have 24 hours in a day.
- You only have so much money.
- You can only borrow so much money.
- You can only manage so many people.

The goal of all attempts at leverage is to maximize efficiency. Efficiency is achieved when leverage is increased to a point where you have approached your capacity without going over. When you exceed capacity, problems occur. This causes you to have to address the method of leverage all over again and possibly repeat certain steps. It is obviously an inefficient process when you have to duplicate any effort. This is why the Savvy Affluent are careful not to exceed their capacity.

You could theoretically increase capacity by working harder, but that is only acceptable if that is the most valuable and profitable use of your time and energy. Leverage is about working smarter, not harder. For this reason, increasing effort is not a viable method of increasing leverage. The rest of this Key will explain the "secret" ways to increase leverage and capacity so you can get even more out of your reduced effort. Getting better results from less effort is the best way to achieve Super Affluence.

Consider This

Leverage makes life easier. Leverage allows you to get more done with less effort or with less money. Once the Savvy Affluent have achieved a measure of leverage, they use their extra time and money to find better methods of leverage. This is a never ending quest to become more efficient and effective in everything they do so that they can build and maintain their wealth and protect their assets.

The next four chapters will specifically discuss how leverage applies to financial transactions, effort, employees, and advisors. The Third Key—Building the Right Team of Advisors—is perhaps the most valuable way to increase the capacity of your leverage. As such, *Wealth Secrets* is filled with practical strategies that can only be employed if you have a team of advisors to help you achieve greater leverage.

CHAPTER 6

Financial Leverage

Now that you understand the basics of leverage and its importance in allowing you to get things done more efficiently and effectively, this chapter will apply those concepts to financial and legal planning. Subsequent chapters in the Second Key will demonstrate how the Savvy Affluent apply these lessons to leverage assets and people to maximize and maintain wealth.

Financial Leverage: The Foundation of Affluence

In every great construction project over thousands of years, levers were required to complete the building process. This was true for moving the large stones to build the pyramids and lifting the stones for Stonehenge. Levers were used to build all the great castles, churches, synagogues, and mosques around the world. Financial projects are very similar to construction projects. They both can seem overwhelming at the beginning, and the success of both types of projects requires significant planning. The implementation of such plans could never be accomplished by one person; instead, the plan requires a host of people who seek to accomplish the same, which in this case is building and maintaining wealth. For every Wealthy Family we interviewed, leverage was fundamental to the building of financial affluence.

> Without exception, every high income earner and Wealthy Family has relied on financial leverage in one way or another.

Once you grasp the concept of leverage and the financial applications of leverage, it becomes impossible to imagine how affluence could possibly be built without it.

Types of Financial Leverage

The Affluent often use different types of financial leverage to create and build wealth. These include:

Leverage of Effort: Leverage of effort is a way to get more out of your financial plans and investments. Since the goal of leverage is to get more done with less effort, all forms of leverage require that you leverage your individual effort by including the effort of others.

Leverage of Assets: Leverage of assets is one way to increase your financial status and get more out of what you currently possess. If you had an unlimited about of money or land, you wouldn't need to accumulate any more wealth; however, this is not generally the case for most people. Since we all have limited resources, we want to get the most wealth/asset accumulation and financial protection out of what we have (with the least amount of effort).

Leverage of People: The Affluent know that they only have the capacity to do so much and that leverage of people is one way to get more than 24 hours out of a day. By leveraging other people's efforts, you can increase the number of tasks you can accomplish in a day. By leveraging people with special skills and expertise you don't have, you can get things done in much less time than it would take you to do these same tasks (if you could do them at all). The goal is to leverage people with as little time commitment and financial expense as possible.

Consider This

Within each of the three categories of leverage discussed above—leverage of effort, leverage of assets, and leverage of people—there are a number of different applications. In the following chapters, we will review each of these categories, discuss how they can be used to generate wealth, and explain which of these types of leverage are more appropriate for creating Super Affluence and which types of leverage will best help maintain higher levels of wealth.

CHAPTER 7

Leveraging Effort

There is no doubt that a willingness to work hard is a key to success. However, this character trait is not one we can teach. Some people become harder workers as they mature, but seldom does a zebra change its stripes. There are generally hard workers and not-so-hard workers. The goal of this chapter on leverage is to help you get the most out of any level of effort. Whether you fancy yourself hard-working or lazy, leverage can help you get more out of your desired amount of effort.

In this chapter, we will discuss the capacity problems of leverage, how education can increase your ability to leverage your effort, and then suggest ways in which the Affluent overcome the barriers of capacity.

You Can Leverage Hard Work . . . but Effort is a Capacity Problem

The basic and inherent problem with effort is that you only have two hands and two feet, and there are only 24 hours in a day. If we consider the case of two landscapers, Lazy Larry and Manic Mike, with very different work ethics, we can illustrate these physical constraints we all have.

Let's assume that Lazy Larry and Manic Mike earn $50 per house per week. If Lazy Larry works five days per week and landscapes eight homes per day, he will earn $2,000 per week before paying overhead, staff, equipment, taxes, and so forth. Manic Mike can work seven days per week and landscape 10 homes per day.

This would give him precious little time off for family or personal time, but he would earn $3,500 per week before all of his expenses.

Both of these landscapers might consider themselves successful (depending on their goals and values). But if hardworking Manic Mike wants to make more money, there aren't enough hours in the day or days in the week for him to make any more money unless he does something that earns him more money per hour or he finds a way to leverage something other than his own effort. The next application of leverage could help Mike do just that.

Leveraging Education

The idea of leveraging education to create wealth is no secret. In fact, it has become part of the American Dream. For over a century, immigrants have come to the United States and taken advantage of the educational system. They have pushed their children to do well in school in the hope that they would get a good job and enjoy a higher standard of living. They have also pushed their children to find careers that pay them more money than a career like Manic Mike chose.

Leveraging education is a key element of fortune building and maintaining wealth. To prove this point, consider the following salaries of highly educated professions. When considering the earning potential of these professions, keep in mind that the median household income for the year 2007 was $48,201, according to the Census Bureau's Current Population Survey dated August 27, 2007. That means that half of all United States households earned less than $48,201 per year. According to an article in *USA Today* (Jan. 18, 2006), the first year salary plus signing bonus for an MBA (two years of graduate school) was $106,000. According to MD Salaries (www.mdsalaries.blogspot.com), the average first year salary of a neurosurgeon is between $350,000 and $417,000 in each of these cities: Houston, New York, Miami, Los Angeles, and Seattle. Neurosurgery requires completion of four years of medical school then a one-year internship and a rigorous five to seven years of residency. Thus, there is no doubt that leveraging education can help you earn more money per year and increase your wealth faster than if you have a job that requires a lower level of education.

Education and Effort Are Not Enough

Would you be surprised to hear that the neurosurgeon mentioned above and Manic Mike have the same problem? While we are not saying that Mike is performing brain surgery, we are suggesting that they both have the same fundamental problem—albeit at a different level of income. Mike doesn't have enough hours in the day, or days in the week to increase his business. Similarly, a neurosurgeon's income is limited by the number of surgeries he can perform, which is also limited by the number of hours in a day and days in a week. Even if you assume that there is an endless supply of patients who need brain surgery and an endless supply of lawns to be mowed, both the landscaper earning $50 per hour and the neurosurgeon earning $500 per hour have the same capacity problem because:

1. They are limited in the amount of money they can earn until they figure out how to leverage what they do.
2. They only make money when they are actually working.

This is a lesson that the Savvy Affluent figured out long ago. As a result, the Savvy Affluent:

- Always focus on the leverage of any business.
- Never consider increasing effort as a legitimate, long-term means to increasing income.
- Never enter into a business that requires them to constantly work to make money.

For these reasons, we prefer to focus our articles, seminars, books, and personal consulting recommendations on strategies that help leverage assets and leverage people.

Consider This

Every teenager has parents, teachers, and coaches who tell them to work harder. We prefer to tell you, and show you, how to work smarter without having to work harder (or having to clean your room or take out the trash). Applications of this smarter working lifestyle will be the focus of Chapter 8 and Chapter 9.

CHAPTER 8

Leveraging Assets

You have undoubtedly heard the phrase, "It takes money to make money." No truer words have ever been spoken. It always takes some investment to generate a return. This chapter will explain how the Affluent successfully leverage assets to create and sustain a high level of wealth. A partial list of assets that can be leveraged includes:

1. Your own money.
2. Other people's money (sometimes shortened to simply OPM).
3. Intellectual property.

In this chapter, we will discuss how the Affluent are able to leverage these three assets.

Leveraging Your Own Money

Leveraging your own money is the oldest and most basic form of leverage. It has been documented all the way back to ancient times of nations, empires, kings, and emperors. These nations had enough money to fund expeditions to discover new lands and acquire even more wealth. A visit to any of the museums of Rome or other ancient city will bear witness to this leverage.

Hundreds of years later, you can witness similar leverage right here in the United States. The Affluent make their capital work for them in various ways. To illustrate this point, let's take a look at one of the nation's most flamboyant and public billionaires—Donald

Trump. If you visit Trump's web site, you will see that he has a significant portfolio of real estate that includes properties in New York, New Jersey, Honolulu, Los Angeles, Chicago, Florida, Las Vegas, Dominican Republic, Seoul, Toronto, Panama, Mexico, and Connecticut. Additionally, he has plans to develop properties in New York's Soho district, Atlanta, New Orleans, and Dubai.

Trump was able to expand his real estate portfolio because he leveraged his assets. His earnings from real estate generated income for him to support expansion into golf clubs in six cities, four casino resorts, various television programs and pageants, a university, merchandise, a travel company, restaurants, skating rinks, and others. Once Trump made money from certain ventures, he was able to leverage those assets into more projects. The profit from those additional projects gave him the capacity to start even more businesses.

You don't have to be a billionaire with a ridiculous haircut to use leverage. If you have money, you can purchase land or real estate and lease it to others who can't afford to buy the property outright. If you have money you don't need to spend to support your lifestyle, you can invest in long-term investments that have higher expected returns than shorter term investments. These may be investments that are unavailable to investors who require a short-term return to pay bills. Lastly, when you have money, you can use it as collateral to borrow money and use other people's money to make money, too. This is what Trump and the Savvy Affluent do all the time to maximize wealth. This is the next application of leverage.

Leveraging Other People's Money

Generally, using other people's money is considered the classic definition of leverage. Recall from Chapter 5 that this is the third definition provided by the Miriam-Webster dictionary. Using other people's money as leverage certainly relates to credit, but we will broaden its definition to include all types of leverage involving OPM.

The most common way to use OPM is debt. Many Affluent people throughout history have achieved their wealth by borrowing at lower rates and reinvesting the loan proceeds at higher levels of investment return. Donald Trump's empire was built in a similar fashion—typical of most real estate investors. They put down a small percentage of the total costs to build properties and use OPM to fund the remainder of the costs. By borrowing money from the bank at rates that may be as low as 6 percent to 8 percent and developing properties that may have an overall return of 15 percent per year, the leverage gives the investor an amazing return on actual dollars invested. Consider the following:

Investor	Amount Invested	Rate	Amount Earned
Total=	$10,000,000	15%	$1,150,000
Bank+	$8,000,000	8%	$640,000
Trump	$2,000,000	25%	$510,000

Based on these numbers, Trump can actually get a 25 percent return on his investment by using OPM leverage to fund a project he anticipates will yield a 15 percent total return. This is a classic example of how leverage works with real estate.

In other situations, like starting a business or making another speculative investment, the Affluent are able to take higher levels of risk because they don't need the money to pay for living expenses. This allows them to take chances and realize higher investment returns than less risky investments offer.

The other way to leverage OPM is called equity; that is, taking someone else's money and giving them a piece of a business or investment in return. In this situation, the investor takes more risk, but also gets a higher expected return than the bank would get with debt. Though this kind of deal ultimately costs the Affluent a higher piece of their total return, it doesn't have monthly or annual payment requirements like a loan does. This gives the Affluent American more short-term freedom with regard to cash flow because no interest or principal payments are due. In fact, even if there is a profit, the Affluent American may be able to effectively borrow the investor's share simply by not distributing it and reinvesting in the next project.

Equity is best suited for deals that are more speculative and cannot guarantee regular short-term income. Even well-established, publicly traded companies like AT&T, Disney, Oracle, and so on do this on occasion. Many wealthy Americans have learned a lesson from these companies and have offered equity positions to investors to help fund the growth of their family wealth while offering participation in the upside.

Leveraging Intellectual Property

Since World War II, the most significant wealth accumulation has resulted from leveraging intellectual property. This intellectual property could be an idea, like McDonald's fast-food assembly line concept, or a patent on a technology millions of people use, like Microsoft Windows. Other forms of intellectual property include copyrights like the *Star Wars* or *Harry Potter* stories. In each of these cases, an individual or a small group of partners comes up with an idea, proves it could work, legally protects the idea, and then attempts to leverage it in ways where they can make money as a result of other people's efforts. Let's consider three examples.

Bill Gates and Microsoft created the Windows operating system. He (meaning his firm, Microsoft) didn't create a desktop or laptop to run his operating system. He just created a system that other people would run on their computers. Every computer that is built that runs Windows results in a license fee to Microsoft. Gates didn't have to drive the increase in the sale of computers. Rather, he found a way to profit from the efforts of all the other companies that were building and selling computers and from the efforts of all of the software manufacturers that were designing products to make the use of a computer a more enjoyable, and necessary, part of life.

The second example of a person who leveraged intellectual property is George Lucas. Lucas created the *Star Wars* concept. He made a few movies that became classics. The interest in the characters and story line didn't end with the movies. It expanded to action figures, lunch boxes, video games, and countless other items that were based on his concept. Lucas could have tried the do-it-yourself technique, but that would have only yielded a fraction of the financial profit the leveraged approach did. Instead, he licensed his intellectual property to other people. Their efforts made Lucas hundreds of millions, if not billions, of dollars.

The last example of leveraging intellectual property is the McDonald's franchise of restaurants. One successful restaurant might have generated $100,000 to $250,000 of annual profit. An international chain of restaurants whose focus is on fast, consistently prepared food has served three billion customers and is worth billions. One of the authors has had a private tour of one of the three facilities that process and package all of McDonald's food worldwide. It is truly an operation designed to create consistency and maximize leverage.

In less extreme cases, every city has a restaurant, dry cleaner, or other business that isn't particularly profitable on an individual basis. However, the owner may be able to take the unique approach, branding, experience or know-how and open additional locations and achieve a higher level of financial success. This is often how Average Americans use leverage to achieve a certain level of affluence.

Consider This

All three categories of leveraging of assets—leveraging your own money, leveraging other people's money, leveraging intellectual property—can be very valuable. Certainly, many have achieved Super Affluence by doing so. The important lesson is that you need to get the most out of your assets if you want to achieve a higher level of wealth. Now that you know how the Affluent leverage assets, you are ready to learn the most powerful leverage technique—leveraging people!

CHAPTER 9

Leveraging People

While leveraging assets and capital are fundamental wealth-building techniques of the Affluent, they cannot succeed without also leveraging people. At the end of the day, every deal, investment, or transaction needs people to manage or oversee it. No matter how rich you are, you still only have 168 hours per week. To our knowledge, no one has figured out how to be in two or more places at one time. As a result, the single most powerful type of leverage is the leverage of people. By properly leveraging people, you can have multiple levers working at once. This is how Super Affluence is created.

This chapter is going to explain why, and how, to get the most out of leveraging people. More specifically, we will focus on:

1. Leveraging employees
2. Leveraging advisors

Leveraging Employees

The most common method of leveraging people is hiring employees. Those with financial means can afford to hire other people to do jobs for them. The employer has successfully leveraged people if the collective group of employees helps the owner earn more money than the amount it costs the employer in employee salaries and benefits.

Simple Leverage: Pay Less than Productivity

The more employees you have, the more potential leverage opportunities you have. Sometimes you hire staff to support these employees. That is an investment that you hope increases the productivity of the other employees by more than the cost of the administrative help.

In order to leverage your employees successfully and yield a profit, a simple rule is to pay people less than the value they provide your firm. Law firms have followed this lesson for years. For example, law firms may bill out attorneys to their clients at $200 per hour and require the attorneys to bill out 2,000 hours per year. Though the firm collects $400,000 for the services of the particular attorney, it may only spend $300,000 for that particular attorney's salary, benefits and allocated overhead. The firm earns $100,000 per attorney. If the firm can afford to hire 10, 20, or 100 less-experienced attorneys and can find enough work to keep them busy, the senior partners of the firm can earn a very nice living—10 to 25 times that of Average Americans and 5 to 10 times that of a less experienced attorney. In doing so, law firms are leveraging their employees productively; that is, they are training less expensive attorneys to do the work, which enables the senior partners to land contacts and build relationships for the firm.

Benefits to Leveraging Employees

In many circumstances it may not be as easy to quantify the financial return on a leveraged person as it was in the law firm example above. Often there may be equally important qualitative benefits in addition to the quantitative ones. For example, consider the benefits of leveraging employees below:

1. **By leveraging some employees, you are able to spend your time performing tasks that create greater profits.** This is a quantifiable benefit. Using the example above, by having associates do the work, the law firm partners can also do what they are best at: bringing in new business. This is likely a "highest and best use" of their time. What is your highest and best use? Is it possible to pay someone to do the least profitable tasks you currently perform? If so, you can take advantage of leverage.

2. **By leveraging an employee, you are able to spend your time doing things you *want* to do.** This is a qualitative benefit. If you

could have employees perform more of your work, perhaps you could spend time doing something you prefer to do, such as playing golf or spending time with family. This is not being lazy; it is using leverage, not for increased profits but for a better life. What is more important than that?

3. **By leveraging experts, you are able to spend time on your own areas of expertise and save money.** As we will see in the Third Key, leveraging people, specifically advisors, because they have more expertise than you have in certain areas is fundamental to long-term success. While it is possible that you could learn to become a CPA, money manager, or an attorney, learning all of these jobs would not be time well spent. This would take you away from things that are a good use of your time.

   Leveraging people who have expertise is very economical. You can pay them less to help you in certain areas than what it would cost you (in time, money, and aggravation) to learn these fields yourself and then try and do the work yourself. Bill Gates didn't learn how to build computers and George Lucas didn't learn how to make action figures, instead they both benefited from someone else's expertise.

Now that you see how important it is to leverage employees, let's learn the importance of leveraging advisors.

Leveraging Advisors

Leveraging advisors is one application of leverage that Savvy and Super Affluent Americans believe is integral to their success, yet Average Americans ignore or undervalue it. Look at any Affluent person's or Wealthy Family's inner circle and you will almost always see key business and financial advisors who are involved in most of their decisions. The advisors' charge is to help their Affluent clients develop a plan, analyze how every step fits (or doesn't fit) into the plan, and help them avoid numerous pitfalls that could arise from straying from the course.

Simply put, most Affluent Americans, and certainly the Savvy Affluent, recognize that it makes much more sense to hire advisors to help them handle their planning than it does to try to do it themselves. Doing it themselves is not only a bad idea because they undoubtedly do not have the experience and expertise in all the areas needed for planning, but it also violates the principles of leverage. (For more information on this point, see the next Key on building the right team of advisors.)

By doing it themselves, Affluent clients would be spending their time on a suboptimal use of their time instead of in the desired highest and best use of their time. In other words, does it pay for a neurosurgeon to spend three hours of his time researching a disability policy, when a disability expert could do it in one hour? Consider that those three hours could have been spent seeing patients and making more money than the disability expert will be paid. Do you think the doctor would enjoy this research more than playing golf or sitting on the beach? Probably not.

Finally, what is the likelihood that the doctor will make the right analysis and decision on the policy? Is he an expert? Has he looked at hundreds or thousands of policies in the past? Why would you think he would do any better job at this task than the disability expert would do examining the neurosurgeon's patient?

Despite these obvious pitfalls of fighting the principles of leverage, some people make the mistake of foregoing advisors and try to do it themselves. They are stuck in the Average American mindset of saving a penny and losing a dollar. Average Americans do not have the funds to hire advisors, nor do they have the financial complexity to necessitate outside advisors. Affluent Americans should know better. The Savvy Affluent do.

This leads us to a very important statement about the Savvy Affluent:

> The Savvy Affluent realize that time is worth more than money.

Average Americans look for ways to save money by doing things themselves. This may include home or auto repairs, preparing their own taxes, driving instead of flying, or handling other tasks. Affluent Americans look for highly qualified people to handle as many tasks as possible so they can focus on the best possible use of their valuable time.

Because the right advisory team has expertise that the Affluent don't have, the right advisors can do the job in much less time than the Affluent or the wrong advisors could. Given that a job done poorly will need to be repeated, doing it right the first time, even at a higher hourly rate can actually save money in the long run. Additionally, when the Savvy Affluent can pay someone to do what he does best, this gives the Savvy Affluent person more time to do what he does best, which undoubtedly is what will make the most money (selling, inventing, finalizing deals, and so on).

Complexity Demands Leveraging Advisors

We have found that, the greater the wealth of the individual or family, the more important the role of the advisor team. As the client's wealth increases, the more complex the comprehensive financial situation becomes. As the situation grows more complex, the client's need to leverage the advisors' expertise and experience to save time and maximize total benefit increases exponentially.

To illustrate how complexity grows exponentially, let's consider the following two situations. Figure 9.1 shows the relationship between two people. Figure 9.2 shows the six different relationships that exist when you have four people in a group.

In Figure 9.1, you can see that Dick and Jane have one relationship. There is only one relationship when you have two people. This seems relatively easy to manage as you have two people and only one relationship. Let us see what happens to the complexity of the interactions when we have four people in a group. This is illustrated in Figure 9.2.

Figure 9.1   Situation 1: Relationship between Two People

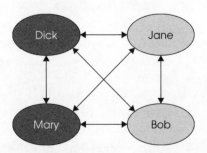

Figure 9.2   Situation 2: Relationships between Four People

In Figure 9.2 you will see Dick, Jane, Mary, and Bob. There are two additional people than we saw in Figure 9.1. Doubling the number of people in the group actually increased the unique interactions by 500 percent—from one interaction to six interactions (Dick and Jane, Dick and Mary, Dick and Bob, Jane and Mary, Jane and Bob, Mary and Bob). That means that it is at least 500 percent more work to manage four businesses or elements of a comprehensive financial plan than it is to manage two businesses or elements of a financial plan. If you have eight businesses or elements of a plan, then you have 56 different interactions to monitor. You can see how the complexity of the situation increases quickly.

To see how this general theory of complexity can be practically applied to the planning of the Affluent, we need to understand what the Affluent's concerns are. Below is a partial list of common financial planning concerns of the Affluent:

- Managing growth of the assets.
- Managing lawsuit risks from employees, customers, and competitors.
- Protecting assets from eventual lawsuits.
- Managing the investment risk while attempting to grow assets.
- Managing tax liabilities to maximize after-tax growth.
- Managing business succession and estate planning concerns.
- Protecting family members against a premature death or disability.
- Protecting family's inheritance against lawsuits, taxes, and divorce.

Surprisingly, the Affluent worry about all of the aforementioned items while continuing to do *everything* they did to help them reach their current level of success. If you think this is impossible, you are correct. It is impossible to do all of these things as a one man show. Leveraging advisors is essential; it is a fundamental precursor of long-term success.

Consider This

This Key explained why leverage is such an important key to achieving Affluence, building your fortune, and protecting your assets. You learned how the Affluent leverage their own assets, other people's money, and people. You learned that the biggest limitation to leverage is one's capacity. This can be limited time or limited money. In either case, the best way to increase your capacity is to build a team of experts to help you efficiently maximize leverage and increase your capacity for leverage. This is the focus of the next part—the Third Key—Building the Right Team of Advisors.

THE THIRD KEY

BUILD THE RIGHT TEAM OF ADVISORS

In the Second Key, you learned how the Savvy Affluent create and maintain wealth by leveraging effort, assets, and people. You also learned that leveraging people is the most powerful method of leverage, and that leveraging advisors is the most powerful way to leverage people. Once you figure out how to use leverage to achieve even a modest level of affluence, learning how to leverage advisors is important if you want to maintain any level of affluence and is integral if you want to achieve Super Affluence.

In the Third Key we will examine the types of advisors that exist, the benefits and limitations of each, point out some common pitfalls that both Average Americans and nonSavvy Affluent Americans face with advisors, and ultimately recommend how to work with the right team of advisors.

CHAPTER 10

The Value of Advisors

Affluent Americans achieve their wealth and income through leverage. As discussed in the Second Key, the Savvy Affluent achieve this profitable leverage by adding employees, making additional investments, and creating new businesses. These additional steps to increase leverage exponentially increase the complexity of their comprehensive financial plans. This complexity necessitates the need for the Savvy Affluent to rely on a team of advisors for assistance. Without a team, Average Americans struggle to find free time in their much less complex lives. On the other hand, Affluent Americans could never manage leverage if they didn't have a team. To illustrate the value of advisors, refer to the equation below:

Affluence can only be achieved through leverage.

+

Leverage can only be managed with a team of advisors.

=

Affluence can only be achieved with a team of advisors managing the leverage.

In this chapter, we will discuss the reason *why* the Affluent need a team of knowledgeable and diverse advisors. Then we will discuss how to maximize the value of advisors and suggest tips for working with your team.

Managing Complexity: The Need for Advisors

Most people realize that wealth creates complexity. What the Savvy Affluent have realized is that the management of complexity and leverage is not the job of a traffic cop. As wealth grows, the number of complicated, technical risks that the investor faces also grows exponentially.

For example, when you go from running a sole proprietorship to having one employee, you may not see a major difference, but that couldn't be further from the truth. The addition of just one employee creates a need for:

- Payroll creation, funding, and payments.
- Regular payroll tax payments (or you can go to jail).
- Withholding tax filings and payments.
- Workers compensation insurance or fund payments.
- Occupation Safety Hazard Association compliance.
- Separate retirement plan (ERISA) regulations and contribution requirements.
- A host of other state and federal reporting requirements.

In addition to all of the aforementioned specific issues, the leverage of assets also increases the need for more general categories of planning, like asset protection, banking (private and commercial), business planning, financial planning, income tax management, investing, life insurance analysis, disability insurance analysis, property and casualty insurance analysis, long-term care insurance analysis, educational funding, retirement planning, family law, gift and estate tax planning, charitable planning, Medicaid planning, and a host of other areas.

Each category of planning has its own technical areas that can be competently handled by an advisor who has expertise in that area. Although it is common to find an advisor who has expertise in a few areas, there is also some overlap where two advisors are needed for one of the categories above. For example, tax issues are typically handled by a both a tax attorney and a CPA. As a result, there is no way that a small team of two or three advisors could possibly handle the needs of a Super Affluent Family or a Wealthy Family. This means that, over a lifetime, a member of the Affluent may need to leverage the services of six or more advisors at the same time and the Super Affluent may need to leverage the services of 10 or more advisors to maintain Affluence.

While this number of advisors may seem overwhelming, consider your personal health. As an adult, you certainly do not see the same obstetrician who delivered you or the pediatrician who treated you as a child for all of your ailments. If you have an injury, you may need to see an orthopedist. If you have a skin problem, you may see a dermatologist. If you develop digestive issues, you may see a gastroenterologist. Most adults receive help from at least 10 to 15 different physicians from a variety of specialties.

Nonetheless, if you are like most people, you would love to be able to keep the same general physician (i.e., internist or family doctor) for as long as possible. Having someone you know and trust as your primary contact is very comforting. This primary care physician can help explain situations to you, find the right specialists if a need for one arises, and help communicate with you as complicated procedures take place. Keep this in mind.

Throughout the book, there will be discussion of your team of advisors. In the Tenth Key, we will discuss the planning process that is necessary to integrate all of the important lessons in this book and the secrets of the Affluent. One of your advisors on this team is going to be the primary contact to help you through it all.

Working with Your Team

Having the right team of advisors is another step in the right direction, but there is still more to do. Having a team that is run poorly is like having an alarm on your house and never turning it on. You have to work with the team for the team to provide any value. In our discussion with the partners of The Founders Group in San Diego, we learned some valuable lessons about the Affluent. The Founders Group only deals with families with businesses or net worth above $25 million. They found that the most efficient Affluent clients and Wealthy Families arranged semiannual, all-day and multiple day meetings with all of their advisors and family members. Sometimes, the costs of flying in advisors to participate in these meetings and paying them their hourly wages can total $50,000 per year.

According to Joe Strazzeri of The Founders Group:

> The families that make this effort to spend time with the experts on their team generally see these meetings as the family's most productive use of time and money all year.

Tips for Working within a Team

As with any collaborative endeavor, the collection of people is not enough to ensure success. Every conference call and meeting must have an agenda and someone to manage the meeting to make sure all important items are handled in the allotted time. It is common to put one of the advisors in charge of organizing and facilitating information flow among the other advisors. This is usually a financial planner and not an accountant or attorney. Within the group, you need to identify roles and responsibilities and make one person accountable for the completion of each task.

When considering different options, it is wonderful when there is a unanimous decision on whether or not to go in a particular direction. However, many decisions will not be unanimous. You need to set the rules (51 percent, 66 percent, 80 percent) concerning how decisions are to be made within the group and share them with the group. If they know how you are going to make decisions, it will make it easier for them to participate in the group and allow them to continue to participate even when the rest of the group disagrees with a particular decision.

Consider This

You can't possibly expect to achieve Affluence while maintaining your sanity unless you build the right team of advisors. Trying to achieve financial success without a team of advisors is like trying to get 100 percent of your healthcare from one doctor. The pediatrician or family care physician you had may have been great. But, without the help of orthopedists, dermatologists, neurologists, obstetricians, and dozens of other specialists, your health would certainly suffer. Society has benefited from the developing expertise in different areas of medicine. The Savvy Affluent have benefited from the development of expertise in different financial planning areas. You can, too.

The Savvy Affluent realize that the process of building and maintaining wealth in today's world brings with it potential challenges from all areas of law, accounting, finance, insurance, and business. They accept this reality and embrace the need to leverage the expertise of advisors in all of the areas mentioned above. They realize that the task of financial planning needs to be a coordinated effort within a multidisciplinary team of advisors.

What types of advisors do the Affluent utilize? How do you divide the responsibilities within the team? How do you choose the actual advisors? In the next two chapters, we will answer all of these questions.

CHAPTER

11

Types of Advisors

Before you can choose your advisors, delegate responsibilities to team members, or begin to benefit from the leverage of advisors, you need to understand the types of advisors who could be part of the Savvy Affluent's advisor team. In this chapter, we provide a list that covers the team members that 90 percent of situations require. Some advisors, like mortgage brokers, are not discussed because they play more of a transactional role at different points in the client's lifetime. The other advisors may review mortgages, but the mortgage broker typically is looking for the lowest price and isn't changing loan offers based on the other pieces of the comprehensive financial plan. In addition, unique circumstances may call for some teams to require additional advisors with very unique skills. Below is the list of the most common advisors:

- Accountant
- Asset Protect Attorney
- Estate Planning Attorney
- Tax Attorney
- Insurance Professional
- Investment Advisor
- Financial Planner

Accountant

The term *accountant* will be used to generically describe an accountant, Certified Public Accountant (CPA), or Enrolled Agent (EA).

What they do: Accountants (and CPAs and EAs) are trained and licensed to prepare tax returns for submission to the Internal Revenue Service. Each state has its own licensing and accreditation procedures for accountants and CPAs. CPAs must pass a multipart exam to earn accreditation. Enrolled Agents complete a federal licensing process. In all situations, these advisors primarily prepare tax returns. In the most desirable client-advisor relationship, the accountants also provide clients with advice on tax matters.

Limitations of an Accountant:

1. The U.S. tax law is the most complex set of rules created by humankind, and significant changes are made to these rules every year. Therefore, it is impossible for any accountant to be well-versed in all areas of tax law. More likely, the accountant will be an expert in one or two areas out of 20 or more potential areas. Tax planning is like medicine—each area has become so complex that one can't possibly expect to become an expert in many disciplines. In the medical arena, most patients and physicians realize that one doctor can't do everything. They both readily accept being referred to, or referring patients to, other physicians. A gastroenterologist would no sooner make diagnoses for skin conditions than a dermatologist would diagnose and treat an intestinal issue. Unfortunately, this is what happens all the time in the tax arena.

2. Some accountants are comfortable acknowledging what they know and don't know. Some accountants feel responsible for answering all tax questions and resist referring clients to other accountants for specific needs for fear of losing the client altogether. This is more of a limitation of an individual than it is a limitation of the profession as a whole, but it should be recognized.

3. Conflict of interest may arise. Many accountants are beginning to look for additional revenue opportunities by getting licensed in life insurance and securities. They then recommend particular investment and insurance products to their clients. This can create significant conflicts of interest with clients who are looking for tax advice but who are getting financial suggestions. Clients should be concerned about how accountants, who deal with very complex tax issues,

find time to become experts in insurance and investments. Revisiting our doctor analogy, how could a practicing dermatologist find the time to learn oncology on the side and offer a high level of cancer treatment to the dermatology clients who develop cancer? Savvy patients would prefer a full-time oncologist in that situation. Despite the conflict and impracticality, many CPAs with years of accounting experience are now trying to increase revenue by advising clients on investments and insurance when they have little or no practical experience in these areas.

Asset Protection Attorneys

The term *asset protection attorney* describes an attorney who has strong working knowledge and experience in the area of protection from creditors. There is no state-specific accreditation for asset protection. All attorneys must be admitted to the Bar Association in the state(s) in which they wish to practice.

What they do: Asset protection attorneys specialize in the field of asset protection. They help clients arrange their personal and business affairs in a manner that protects their wealth from potential future lawsuits and other creditor risks. Because many of the tools used in asset protection are the same tools used in estate planning and business planning, it is common for asset protection attorneys to also have a strong working knowledge in those areas as well.

Limitations of Asset Protection Attorneys:

1. Because asset protection is a relatively new field of law and most attorneys are overwhelmed in their primary fields of interest (litigation, business law, estate planning, and so on), few attorneys have found the time and had the interest to study this important field of law. As a result there are very few attorneys who are experts in this area. Though one of the co-authors (Mr. Mandell) specializes in this area, he is one of fewer than 50 attorneys in the country whose focus is exclusively on asset protection. If we had the time to research this point, we might find the total number of asset protection attorneys to be closer to 25.

2. Asset protection attorneys are not estate planning or tax attorneys—or any other type of attorney, for that matter.

Do not expect that you will get estate planning or tax advice from these attorneys unless they also have specific training in these areas. However, your asset protection attorney should be willing to interact with attorneys from the other fields who will be necessary to help you complete your planning.

Estate Planning Attorneys

An estate planning attorney has strong working knowledge and experience in the area of trusts, probate, and estate planning. There is a state-specific accreditation for estate planning in many states. All attorneys must be admitted to the Bar Association in the state(s) in which they wish to practice.

What they do: Estate planning attorneys focus on helping families address the financial needs that arise at death or as death approaches. Estate planning attorneys are required to draft estate planning documents such as wills, limited partnerships, and various types of trusts. They have a strong working knowledge of gift, estate, and generation-skipping tax issues. Though many estate planning issues are federal issues, there are some state-specific issues that require a local attorney. For very complex issues, the Savvy and Super Affluent will often use the best estate planning attorney they can find (anywhere in the United States) and have a local attorney co-counsel the case so state-specific issues can be addressed.

Limitations:

1. We have seen many estate planning attorneys who create estate plans using almost exclusively legal tools they can be paid to create. They have little experience or knowledge of important financial vehicles that can play a significant role in the estate planning of Affluent Families. By excluding entire categories of planning tools (most often cash value life insurance), these attorneys often fail to help their clients create the liquidity necessary to handle the financial obligations that arise at death. Sometimes attorneys shy away from recommending financial and insurance tools because they do not properly understand these tools and they fear the potential liability of recommending products they don't understand. The response to this limitation is to do what the Savvy Affluent do—make sure there are attorneys and insurance

experts on the financial planning team so the clients can get the best combination of planning tools to most efficiently meet their needs.

2. Estate planning attorneys generally are not asset protection or (income) tax attorneys either. While attorneys in these different fields may use similar legal tools from time to time, that is not enough. A scalpel in the hands of a surgeon can be an important tool to help save a life. A scalpel in the hands of a mugger is a knife that can kill someone. We are not suggesting that one type of attorney is an angel and one is a devil (readers are encouraged to insert their own jokes here, now). We are merely saying that tools used differently can have very different outcomes and can offer varying benefits. For this reason, it is best to involve specialists in asset protection and income tax to work with the estate planning attorney, if needed.

Tax Attorney

A tax attorney has strong working knowledge and experience in the area of income tax and possibly estate tax. There is a state-specific accreditation for tax attorneys in many states. Most tax attorneys have added another year of school beyond law school to earn a degree in taxation called an LLM. All attorneys must be admitted to the Bar Association in the state(s) in which they wish to practice.

What they do: Tax planning attorneys are required to give advice on the tax ramifications of certain transactions (i.e., selling an appreciated asset) or strategies and to assist with the creation of the legal documents used in these transactions. These specialized attorneys have a strong working knowledge of income and capital gains tax issues, as well as taxation of corporations, partnerships, and other entities. Since most state taxes are based on federal taxes, most tax attorneys can handle all of the clients' tax issues.

Limitations:

1. Tax attorneys do not generally prepare tax returns. Though they have a very strong working knowledge of tax law, the preparation of tax returns is a specialty that is generally left to the accountant (discussed previously).

2. Though some of these attorneys are also experts in estate planning, most do not work in this area regularly. This results in two limitations:

   a. Tax attorneys may not be aware of potential estate planning solutions that are more appropriate for Affluent and Super Affluent clients.

   b. They are likely to have very limited knowledge of financial and insurance vehicles and their place within an estate plan because they are tax attorneys first and estate planning attorneys second. If full-time estate planning attorneys don't have time to fully understand financial vehicles, how could you expect part-time estate planning attorneys with another full-time focus to have time?

3. In addition, tax planning attorneys generally are not asset protection attorneys. While they may know a bit about this area, the same comparison of the surgeon and the mugger needs to be revisited here—a little knowledge can be dangerous. It is best to involve specialists in asset protection and estate planning to work with the tax planning attorney.

Insurance Professionals

Insurance professional is a term used to describe life and health (life) or property and casualty (P&C) insurance agents. Life and P&C agents must have a resident agent license in the state in which they reside. In some states, a week-long course and a state-sponsored exam are required to earn a license. They can apply for nonresident licenses in the other states so that they can provide insurance to clients in those states as well. Certified financial planners, accountants, investment advisors, and attorneys can all secure life insurance licenses. Many of their regulatory agencies require those advisors to disclose the potential conflict to clients when the advisor could benefit from multiple income sources (professional fees and insurance commissions).

What they do: At the most basic level, insurance professionals provide various types of insurance policies to clients. Some insurance professionals also offer financial planning or investment solutions. The life insurance professional works closely with the estate planning attorney to help clients meet their estate planning needs. If you are interested in purchasing any type of insurance, it is imperative that you consult with a licensed insurance professional experienced in the insurance area at issue. Typically, one person can only be an expert in one area of insurance. If you look at the list of types of insurance below, you can see why it is so important to work with a firm (like our firm O'Dell Jarvis Mandell—www.ojmgroup.com) that has a number of insurance and investment experts on staff to help clients with their various insurance and investment needs.

Life Insurance   In the Ninth Key, you will learn why life insurance is a fundamental building block of wealth planning for the Savvy Affluent. By offering tax benefits, wealth accumulation, liquidity, and protection against financial disasters, life insurance should play a role in every affluent client's financial plan.

Disability Income Insurance   In the Eighth Key, you will learn how to protect your family from financial disasters. For the Working Affluent, the single greatest asset may be one's earning potential. Disability income insurance is required for every person whose income is needed for the family to pay bills or meet other financial needs. Disability income insurance should be handled by a life and health insurance agent who specializes in disability.

Long-Term Care Insurance   Also in the Eighth Key, you will learn that long-term care insurance (LTCI) is an important tool for Affluent Families who want to avoid losing their hard-earned wealth to a Medicaid spend-down to pay for nursing home care, home care, hospice, and a host of other services most of us will need in our final years. Long-term care insurance covers health-related expenses that will not be covered by social or private insurance in retirement. In addition, some families use long-term care insurance to protect retirement savings for their heirs (as an inheritance). LTCI can be handled by life insurance agents; some states require the completion of additional LTCI-specific training.

Property and Casualty Insurance   Property and casualty (P&C) insurance is a separate set of insurances that require different training and licensure from that required for the aforementioned types of insurance. P&C insurances are very common even though you may not have heard the acronym P&C before. These coverages include: homeowners, personal auto, commercial auto, professional liability insurance, worker's compensation, umbrella, premises, product liability, flood, hurricane, and many other policies. To protect wealth, the Affluent need to address P&C concerns by adding an insurance agent who is an expert in these areas.

Limitations of Insurance Professionals:

1. Some are working for the insurance company or themselves and not for you. Some insurance agents have "career agent" contracts with certain insurance companies like Mass Mutual or The Principal. These agents are highly motivated to sell a specific company's products because they must sell a certain amount of these products or lose their health and financial benefits. Other insurance companies, like Northwestern Mutual, have "captive" agents who can only offer you products from one company. They can't shop for the best policy or even pretend to have an unbiased position or to have your best interests in mind. Many insurance agents are neither career nor captive agents. Even independent agents will have a personal preference for certain companies or products. The Savvy Affluent always work with independent insurance professionals who have a range of options they can offer and can display a track record of using different companies to meet their clients' best interests. The Savvy Affluent also look for agents of the highest moral character who are experienced and successful enough not to be influenced by slightly higher commissions or other incentives insurance companies offer. One client said about his choice of an agent: "I wanted an agent who wanted my business, but not one who needed my business." Another client said, "I feel comfortable knowing that my agent doesn't need to sell me anything to pay the bills."

2. Many agents work only for commissions. The Savvy Affluent realize that insurance professionals, like all of us, need to make a living. They do not begrudge the insurance professional earning a commission that is inherent in the insurance product (or the real estate agent or any other commission-compensated person). However, when asking for advice and recommendations on how to address a financial need, you have to expect a commission-based advisor to suggest only commission-based products. You may get the

best commission-based solution, but are not likely to receive a recommendation of the best possible solution if that solution doesn't involve a commission. This is the converse limitation to the estate planning attorney who only recommends legal solutions. The Savvy Affluent want independence. This is much more important for certain products, like life insurance, than for less expensive products such as homeowner's or even disability insurance.

Unfortunately, it is true that many of our colleagues in the financial planning and insurance industries allow commissions to bias their view of insurance products. That is why our firm (www.ojmgroup.com) insists that it be compensated on a fee basis for any advice, planning, or product consulting we do. If an insurance professional works like this, he is much less likely to be biased toward lucrative commissions or to *sell* a product at all. Insurance agents who are commission only, need the sale or commission to stay in business and their business model is impacted accordingly. Therefore, the Savvy Affluent prefer to work with fee-based advisors when evaluating insurance products and wealth planning strategies involving insurance.

3. Few have significant training in other areas. To get an insurance license in most states for any of these types of insurance, one typically only, needs to take a weeklong class and pass an exam. Contrast that to earning an MBA (two years); a law license (three years plus bar exam); or a medical license (four years medical school, four to eight years of internship/residency plus board exams).

Because of this limited training, many insurance professionals are simply salespeople without the sophistication or training to do more than sell. The Savvy Affluent look for more in their insurance advisors. This "more" they seek includes education, training, years of experience, and the professional's team. Again, as an example, our firm has three MBAs, two attorneys, and a CPA among its team designations. Our firm is certainly not the only firm with very highly qualified professionals. We just believe it is a good example of what you should look for in a firm if you are looking for well-educated professionals who can help you with many facets of your planning.

Investment Advisor

We use the term *investment advisor* to include money managers and stockbrokers. These advisors have to study and pass a three-hour securities exam and a 90-minute ethics exam or file as an independent Registered Investment Advisor directly with the U.S. Securities and Exchange Commission.

What they do: Investment advisors essentially handle investments for clients. They typically take a fee based on the amount of assets they manage. Stockbrokers may be paid based on the number and size of the trades they make as well.

Limitations:

1. Most fail to adequately manage taxes. The overwhelming majority of money managers primarily handle pension or corporate (institutional) assets, which are not as sensitive to taxes as are the nonpension assets of the Affluent. As a result, these advisors focus on their gross, pretax investment returns. This gross number is what they publish in their marketing material, how they are measured against their peers, how they are compensated, and what they care about. This would be acceptable, except this is exactly what affluent clients are trying to avoid. The affluent client is interested in the *post-tax* return of the investment. We will discuss this in greater detail in the Seventh and Eighth Keys.
2. Most have very little knowledge or interest in any kind of planning. Like most specialists, investment managers have to focus on their craft. Because the world markets are now integrated, investment management is practically a 24-hour-per-day job. When Japan is closing, London is opening. When London is winding down, New York is ramping up. It isn't easy for investment advisors to be well-versed in other planning areas, and it is basically impossible for these advisors to be the quarterback because of their limited knowledge of the other areas.

Financial Planner

We use the term *financial planner* to describe someone who charges a fee to create a financial plan for a client. Sometimes, this is a certified financial planner who has taken six courses and passed an exam. Other times, this person is an accountant who has financial training and may have passed an exam in addition to training as an accountant and possibly passing the CPA exam. Still other times, this could be someone with a master's degree in business administration with a concentration in finance, who has professional experience and has spent two years learning about business, business law, economics, and finance.

What they do: Ideally, a financial planner is someone who uses a planning process to help a client leverage the other planning areas above. The planner integrates all of the planning of the other advisors into one comprehensive plan to help the client's family meet its planning needs. A financial planner should have a strong working knowledge of many of the disciplines. His level of proficiency should be enough to allow him to interact at a high level with the various specialists and add some value in his areas of expertise from time to time. More often than not, this advisor will also act as the coordinator or quarterback for all of the other specialists (like the family doctor in the analogy used earlier). The financial planner provides motivation, understanding, and a disciplined periodic review to make sure all of the various planning areas stay on track. We will develop the discussion of a quarterback for your financial planning team at the end of this Key and in the Tenth Key.

Limitations:

1. Can be a salesperson in disguise. It can be hard to decipher between the true planner and the disguised salesperson who is really focusing on selling something. It is okay for a planner to be used in the implementation of a plan, but you must focus on the plan itself first. Beware of financial plans offered for free. You should know that anything you get for free is not worth much. Further, the business model of such planners is simply to use the plan just to sell you something. How else could they recoup whatever little time they spent on such a plan?

2. Weak knowledge of disciplines. This could be the biggest potential problem. If your financial planner is acting as the quarterback of your planning team, the planner has to understand what the other advisors can and will do and be able to spot important issues in all disciplines. In working with hundreds of insurance agents and financial planners, we

have only met a couple who have a strong working knowledge of asset protection and tax. Insurance and investment (the products they typically sell) knowledge is not sufficient to be a good financial planner. The top four planners at O'Dell Jarvis Mandell have three MBAs, a law degree, and a CPA between them. The best way to test the knowledge of a planner is to have a meeting with the planner, your attorneys, and your accountant. After that meeting, you can ask the other advisors if they think the planner will add much to the team.

Other Advisors

In addition to the list of advisors provided, there are other advisors who may be valuable to leverage including business or corporate attorneys, real estate attorneys, private bankers, charitable planners and attorneys, Medicaid attorneys, and family law attorneys. Each of these experts may have a specific role to play in your planning at some point.

Consider This

You now have an understanding of what types of advisors you could add to your financial planning team. You may even foresee some of the benefits you and your family may achieve from working with the specialists on your team. Before you jump into hiring team members, it is important to learn from the mistakes of thousands of people before you. Read Chapter 12 on the seven mistakes to avoid when building and working with your team. This could save you a lot of time, money, and aggravation in the long run.

CHAPTER 12

Seven Mistakes to Avoid

In our many years as financial planning professionals, we have seen many clients make mistakes when choosing and working with their advisors. These mistakes are as common with Average Americans as they are with Affluent Americans. However, these mistakes seldom occur with the Savvy Affluent. We know this because many of our clients are members of the Savvy Affluent or Super Affluent and have effectively built their fortunes and protected their assets by building the right team of advisors. There are seven pitfalls of choosing and working with advisors on your financial plans. The seven pitfalls to avoid are:

1. Friends and family as advisors.
2. Choosing only local team members.
3. "If it ain't broke, don't fix it."
4. Never getting a second opinion.
5. Hiring yes-men and women.
6. Not accepting that complexity requires outside experts.
7. Failing to insist on advisor coordination.

In this chapter, we will examine these seven pitfalls and explain how each can be avoided.

Pitfall #1: Friends and Family as Advisors

One of the biggest mistakes we see is the inclusion of friends and family in the planning team. We can't fault people for thinking that trust is important when choosing people to help manage money.

Trust is very important. However, unless you are willing to lose the relationship to achieve your financial goals, you should avoid hiring friends and relatives. It is okay to become friendly with your advisors. This can work because the relationship starts as a business relationship. However, when the relationship starts as a friendship, there can often be problems later when you disagree on a course of action or when the advisor makes a mistake.

Pitfall #2: Choosing only Local Team Members

The best available team members need not be the best available advisors in your neighborhood. We have helped clients who built their teams with advisors from all four corners of the country. In today's age of technology, information is easily shared through e-mail, fax, and more recently, online data sharing applications. A surgeon needs to be in the room to do surgery. Financial or legal professionals don't need to be in the room to do what they do. Don't be afraid to enlist the best advisors you can find—even if they are not in your backyard.

Pitfall #3: "If It Ain't Broke, Don't Fix It"

Just because you have worked with the same advisor for 10 or 20 years does not mean you should continue to do so indefinitely. If you applied that logic to medicine, you would still see your pediatrician long after you turned 18 years old. There is a high likelihood that, as you have accumulated wealth, your needs have changed. Though your advisor was there for you when you had simpler needs, you are not required to stay with that advisor when you have outgrown the advisor's or firm's capabilities and expertise.

The first mistake that the overwhelming majority of business owners make in the financial, legal, or tax aspects of their careers is the method they use to choose their initial professional advisors. Whether it is their CPA, investment professional, or attorney, many business owners make a poor choice because their method of choosing an advisor is flawed.

When you consider the typical pattern, this is not surprising. Clients choose their advisors when they are just starting out. The client may need some life or disability insurance, a will, and someone to prepare and file tax returns. Working long hours and without the means to evaluate an advisor, they typically do what other busy people do and take the path of least resistance. They use the advisor their parents or friends use or hire a friend or family member.

Though this unscientific approach is obviously flawed, it serves its purpose when there are bigger challenges at hand (like 20-hour work days). When life is so hectic people feel they just need to make a decision quickly. Often the only criteria clients use when choosing their first advisor is competency and affordability. Like triage nurses in an emergency room, they do not have to be top-trained specialists when all that is needed are some basic stitches. This approach is quite understandable.

What is so alarming to us is not this initial choice of advisor, but the fact that most clients stay with the same advisors who handled their initial financial planning for the rest of their careers. The typical justification for this is rarely anything concrete or acceptable. Answers like, "We have been together so long, I'd hate to change now," or "If it ain't broke, don't fix it," are unpersuasive. Further, this begs the question: "How do you know it ain't broke if you don't get a second opinion?"

Most alarming to us is when a client stays with an advisor when the client has clearly outgrown the expertise of the advisor. Consider the case study of Oscar the Boat Builder.

Case Study: Oscar the Boat Builder

Oscar, a boat builder in Florida, contacted our firm after reading our last book. While his income was more than $1 million per year and he was part of an extremely successful business, Oscar used the same local lawyer who created his wills 20 years ago when he was just starting out. When in Florida, we had a meeting with this attorney.

Not only was this attorney not a tax specialist (yet he was advising Oscar regarding tax law), but he also advised Oscar in other areas that were clearly beyond his expertise. While he was certainly a nice gentleman, and perhaps competent to handle basic planning for someone with minimal tax or estate planning concerns, he had no concept of the advanced techniques that a business owner making more than $1 million per year should be considering. He had no knowledge of asset protection planning or other fairly routine planning that we implement for high-income business owners. While this attorney may have been an acceptable choice for Oscar when he was just starting out, his lack of expertise in more complex areas of financial planning made him a poor choice to continue serving this successful business owner.

Self Test

How did you choose the professional advisors you work with today? How many other professionals did you interview prior to choosing one? Have you periodically interviewed others as your needs have changed?

Pitfall #4: Never Getting a Second Opinion

A good way to grade your existing advisors and test the competencies of potential team members is to get a second opinion. Good advisors are busy helping clients like you. They are professionals and will expect to be paid for the analysis. Sure, there are plenty of advisors who will analyze your situation for free, hoping to dazzle you with their recommendations to earn your investment, insurance, or legal business. However, the goal of these people is to sell you something. If you find good people who could be valuable members of your planning team, they won't need your business, but they will want your business. Treat them fairly by paying for their time and advice. You will learn how organized their firms are and how well they communicate by going through this exercise.

Of the flaws discussed here, never getting a second opinion is the most damaging. Unfortunately, it is also the most common. It is most damaging because a second opinion is the primary way of identifying planning mistakes or noticeable omissions from your planning.

Just as good physicians encourage patients to get second opinions, good advisors should encourage their clients to do the same. This is the only way for you to adequately judge an advisor's performance. You are no more qualified to look at a trust document or tax return and see flaws than we are to examine a report on a chest CT scan and identify a misdiagnosis. With your entire financial future banking on the success of your professional advisors, it amazes us how few of you have paid another professional to review your existing advisor's work. If your life were in jeopardy, wouldn't you get a second opinion? Isn't your financial life important as well?

Consider this true story:

In 2000, David Mandell's prior law firm was retained to perform a self-audit by a longtime client. The client, an extremely successful businessman, was concerned that he might become an

IRS target. He hired the firm to do an audit of his personal and various businesses' income tax returns for the prior five years. What the firm found was shocking.

Even though this client had used four different accounting firms for his various returns (including a well-known 500-plus person firm), the taxes he had paid were far from what he owed. Luckily for him, he had overpaid—by millions of dollars.

That is a true story. Because of the self-imposed audit that David's firm oversaw, the client was able to file for a huge refund from the IRS and state tax agency. Luckily for him, he was concerned about poor tax advice and spent the money to hire the firm to perform the audit.

Self Test

Have you ever paid an outside advisor to review your attorney's work? Your CPA's work? Your investment advisor's work? If not, why not?

Pitfall #5: Hiring Yes-Men and Women

When we asked numerous Affluent clients what advice they would give, we received many suggestions. They included: "Find experts," "Don't look for yes-men," and "Hire people smarter than you are." We put them all in the same category because the end result is the same. The Affluent have wealth because they did something very well. The very successful ones realize that they can't be experts at everything. Some rightfully believe that they could focus on finance or law and probably be just as skillful as some of their advisors. They also realize that it would take many years to achieve that level of expertise. To leverage their time, they choose to hire experts in different disciplines to work for them. They are likely paying someone less per hour than they earn running their businesses, and the advisors are getting it done in less time.

Our Affluent clients have told us that they have enough yes-men in their lives. Interestingly, they cherish the moments when advisors stand up to them and challenge their positions or question their decisions. They see this as an opportunity to improve their position. Some even enjoy the challenge.

Pitfall #6: Not Accepting that Complexity Requires Outside Experts

If you needed a stent put in your aortic valve, you would not go to a general practitioner. Moreover, you would not consult with any specialists outside of cardiology. In fact, you would not even settle for seeing a regular cardiologist. You would seek the help of an interventional cardiologist to handle this procedure. The point is that medicine is highly specialized. If you have a specific issue, you want a physician properly trained and experienced with that particular issue.

Seeking a specialist to help you with your health concerns may be obvious. However, we can attest that in the areas of law, taxation, and finance, business owners completely ignore this lesson. To illustrate this, consider the area of taxation. The ever-changing United States tax law is the most complex set of rules ever created by one society. The lengthy and confusing Internal Revenue Code is only the beginning. IRS revenue rulings, private letter rulings, tax memoranda, announcements, circulars, as well as tax court and federal court cases only make the field all the more difficult to understand. If you step foot in any law library, you may see an entire floor dedicated to tax materials. Suffice it to say, no one person can possibly be an expert in all areas of tax law.

Nevertheless, many business owners will rely on one CPA to serve as a tax advisor in all areas of tax. The taxation issues that require guidance typically include: retirement planning, income structuring (salary vs. bonus), payroll tax, whether to be an "S" or a "C" corporation, whether or not to implement a deferred compensation plan, estate tax planning, taxation on sales of real estate, individual tax returns, corporate tax returns, and buying or selling the practice. All of these areas are actually particular sub-specialties that require a unique knowledge base. If this isn't bad enough, we have seen many business owners ask their tax advisors to guide them in areas that are far outside the realm of tax issues altogether—such as asset protection or investing.

We cannot tell you how many times we have tried to work with a business owner's CPA or attorney to implement a particular strategy and run into the same problem. It was patently obvious that this advisor had little experience in the business owner's area of concern. Ninety-nine percent of the time that this situation occurs, the business owner suffers needlessly.

Because the advisor is so fearful of bringing in another advisor who may steal the client, the attorney or CPA will not admit his shortcomings to the business owner and recommend another specialist. One reasonable alternative would be for the advisor to admit his lack of experience in the area and agree to review the area in question and charge the client for the time needed to get up to speed. Most advisors are afraid to do this. Possibly, they are afraid of the client seeing them as inadequate. Instead, the advisor will tell the client the idea doesn't work without providing any substantial explanation (see the warning signs following). In the end, the business owner remains clueless as to what is really going on and the problem is not solved.

Self Test

Ask your CPA or attorney which tax areas noted above are within his field of expertise. Ask him how he would handle an issue for you beyond this area.

Self Test

Ask your tax advisor if he does asset protection planning. If the answer is yes, ask a follow-up question: "Have you ever created a self-settled foreign asset protection trust?"

Pitfall #7: Failing to Insist on Advisor Coordination

Even if you have a team of highly experienced advisors in the fields of tax, law, insurance, and investments working for you, your plan can still be in complete disarray. If the advisors are not collaborating to utilize their collective expertise to implement a comprehensive, multidisciplinary plan for your benefit, your planning will suffer significantly.

All too often, we see the symptoms of such a lack of coordination. Clients who come to our offices often have paid a technically sound attorney to create a very comprehensive living trust, but the family's assets have not yet been titled to the trust (perhaps making the document useless). We see life insurance policies and life insurance trusts, but the proper steps were not taken to combine the two so the death benefit of the insurance policies may be unnecessarily taxed at a rate of 50 percent. We see investment accounts that are managed like they are in a pension, with no regard for taxation, and the end result is often a 20 percent to 45 percent reduction in the gain of the investments. Conflicting advice from professionals in different areas or a lack of respect for what the other professionals do often leads to planning inertia or just plain bad planning.

Like the radiologist, surgeon, and anesthesiologist, your CPA, attorney, and financial advisors *must* work together. If the surgeon never saw the films or charts and the anesthesiologist and surgeon didn't speak, it would be pretty difficult to successfully treat a surgical patient.

Self Test

How often do your CPA, attorney, financial and insurance advisors sit down to discuss and coordinate your planning? Once per quarter? Once per year? Never?

Warning Signs That You Are Ill-Advised

Do any of these warning signs that you are ill-advised seem familiar? If so, you are likely suffering from flawed professional advisory relationships:

- You have had the same advisors for years—and never interviewed prospective competitors.
- Your advisors don't bring you detailed analyses of your practice and personal situation, complete with helpful suggestions, annually.
- You have no idea what the true subspecialties of your advisors' professions are.
- Your current advisors reject your ideas without detailed written explanations of why they don't make sense for you.
- Your current advisors have never told you that a certain idea required further research for which they would need to charge you.

- You rarely, if ever, have paid for second opinions from other professionals.
- You have trusts, partnerships, or other legal entities that may not be funded.
- Your CPA, attorney, and financial advisors do not meet periodically to coordinate your planning.
- You stay with your current advisor(s) out of lethargy, guilt, or an "if it ain't broke, don't fix it" mentality.

Consider This

In the first Three Keys of *Wealth Secrets,* you have learned very valuable philosophical lessons. The misunderstanding and misuse of these lessons have been the major roadblocks to financial success for most people. Now that you are in the proper mind frame—you are open-minded, you understand the need for leverage, and you understand why you need advisors to help you—you are ready to learn the practical lessons and applications that *Wealth Secrets* offers.

The next Seven Keys to fortune building and asset protection are important lessons we have learned from our most successful clients. Inside each Key, there are many chapters with specific suggestions, strategies, or tools that may or may not be appropriate to help you achieve that goal. One strategy might be perfect for one family and detrimental to another. The proper choice of technique or tool can only be determined by working with your team of advisors to identify your needs, analyze all available options, make a decision, and implement that strategy.

You are now ready to continue. There is no use in focusing on accumulating more wealth if you will only lose it. This is why we want to start by teaching you how to protect your existing and future wealth. The next section—The Fourth Key—will teach you how to your protect assets. Having a team is another step in the right direction, but there is still more to do. Having a team that is run poorly is like having an alarm on your house and never turning it on.

THE FOURTH KEY

PROTECT ASSETS

In the Second Key, you learned how hard it is to make money and build your fortune. In the Third Key, you learned how hard it is to manage the increase in wealth. Since it is so hard to gain wealth, the Affluent want to preserve what they have. Think about the Middle Ages. Kings would build impressive castles. Some would build walls around the towns that surrounded their castles. Others would even build moats around those walls. This is exactly what the Super Affluent do with their wealth. Since affluence is so hard to attain, the protection of wealth is paramount to maintaining wealth over time.

The last 25 years, the most significant period of wealth accumulation in the United States, has fueled the growth in the field of asset protection. Asset protection is the structuring of one's assets in a way that shields them from lawsuits and other creditors. The goal of asset protection planning is simple, but achieving this goal is quite difficult. Asset protection requires expertise from a number of disciplines and must be managed on an ongoing basis to be successful. As a family's wealth or investment portfolio changes, so too, will the plan need to change to adequately protect the wealth.

In this Key, we will begin by explaining the importance of asset protection, the sliding scale of asset protection, and common asset protection myths. Then, we will explain a number of tools and strategies that have helped the Affluent and Super Affluent protect their assets, such as:

- State and federal tax exemptions.
- Business and personal insurance.
- Family limited partnerships and limited liability companies.
- Using trusts to shield wealth.
- Strategies for protecting your home.
- Strategies for protecting against divorce.
- Captive insurance companies.

The last tool, captive insurance companies, is reserved only for the most successful business owners. This can be the most efficient and flexible asset protection, risk management, tax and estate planning tool. The Super Affluent use this tool to address many of their planning challenges.

To see which tools work best for protecting your assets, you will have to work with your advisory team and make sure there is at least one asset protection specialist in the group.

CHAPTER 13

The Importance of Asset Protection

Until the last part of the twentieth century, it might have seemed excessive to be concerned with protecting assets from potential lawsuits. Lawsuits were not particularly common and jury awards were reasonable. In the 1980s, the number of lawsuits in the United States skyrocketed and outrageous jury awards became commonplace. Affluent Americans realized that protecting their assets from lawsuits needed to be a focus of any financial plan. Why did lawsuits get out of hand? Why shouldn't we count on any true tort reform? This chapter will answer those questions and should motivate you to take asset protection very seriously.

The Lawsuit Explosion

Why are there so many more lawsuits today? It may be because many Americans see a lawsuit as a way to get rich quick rather than as a way to make someone whole and achieve justice for someone who was wronged by another. In our society, many people believe that misfortune is an opportunity to place blame and seek financial reparations—even if another person wasn't at fault for the misfortune. Unfortunately, juries routinely accept the idea that someone must pay for alleged wrongdoings and often disregard the facts of the case when reaching a verdict. Swayed by emotion and bias, juries sometimes give away large sums of money to unfortunate victims—even when the defendants were not to blame for the misfortune.

To illustrate this point, let's consider the decisions reached in some cases you may have read about in your daily newspaper:

> **Lawsuit:** A woman sues a franchise eatery because the coffee she spilled in her lap was too hot.
> **Decision:** Woman receives $2.6 million.
> **Lawsuit:** A trespasser is injured while burglarizing a home.
> **Decision:** Burglar receives thousands of dollars.
> **Lawsuit:** A Pennsylvania woman sues a physician claiming to have lost her psychic powers during a routine set of tests.
> **Decision:** Woman receives a jury award for $690,000.

After reading the large settlements these ordinary people receive, it seems rational that other people would begin to ask themselves, "Why not me?" The more press these cases receive, the greater the reinforcement of this belief. The greater the number of people who try to work the system, the more people who will actually succeed. Each new outrageous success gains more press and the vicious cycle of lawsuits continues to grow.

The Savvy Affluent realize that this lawsuit trend cannot be ignored. They insist on having their advisors devise financial plans that address the protection of their assets. They realize that they have something to lose if they are sued, and the plaintiff often has nothing to lose. This is especially true in the United States' legal system.

American Rule of Legal Fees

Did you know that in virtually every other legal system in the world, a plaintiff who sues unsuccessfully has to pay the defendant's legal bills? That is correct. This rule, called the "British Rule" regarding civil legal fees, effectively keeps people from suing others unless they truly think they have a case with merit. If a plaintiff does not have a very good case, he risks not only paying his own attorney's fees, but also those of the defendant.

This is not the situation in the United States. In U.S. courts, we follow the "American Rule" that dictates that each side pays its legal fees regardless of the outcome of the case. This rule was originally created so that people wouldn't be discouraged from suing big business. Though this rule may have had some positive impact, it has created two negative consequences:

1. As a plaintiff, you have a lot less to lose if you bring a meritless case. In fact, with the prevalence of contingency fee attorneys, plaintiffs literally are in a no-lose situation as they have no skin in the game. This is because contingency fee attorneys do not charge their clients hourly fees. Their only compensation is a percentage of the judgment awards of the cases they win.
2. As a defendant, a winning outcome is still a losing proposition. We say this because a successful defense of a lawsuit still results in significant out-of-pocket defense costs and legal fees. In addition, a legal defense results in time out of work and an unquantifiable amount of stress.

Evidently, the American Rule of legal fees encourages civil lawsuits. Proponents of the system still claim that it allows the poor access to the legal system and is a method for Americans to redress injustices. They may be right. Nonetheless, an unwanted side effect of this rule is that it also allows thousands, if not millions, of frivolous and dubious lawsuits to be filed each year.

People Abuse the Legal System

Whether encouraged by the American Rule of legal fees or not, it is clear that many people simply abuse the legal system for personal gain. This trend is so severe in California that the legislature passed the Vexatious Litigant Act, a law establishing a list of people who routinely abuse the legal system by filing too many frivolous lawsuits. These individuals cannot be denied their constitutional right to sue. However, this act restricts them from filing suits without attorneys unless they receive a judge's permission. This list is available to every lawyer in the state.

Who is on this list? The people on this list are those who, in the court's opinion, have repeatedly filed lawsuits lacking merit or have engaged in other frivolous and abusive tactics. Two offensive examples of people on this list include the following:

1. A Los Angeles claimant who filed more than 200 lawsuits in seven years. Very few of the suits were successful.
2. Defensive plaintiffs. A court clerk recommended certain individuals for this list. These individuals made the clerk a lawsuit target and the clerk was then sued 11 times in two years—unsuccessfully. The clerk's reaction: "I do not exaggerate when I say I am extremely frightened by these people." (*The Sacramento Bee*, November 26, 1995.)

Consider This

At this point, we hope you realize what the Savvy Affluent have known for years. In our litigious society, asset protection planning is an integral part of any comprehensive financial plan. Asset protection planning can be integrated into a financial plan to protect assets from lawsuits, allow the Affluent to spend more time making money, and provide peace of mind. In the following chapters, you'll learn about the various tools and techniques you can implement to shield your wealth from lawsuits and other claims.

14

The Sliding Scale of Asset Protection

The most common misconception regarding asset protection is the idea that an asset is either "protected" or "unprotected." This black or white analysis is no more accurate in the field of asset protection than it is in the field of medicine. In fact, asset protection attorneys are very similar to physicians in how they approach a client. In this chapter, we will discuss the way in which advisors measure a client's assets by using a sliding scale. Then, we will suggest ways to protect assets, avoid high-risk assets, and achieve a high level of protection.

The Sliding Scale and Scores

In order to measure the assets of a client, advisors use a sliding scale that rates the client's good and bad financial habits. Like physicians, asset protection professionals will first try to get a client to avoid bad habits. For a medical patient, bad habits might mean smoking, drinking too much, or eating a poor diet. For a client of ours, bad habits might include owning property in their own name, owning property jointly with a spouse, or failing to maximize the percentage of exempt assets in an investment portfolio.

Like a doctor who judges the severity of a patient's illness, asset protection specialists use a rating system to determine the protection or vulnerability of a client's particular asset. The sliding scale runs from −5 (totally vulnerable) to +5 (superior protection).

As you have probably already guessed, the Savvy Affluent and Wealthy Families generally score closer to the +5, superior protection, end of the scale. Those who do not have efficient and savvy financial plans or who are averse to planning generally score on the negative side of the scale.

When most clients initially come to see us, their asset planning scores are overwhelmingly on the negative side of the scale. The reason for this score varies. Typically, personal assets are owned jointly (−3) or in their individual name (−5). Both of these ownership forms provide little protection from lawsuits and may also have negative tax and estate planning implications.

Many businesses also have asset planning scores that are overwhelmingly negative. The worst way to operate a business or title assets is a general partnership (−5). For all other business entities, liability from operations is always a concern. For this reason, owning any business assets within an operating business is extremely unwise (−3).

Before asset protection specialists can achieve a high level of protection for their clients, they must first eliminate the high-risk assets. There are many ways to protect assets, but the most efficient way to avoid high-risk assets and achieve a high level of protection is to utilize exempt assets. This is mentioned briefly next then discussed in greater detail later in the Key.

The Best Protection: Federal and State Exempt Assets

Each state law identifies assets that are absolutely exempt from creditor claims in that state. Federal law also exempts certain assets. Because these assets are inherently protected by law, they enjoy the highest level of protection, a +5 score on the sliding scale. These will be discussed in detail in Chapter 18. For the purpose of *Wealth Secrets*, every asset protection tool or strategy will be compared with exempt assets.

A good example of how state laws can protect assets is found in Texas and Florida, where the homestead exemptions are generally unlimited for personal residences with certain time frame and size limitations or exceptions, and the cash value in life insurance policies is completely protected. At the federal level, bankruptcy law generally affords protection for retirement plans, like pensions and 401(k) plans (+5).

Basic Domestic Legal Tools

In many states, the list of state exemptions is not very generous. Even in those states where the exemptions are broad, we need to make sure that the asset protection goals are balanced with wealth accumulation and investment goals. For these reasons, there will almost always be nonexempt assets in a client's asset mix. For these assets, we must use other protection tools.

In such a situation, the basic asset protection tools are family limited partnerships (FLPs). FLPs provide good asset protection against future lawsuits, allow you to maintain control, and can provide income and estate tax benefits in certain situations. For these reasons, we call FLPs one of the building blocks of a basic asset protection plan.

FLPs provide adequate asset protection and afford asset protection scores somewhere between +1 and +3, depending on the circumstances. Later in this chapter and Key, we will discuss the other building block of a basic asset protection plan—the limited liability company (LLC).

Advanced Strategies

For many clients, a basic asset protection plan is not good enough. For example, a +2 asset protection score is not satisfactory for many Affluent clients. Many of these clients feel the extra expense of an advanced asset protection structure is worth it when significant tax benefits may also be achieved by using these tools. For this reason, these clients use advanced structures to put themselves at a +4 or +5 asset protection score. Like a doctor giving the ultimate medicine or recommending the most effective surgical procedure, asset protection advisors rely on a number of tools to provide ultimate asset protection. These advanced tools include:

Captive insurance companies. Structured offshore or domestically, captive insurance companies can also reach the +5 status when the shares are owned by a second entity such as an irrevocable trust. Successful businesses can use such insurance companies to provide superior asset protection in addition to risk management and potential tax benefits. This is discussed in greater detail in Chapter 24.

Debt shields. Debt shield strategies are ideal for protecting equity in real estate, especially a personal residence. This technique helps achieve a +1 to +5 rating. The exact score depends on the funding vehicles used in this technique. When structured properly, after-tax wealth can be built while protecting the real estate equity in a superior way.

Consider This

Asset protection planning, like any sophisticated multidisciplinary effort, has degrees of success. Nothing in life is 100 percent certain (except perhaps death and taxes—both of which are discussed in the Fifth and Sixth Keys). For asset protection planning, this adage holds true. In your asset protection plan, make sure you understand the cost and benefits of the various tools you employ. It will not only help you protect the wealth you have already built, but may assist you in building greater after-tax wealth for your retirement and beyond.

15

Asset Protection Myths

Every day, we speak to Affluent clients who harbor significant misconceptions of what asset protection means and how they can achieve the protection they desire in order to maintain their wealth. Perhaps, you also have some of these false beliefs. Five common myths include:

1. My assets are owned jointly with my spouse, so I'm okay.
2. My assets are owned by my spouse, so I'm okay.
3. I am insured, so I'm covered.
4. I can just give assets away if I get into trouble.
5. My living trust (or family trust) provides asset protection.

These myths are dangerous because they lull the individual or family into a false sense of financial security. When you combine these risks with the increased risk of lawsuits, you can see how this false sense of security and lack of adequate planning could hinder the protection of your assets and ultimately be financially devastating.

Myth #1: My Assets Are Owned Jointly with My Spouse, So I'm Okay

Most Affluent clients own homes and other property in joint ownership. As mentioned in Chapter 14, this ownership structure provides little asset protection in both community and noncommunity property states.

In community property states, community assets will be exposed to community debts regardless of title. Community debts include any debt that arises during marriage as a result of an act that helped the community. Certainly any claims resulting from a family business or from an auto accident would be included.

Even in noncommunity property states, joint property is typically at least 50 percent vulnerable to claims against either spouse. Therefore, in most states, at least 50 percent of such property will be vulnerable, and all the other problems associated with joint property still exist in noncommunity property states.

Myth #2: My Assets Are Owned by My Spouse, So I'm Okay

One of the most common misconceptions about asset protection is that assets in your spouse's name can't be touched. We can't tell you how many people have come to us with their assets in the name of one spouse and assumed those assets were protected against claims against the other. This often happens when one spouse has significant exposure because of a high-liability job, such as a physician or real estate developer. Unfortunately, simply transferring title of an asset to the nonvulnerable spouse does not protect the asset. The creditor is often able to seize assets titled in the name of the spouse of the debtor by proving that the asset was purchased by funds earned by the debtor. In order to determine if the asset is reversible, three questions can be asked:

1. Was the vulnerable spouse's income used to purchase the asset?
2. Has the vulnerable spouse used the asset or benefited from it at any time?
3. Does the vulnerable spouse have any control over the asset?

If the answer is "yes" to any of these questions, then the creditor has a strong claim that the "substance" of the arrangement is that the vulnerable spouse owns half the asset, rather than the "form." A winning "substance over form" argument would allow the creditor to attach, lien, or levy the asset.

Important Note

If you think holding assets in your child's name will protect those assets, you are wrong. Please consider implementing the strategies discussed later in this Key.

Myth #3: I Am Insured, So I'm Covered

While we strongly advocate insurance as the Affluent's first line of defense, an insurance policy is 50 pages long for a reason. Within those numerous pages, there are a variety of exclusions and exceptions to exclusions that most people never take the time to read, let alone understand. Even if you do have insurance and the policy does cover the risk in question, there are still risks of underinsurance, strict liability, and bankruptcy of the insurance company. In any of these cases, you could be left with the sole financial responsibility for the loss. Lastly, with losses that are covered within coverage limits, you still may see your future premiums go up significantly.

Myth #4: I Can Just Give Assets Away if I Get into Trouble

Another common misconception of asset protection is that you can just give away or transfer your assets if you ever get sued. If this were the case, you could just hide your assets when necessary. You wouldn't need an asset protection specialist; you would only need a shovel and some good mapmaking skills so you could find your buried treasure later.

To prevent debtors from simply giving away their assets if they get into trouble, laws against fraudulent transfers (or fraudulent conveyances) have been enacted. In a nutshell, if you make an asset transfer after an incident takes place (whether you knew about the pending lawsuit or not), the judge has the right to rule the transfer a fraudulent conveyance and order the asset to be returned to the transferor.

If you have been sued or suspect that you may be sued, there are other ways you can protect yourself. If you have a problem and fear that you may lose a sizeable judgment, then we recommend you implement some type of proactive planning as soon as possible. Typically, reactive last-minute strategies are riskier and may be much more expensive than the highly successful strategies that can be implemented when there are no creditors lurking.

Myth #5: My Living Trust (or Family Trust) Provides Asset Protection

There have been countless instances where clients have come to us with the impression that their revocable living trust provides asset protection. While you are alive, this is simply not true. Revocable trust assets are fully attachable by any creditor. Later in this Key, you will read about irrevocable trusts and how they provide varying levels of asset protection for you and your heirs in addition to the estate planning they are primarily designed to facilitate. A living trust does provide some asset protection, but that protection does not exist until one spouse dies. No matter how much your attorney charges, dying seems to be too big a price to pay for asset protection planning.

Consider This

Don't be concerned or alarmed if you believed any of these asset protection myths. Don't be disappointed if your perceived protection has just been proved inadequate. With the myths dispelled, you can now focus on how the Savvy Affluent implement asset protection plans. The next chapters should be very helpful in this regard.

16

The Mixed Blessing of Property and Casualty Insurance

As principals of a financial firm that provides all types of financial planning, business consulting, insurance analysis, and product implementation, we see that various types of insurance policies are required in every Affluent client's financial plan. Certainly, property and casualty insurance is one of the tools for asset protection. In this chapter, we will define property and casualty insurance coverage and discuss its uses and limitations in the context of asset protection planning.

What Is P&C Insurance?

There are two categories of insurance: life and health (L&H) and property and casualty (P&C). L&H insurance includes all life insurance and health insurance, as well as disability insurance and long-term care insurance. P&C insurance is designed to protect against property and casualty losses. Often P&C insurance is referred to as "property and liability" insurance because it protects people from all types of liabilities. Examples of P&C coverage include: automobile, homeowners and renters, umbrella liability, professional liability, medical malpractice, general liability, flood, earthquake, premises liability, errors and omissions, product liability, and others.

P&C insurance is designed to indemnify the insured. The insurance industry's definition of indemnify is to "make whole" or to restore the status quo. In other words, if you suffer a loss and have P&C coverage, you will be returned to the same financial place you were before the loss (minus any applicable deductibles or copayments). P&C coverage covers your legal bills and other loss adjustment expenses as well as the actual loss. These other expenses may include the costs of adjusters, estimates, expert testimony, or other associated costs.

P&C insurance coverage is very important given today's litigious society and the American Rule of legal fees. As mentioned in Chapter 13, there is no out-of-pocket cost (or deterrent) to the plaintiff under this system, and the defendant is responsible for the actual loss and associated fees. Therefore, if you didn't have P&C insurance and won your case, you still might have tens, if not hundreds of thousands of dollars in legal fees and related expenses. Therefore, it is usually worth buying insurance to avoid these costs and the inconvenience and aggravation let alone the potential judgment or loss.

Best Uses of P&C Insurance

As we mentioned previously, there are various types of P&C insurance. The most common kinds of P&C insurance are homeowners (or renters) and automobile. Average Americans generally have these forms of coverage because they have a mortgage on their home or because they have a loan or a lease on a car. Yet, someone with a mortgage or car loan does not actually own the home or car yet—the bank or credit department does. As such they require collateral. Buyers must insure the asset while they are paying for it. Once the debt on a home or car is paid off, there is no bank or finance company requiring insurance protection. Of course, the Savvy Affluent never completely drop all insurance on the home. The odds are very slim that they will suffer a house fire or burglary, but they realize the costs of insurance are very small relative to what they could lose.

Another common P&C insurance is the umbrella liability policy. For a very reasonable premium, you can get an additional one to five million dollars of excess liability insurance on top of the liability protection you may have from your homeowner's or auto policies. If you are a member of the Affluent or are in a high liability profession, you should seriously consider an umbrella policy.

Other popular P&C coverages are professional liability insurance and premises and product liability insurance. Depending on your occupation, you may have medical or legal malpractice insurance, which is a form of professional liability insurance. If you own your place of business, you should have premises liability insurance. If your business makes a product (toy, part, widget, and so on), then you should have product liability insurance. This type of P&C insurance will protect you from the losses that might result if a product you place into the stream of commerce malfunctions and causes bodily injury and damages.

Four Limitations of P&C Insurance

While some P&C insurance always makes sense as part of the asset planning for every Savvy Affluent, there are significant limitations to this tool. That is why we typically recommend using the other asset protection tools we describe in this Key in addition to any insurance. Let's examine these limitations individually.

1. **Policy exclusions:** Often we find that clients are completely unaware of the fine print that describes P&C exclusions and policy limitations. Of course, they often become aware of such exclusions after it is too late. For example, many clients fail to realize that their umbrella policy only applies if certain underlying insurance coverage amounts are in effect. If your liability limits on your homeowner's policy or auto policy are too low, then you'll have to pay out of pocket before the umbrella coverage goes into effect.

Case Study: Andy's Daughter's Car Accident

Andy was sued for more than $150,000 when his teenage daughter was involved in a car accident driving his car. Andy was certain that his insurance policy covered his daughter. Only after the accident did his insurance agent tell Andy that the policy no longer covered his daughter, because she had recently moved out of the house. There was an exclusion of coverage for child drivers if they did not reside in the same residence as the parents. Now, Andy alone faced a lawsuit that cost him more than $150,000.

The lesson to be learned from Andy's story is simple: Know your policy!

2. **Inadequate policy limits:** Even if your insurance policy does cover you for a particular lawsuit, the policy coverage may be well below what a jury will award. You must pay any excess above the coverage out of your own pocket. Juries routinely hand out awards in excess of the coverage limits of traditional auto, medical malpractice, employee harassment, and other common P&C insurances. If you were hit by a large judgment, would your policy cover you completely?

3. **Insurance forces you to lose control of the defense:** Even if your insurance policy covers against a specific claim, you must consider the consequences of filing a claim. You have lost negotiating power because your insurance company will dictate when the case is settled and how much the case settlement will be. While this may not matter with a personal injury lawsuit deriving from a car accident, a case against you professionally is another matter. Here you may not want to admit liability and settle, while your insurance company does.

   If the claim involves your professional reputation, you may want to settle the case out of court and away from the public view. There is no guarantee that your insurer will see things the same way. In these situations, if you rely solely on insurance, you lose all ability to negotiate effectively.

4. **Claims bring ever-higher premiums:** An additional consequence of relying solely on insurance to protect you from lawsuits is that once you make claims on the policy, your premiums rise. Given the dismal statistics, you will probably endure a number of lawsuits over the course of your lifetime, and your insurance costs will rise with every claim, even if you are not at fault. Consider the following solution for a construction company owner who, before protecting his assets, relied solely on insurance. After his insurance company defended four unsuccessful lawsuits against him, three of which went to trial, his insurance premiums rose to more than $100,000 per year. Insurance cost him more over the next five years than any one lawsuit. This is not an extreme or atypical example.

Recommendations to Managing Limitations

In order to manage the four limitations of P&C insurance as outlined above, we recommend the following preventive measures:

1. Know your policy.
2. Don't skimp on coverage.
3. Consider an umbrella policy.
4. Utilize other asset protection tools.
5. Own your own insurance company if you have significant risk (read Chapter 24 for more information on this idea).

Consider This

P&C insurance should be a part of every Savvy Affluent client's financial plan. Certain types of coverage, such as homeowner, auto, umbrella, and medical malpractice for physicians, are compulsory. Beyond this, much more must be done if you want to adequately shield assets and discourage claims from the outset. In the next chapters, you'll learn about powerful tools that you can use to protect all assets and enjoy significant tax benefits.

CHAPTER 17

Business Protection Often Ignored

As discussed in the Second Key, the Savvy Affluent use leverage in the form of a business or professional practice to build wealth. The business or practice may be leveraging employees, capital, or even ideas. Regardless of what the business is leveraging, it is typically the critical wealth-building vehicle of the Affluent. Since businesses have valuable assets in addition to their income potential, it makes perfect sense to shield the business from lawsuits and creditor threats. It is completely reasonable for most business owners to focus their asset protection planning on their businesses rather than their personal assets.

In this chapter, we will discuss the importance of shielding your business and protecting your assets from potential financial threats. Then, we will suggest two ways that you can protect your business:

1. Asset segregation using multiple legal entities.
2. The buy-sell agreement.

Is Your Business Protected?

Despite the importance of shielding the business and its assets from potential threats, most business owners are so busy building the business that they ignore protecting the assets of the business. Most asset protection specialists focus their efforts on shielding personal assets from potential threats. Whether the blame falls on the business owner's failure to plan or the attorney's focus on personal assets, the protection of the business assets cannot be ignored.

Would you believe that most businesses we see have maximum lawsuit exposure? If you think we are kidding, let's take a little quiz and see how you fare.

- Is your equipment owned by your business or by you personally?
- Is business real estate owned by your business or by you personally?
- Are any other business assets owned in the name of the operating business?

If you answered "yes" to any of these questions, your business is vulnerable. This is only the beginning of the lawsuit risk quiz. Consider the following questions as well.

- Do you have an employee manual?
- Have you complied with all of OSHA's regulations and state and federal guidelines for worker's compensation, discrimination, harassment, and so on?
- Do you have insurance to cover such violations?

If you answered "no" to any of these questions, you and your business are vulnerable to financial risk. Knowing you are vulnerable is not a problem, unless you don't do anything about it. Now that you know you are vulnerable, you can seek the advice of professionals to help you remedy your situation and protect your assets.

Asset Segregation Using Multiple Entities

If you have read the preceding chapters in this Key, you should have learned the following:

1. Why there is a need to protect assets in a highly litigious society, such as that of the United States.
2. How little asset protection is offered by traditional financial planning.
3. Business owners and real estate investors have significantly more asset protection risk than those who do not own a business or rental properties.

As a result of these facts, there is an increased need to protect multiple assets or multiple properties from the various financial risks that threaten them. This can be done through asset segregation using multiple legal entities.

In order to understand the importance of asset segregation using multiple legal entities consider the example of separating ownership of real estate and equipment from the operating business. There are three reasons to separate the ownership of the real estate and equipment (RE) from the operating business. First, the RE is a valuable asset that should be isolated from any liability created by the business. Second, the RE itself may cause liability. That liability could be in the form of slip and fall claims from people coming and going on the premises or claims deriving from the equipment injuring someone. If the RE and the business are operated by the same legal entity, all eggs are in the same basket. This means that the claim will be against an entity that has something to lose—those assets.

By separating the RE from the business, you have asset-protected the business. By isolating the business from the real estate, you may have removed the premises liability and equipment liability created by the business's real estate. In doing so, each entity is protected from the other. This is the kind of planning the Savvy Affluent do.

What Separation Involves

Separating ownership simply involves creating a new limited liability company and transferring ownership of the real estate to the new LLC. Because the RE is no longer owned by the operating business, employees suing the business have no claim against this RE or the LLC that owns the RE. So long as the transfer to the LLC is done properly and the formalities of the new arrangement are respected, this protection will hold.

Your Financial Incentive

For simplicity's sake, we will assume that you have a single-owner business even though these techniques work equally well for businesses with multiple owners.

Let's say that you own your business RE through an LLC that is initially owned by you and your spouse. Over time, you can gift ownership interests to children, while maintaining 100 percent

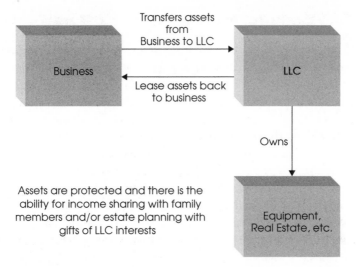

Figure 17.1   How to Structure Assets of the Business for Maximum Lawsuit Protection

control of the LLC and the RE. Once the child is over the age of 18 (24, if he or she is a full-time student), their percentage of the LLC income will likely be taxed at their lower income tax rates. If you can take full advantage of this strategy like the Savvy Affluent do, you can save tens of thousands of dollars in income taxes each year. Stretched out over a career, the savings, and growth on saved dollars, can reach well into the six figures. (See Figure 17.1.)

Obviously, this asset segregation strategy helps you protect the assets of the business from lawsuits against any of your partners or employees. An additional benefit of this strategy is that it can be used to reduce your income taxes through income tax sharing strategies. Lastly, this strategy can also help you more efficiently structure the buyout of retiring owners. By letting retired owners retain ownership of the LLC, they can still receive rental payments after they retire.

This Technique Can Be Used for a Business's Accounts Receivable

While the details go beyond the scope of this chapter, it is possible to use a leaseback with an LLC to shield a company's accounts receivable (AR) as well. As the AR is often the company's greatest asset, this can be a valuable strategy as well.

The One Contract Every Business Must Have: The Buy-Sell Agreement

As an owner of a privately held business, professional practice, or other venture, you likely spend 10 hours per day and six or seven days per week growing your business to the point where it can provide a measure of security for your family. We know this because we have been there ourselves. Nonetheless, if you ignore one fundamental legal contract, all of your work may be in jeopardy. That contract is the buy-sell agreement. The Seventh Key—Avoid Financial Disasters—offers an entire chapter on protecting yourself from the loss of a partner by implementing a buy-sell agreement. Please make sure you read that chapter if you want to protect your business, your family, and yourself from unnecessary aggravation and increased costs.

Consider This

Most businesses focus on making money. Many business owners fail to protect their businesses from business or personal lawsuits. It is important to protect your business as it can be the main source of income for you and your family. While you and your partners are handling the business protection needs, you can concurrently address your personal asset protection concerns. Read the next chapter to learn the quickest, easiest, and most effective tools for your personal planning so that you can maximize the protection of your assets.

18

Maximizing Exempt Assets

In the following chapters, we will explain a number of legal entities and techniques we use to protect the assets of Affluent clients and Wealthy Families. This chapter on maximizing exempt assets precedes the following chapters because, in our view, clients should always reasonably maximize their use of exempt assets before moving on to legal tools, legal entities, and other techniques.

Despite their superiority to other asset protection strategies, exempt assets are not universally used or even understood by Average Americans or by most of the Affluent. This chapter will explain why most advisors don't recommend exempt assets as often as they should. Then, there will be discussions of all of the exempt assets that can be valuable components of a comprehensive financial plan. Throughout the book, you will revisit many of these exempt assets as they provide additional benefits to the asset protection. In the Ninth Key, you will learn how the Savvy Affluent save time and money by leveraging exempt assets that also offer additional benefits. For now, let's begin discussing why exempt assets are considered the best asset protection tool and then discuss the reasons why they remain a secret of fortune-building and asset protection.

Exempt Assets: The Best Asset Protection Tool

We consider exempt assets to be the best asset protection tool for the following reasons:

- **No legal or accounting fees.** Most of the tools in subsequent chapters involve the creation of legal entities that require both one-time and ongoing legal fees, state fees, accounting fees, and even additional taxes. Using the exempt assets described in this chapter involves none of these significant costs and affords better protection as well.
- **No loss of ownership or control.** The legal tools described in the following chapters typically require giving up some level of ownership or control to family members or even third-party trustees. By using exempt assets, you can own and access the asset at any time while enjoying the highest (+5) level of protection.
- **Superior protection.** The legal tools explained later offer protection that ranges from +1 to +5. Exempt assets always enjoy the top (+5) protection.

Conflict of Interest: You vs. Your Advisor

Given the clear benefits of exempt assets, one would think that exempt assets would be preferred over other tools in an asset protection plan. Surprisingly, this is often not the case. The reason for this may be that most asset protection planning is implemented by attorneys who are not familiar with the financial tools a multidisciplinary team could offer.

There are various planning pitfalls that can arise when you do not have the benefit of a coordinated, multidisciplinary team to help implement your plan. Attorneys generally do not understand many of the exempt asset classes such as cash value life insurance and annuities. You cannot expect an advisor to recommend something he doesn't understand. This doesn't mean that one attorney could not recommend an adequate asset protection plan. What it does mean is that the plan created by one attorney may not be efficient because the plan may be limited only to legal solutions. If you were more skeptical, you might point out that attorneys are generally not licensed to sell such financial products. Is it unrealistic to expect an attorney to have a bias against the use of exempt assets for asset protection when these assets do not require any legal work? Is it unreasonable to expect attorneys to focus their asset protection recommendations around the use of legal documents that may generate thousands of dollars of legal fees? This is not a conspiracy nor is it an indictment of attorneys. The Savvy Affluent see this as a reality that cannot be dismissed.

In our practices, we have seen Affluent client after Affluent client come to us after paying an attorney $10,000, $25,000, and in one case more than $75,000 to implement a complex set of legal tools to meet their financial planning needs. These tools included significant annual costs such as trustee fees, legal fees, accounting costs, tax preparation costs, government fees, and others. In one case, the collection of legal tools was used in a way that required the client to put his faith in a trust company that would serve as the custodian of the family's assets and be responsible for carrying out the family's estate planning. The structure was complex and difficult for the client to understand, let alone monitor. After all of this cost and complexity, the structure only provided +2 protection for part of the client's wealth and +5 for the remainder.

When we explained to the client that he could have achieved better protection (+5 across the board) *and* eliminated annual costs and fees while maintaining 100 percent ownership and control by using exempt assets instead, the client was livid! How could we disagree with him?

The lesson here is simple. Your asset protection plan, like the rest of your financial plan, *must* be handled by a coordinated, multidisciplinary team that considers all planning options to help you efficiently achieve your goals. The absence of exempt assets in a plan is always a warning sign that the planning is not coordinated.

Federally Exempt Assets

Federally exempt assets are those assets that are protected under federal bankruptcy law. Federal law protects certain assets from creditors and lawsuits if the defendant is willing to file bankruptcy to eliminate the creditor. In a Chapter 7 bankruptcy, the debtor will be able to keep any assets that the federal law deems exempt after dismissing the creditors. The two significant asset classes that the federal law protects are qualified retirement plans (QRPs) and IRAs. There are limitations on these protections that are very specific—which your advisory team should understand well.

The term *qualified retirement plan* means that the retirement plan complies with certain U.S. Department of Labor and IRS rules. You might know such plans by their specific type, including profit sharing plans, money purchase plans, 401(k)s, or 403(b)s. IRAs are very similar to such plans but are technically different. IRAs are now given exempt status under the federal law as well.

While this protection is +5, you must recognize that this federal protection only applies if you are in a bankruptcy situation. If you were simply sued and a creditor was trying to take the funds in your pension or IRA, bankruptcy protection would not apply. You would have to take the step of filing for bankruptcy to shield the asset. This might be too great a cost for the protection.

If you do not file for bankruptcy, this federal protection would not apply. The amount of value in the QRP or IRA that would be protected outside of bankruptcy is controlled by state law. While many states do provide the same +5 shield for QRPs and IRAs, not all do.

State Exempt Assets

State exemption leveraging is a fundamental part of a financial plan and one that every Savvy Affluent client takes seriously. The most significant state exemptions are:

1. Qualified retirement plans and individual retirement accounts.
2. Primary residence (or homestead).
3. Life insurance.
4. Annuities.

In this section, we will examine each state exemption separately.

Important Note

We will make general comments regarding state exemptions below. If you are interested in exactly how your state exemptions work, please call us at 800-554-7233.

QRPs/IRAs

Outside of bankruptcy, any protection for QRPs or IRAs is provided by state law. Most states provide +5 protection for QRPs. Fewer states shield IRAs at a +5 level. For IRAs, a number of states will only protect the amount reasonably necessary for support, leaving it up to a judge to decide how much should be shielded in any particular case. While this may be adequate for Average Americans who generally have not accumulated much in such accounts, it certainly will not provide a shield for the IRAs of the Affluent.

Primary Residence: Homestead

Many Americans consider their homes to be their most valuable asset. You may have thought you understood the laws that protect your home. Perhaps you have heard the term *homestead,* and assumed that you could never lose your home to bad debts or other liabilities because of this homestead protection. The reality is that few states provide a total +5 shield for the home.

Most states only protect between $10,000 and $60,000 of the homestead's equity. Some states, such as New Jersey, provide no protection, while other states provide unlimited protection. Given today's real estate values and the equity that many Affluent have in their homes, it is clear that most states' homestead exemptions provide inadequate protection.

To determine how well a homestead law protects your home, you should compare the protected value to the equity. In order to do so, subtract the value of any mortgages from the fair market value of your home. For example, if you live in a home with a $300,000 fair market value and have a $150,000 mortgage, then your equity is $150,000. If your state protects only $20,000 through its homestead law, then you still have $130,000 ($150,000 of equity minus $20,000 homestead) of vulnerable equity.

Homestead protection is often automatic but may require additional action in some cases. Each state has specific requirements for claiming homestead status. In some states, you must file a declaration of homestead in a public office. Other states set a time requirement for residency before homestead protection is granted. Never assume your home is protected. You may be wrong and your inaction may cost you the protection you deserve. Your asset protection advisor can show you how to comply with the formalities in your state.

Life Insurance: Protected Everywhere

All 50 states have laws protecting varying amounts of life insurance. For example:

- Many states shield the entire policy proceeds from the creditors of the policyholder. Some also protect against the beneficiary's creditors.

- States that do not protect the entire policy proceeds set amounts above which the creditor can take proceeds.
- Many states protect the policy proceeds only if the policy beneficiaries are the policyholder's spouse, children, or other dependents.
- Some states protect a policy's cash surrender value in addition to the policy proceeds. If you have substantial cash value in a life insurance policy, be sure to consult your asset protection advisor who will check the state exemptions and recent cases to determine how well protected you are.
- If the policy is purchased as part of a fraudulent transfer, a court can undo the policy. This is the same for any other fraudulent transfer.

Annuities: Shielded in Many States

Another exempt asset in many states is an annuity. Annuities are insurance contracts that offer the upside of investment appreciation, tax-deferred growth, and principal protection. This diverse list of benefits makes annuities important components of asset protection and wealth accumulation plans.

Consider This

It should be clear that exempt assets should be a central component of any client's asset protection planning. However, to use them in the right way, you may need insurance product, home loan, qualified plan, tax, and asset protection expertise. This is another example of why you need a multidisciplinary team to help you achieve your financial goals. Because you can't practically place every dollar of your wealth into exempt assets, you will have to use legal strategies as well. The next chapter will discuss the two most common asset protection tools of the Savvy Affluent—the family limited partnership and the limited liability company.

19

Family Limited Partnerships and Limited Liability Companies

While exempt assets may be the most effective asset protection tools, most clients will need to go beyond the use of just exempt assets in their quest to protect assets. They will make use of legal tools as well. Of all the legal tools we use to shield assets, the two we use most are family limited partnerships (FLPs) and limited liability companies (LLCs). Of course, having family members play a role in these tools is common—that's why we use the word "family" in front of the LP. However, using family members in this way is not required. Whether you use family members or nonfamily members, these entities can provide you extraordinary asset protection. In this chapter, we will discuss the similarities between the two tools, how they protect assets, and three tactics the Savvy Affluent use to incorporate FLPs and LLCs into their plans to build and preserve wealth.

FLPs and LLCs: Similarities and Differences

We have combined FLPs and LLCs in this chapter because they are very similar. You can think of them as closely related, like brothers and sisters, as they share many of their best characteristics. In fact, unless we make the point otherwise, we will use these tools interchangeably; if a case study refers to an FLP, you can generally assume that an LLC could have been used and vice versa.

Similarities between the FLP and the LLC include the following:

1. **They are both legal entities certified under state law.** Both FLPs and LLCs are legal entities governed by the state law in the state where the entity is formed. Many of these laws are identical, as they are modeled after the Uniform Limited Partnership and Limited Liability Company acts, which have been adopted at least partially by every state. As state-certified legal entities, state fees must be paid each year to keep an FLP or LLC valid.

2. **They both have two levels of ownership.** FLPs and LLCs allow for two levels of ownership. We'll call one ownership level "active ownership." Active owners have 100 percent control of the entity and its assets. In the FLP, the active owners are called general partners, while in the LLC the active owners are called managing members.

   As you may have already guessed, the second ownership level is "passive ownership." Passive owners have little control of the entity and only limited rights. The passive owners are called limited partners in the FLP, and members in the LLC.

   This bilevel structure of ownership allows a host of planning possibilities because clients can then use FLPs and LLCs to share ownership with family members without having to give away any practical control of the assets inside the structures. Why is it optimal to be able to give away ownership but still maintain control? The asset protection reasons will be discussed in great detail in this chapter and the estate planning benefits will be explained in the estate planning section—the Sixth Key.

3. **They both have beneficial tax treatment.** In terms of income taxes, both tools can elect pass-through taxation, meaning neither the FLP nor the LLC is liable for income taxes. Rather, the tax liability for any and all income or capital gains on FLP and LLC assets passes through to the owners (partners or members). Also, as discussed in the income tax and estate planning Keys, both entities allow the participants to take advantage of income sharing and discounting techniques in the same ways.

4. **They both have the beneficial "charging order" asset protection benefit.** While state laws do vary, those based on the Uniform Acts provide charging order protection to FLP and

LLC owners. The charging order will be discussed later in this chapter.

5. **They both cost about the same in terms of legal fees.** To create an FLP or LLC requires designing how the entity will work in a client's plan, drafting the operating or partnership agreement, writing minutes, and preparing tax forms, assignments, and so forth. Experienced attorneys in the field will charge between $2,500 and $7,500 for these basic services, depending on the complexity of the ownership and a number of other factors. Of course, a complex business or significant estate planning effort for the Super Affluent may require an extremely complex operating agreement and may cost many times the amount quoted above.

Two big differences between the FLP and LLC are:

1. **Only the LLC can be used for a single owner.** Most states now allow single-member (owner) LLCs, while a limited partnership in every state must have at least two owners. Thus, for single clients, the LLC is often the only option. Also, if we are considering having an FLP or LLC protect a home, then the single-member LLC is one alternative. Because the home is a significant asset both financially and emotionally, there is an entire chapter devoted to protecting it.
2. **The FLP's general partner has liability for the FLP.** While a general partner has personal liability for the acts and debts of the FLP, a managing member has no such liability for his LLC. For this reason alone, asset protection experts always recommend using an LLC rather than an FLP when the entity will own dangerous assets.

Dangerous assets are those that have a relatively high likelihood of creating liability. Common dangerous assets included real estate (especially rental real estate), cars, recreational vehicles, trucks, boats, airplanes, interests in closely held businesses, and others.

Safe assets, conversely, are those that are unlikely to lead to lawsuits. Common safe assets include cash, stocks, bonds, mutual funds, CDs, life insurance policies, checking or savings accounts, antiques, artwork, jewelry, licenses, copyrights, trademarks, and patents, among others.

Because FLP general partners have liability exposure and LLC managing members do not, it usually makes sense to use an LLC rather than an FLP to own dangerous assets.

How FLPs and LLCs Protect Assets

FLPs and LLCs are outstanding asset protectors because the law gives a very specific and limited remedy to creditors coming after assets in either entity. When a personal creditor pursues you and your assets are owned by an FLP or an LLC, the creditor cannot seize the assets in the FLP or LLC. Under the Uniform Act provisions, a creditor of a partner or LLC member cannot reach into the FLP or LLC and take specific partnership assets.

If the creditor cannot seize FLP/LLC assets, what can the creditor get? The law normally allows for only one remedy: the charging order. The charging order is something a creditor can have served to a debtor. In other words, the creditor must legally be paid any distributions that would have been paid to the debtor. The charging order is meant to allow the business to continue operating without interruption and provide a remedy for creditors to be paid. Oftentimes, the best the creditor will be able to do is obtain a charging order when assets are owned by an FLP/LLC. You will see that the charging order is generally a very weak remedy.

Of course, this discussion assumes that in transferring assets to an FLP or LLC, you do not run afoul of fraudulent transfer laws. We introduced the concept of these laws in the introduction to this Key. It also assumes that one remain in compliance with state laws and not use the FLP/LLC as an alter ego of one's personal business affairs.

The Limitations of the Charging Order

As mentioned earlier, the charging order is a court order that instructs the FLP or LLC to pay the debtor's share of distributions to his creditor until the creditor's judgment is paid in full. Importantly, the charging order does not:

- Give the creditor FLP/LLC voting rights.
- Force the FLP general partner or LLC managing member to pay out any distributions to partners or members.

While the charging order may seem like a powerful remedy, consider its limitations:

1. **It is only available after a successful lawsuit.** The charging order is only available after the creditor has successfully sued you and won a judgment. Only then can your creditor ask the court for the charging order. It must be noted that once the threat of a charging order exists and even while a lawsuit is proceeding, FLP/LLC assets are completely untouchable and available for you to use (so long as you avoid fraudulent transfers).

2. **It does not afford voting rights—so you stay in complete control.** Despite the charging order, you remain the general partner of your FLP (or managing member of the LLC). You make all decisions about whether the FLP/LLC buys assets, distributes earnings to its partners or members, shifts ownership interests, and so forth. Your judgment creditor cannot vote you out because he cannot vote your shares. Thus, even after the creditor has a judgment against you, you still make all decisions concerning the FLP/LLC, including the decision to refuse to pay distributions to the owners.

   Why would you decide to pay distributions when you know that the creditor will get them? Perhaps you want to compensate yourself and your spouse as general partners (or managing members) by paying yourself a reasonable salary for running the FLP/LLC. This is generally permissible, and your creditor still won't be able to interfere.

   Keep in mind that a charging order may have no impact on most FLP/LLCs. If your FLP/LLC simply owns cars, vacation homes, antiques, or other nonincome-producing assets, your FLP/LLC would likely have little or no income to distribute.

3. **The creditor pays the tax bill.** The real kicker is how the charging order backfires on creditors for income tax purposes. Because taxes on FLP/LLC income are passed through to the parties that are entitled to the income, the FLP/LLC does not pay tax. Each partner/member is responsible for his share of the FLP/LLC income. This income is taxable whether or not the income is actually paid out.

   A creditor who does not understand the tax law here may foreclose upon their charging order interest—thinking that this puts them in a stronger position to negotiate. Unfortunately for them, a creditor who forecloses on a charging order against your FLP or LLC interest will step into your shoes for income tax purposes with respect to the FLP/LLC income. Therefore, your creditor will receive your tax bill and owe income taxes on your share of the FLP/LLC income. This tax liability exists even though the creditor never received the income. (Remember, you and your spouse decide if and when to make distributions, and you certainly won't make any when there is a creditor with a charging order.)

With this extraordinary poison pill, you may ask the creditor to sue your wife and kids, too, so your family never pays any taxes again! Perhaps the real beauty of this predicament lies in the fact that once the creditor realizes that he will get more money out of a cheap settlement than from the foreclosed charging order interest, he will likely opt to settle cheaply.

Case Study: Woody and Marge Are Protected by Their FLPs

Return to the example of spouses Woody and Marge. Assume that Woody is an oncologist. After two years of employment, Woody's assistant, Maribel, sues Woody for sexual harassment, and wins an award of $750,000. Woody's general business insurance package does not cover this type of lawsuit. Once Maribel discovers, through a debtor's examination, that Woody and Marge's assets are owned by their FLPs, what can she do?

She cannot seize the vacation home, stocks, and cars owned by the FLPs. The Uniform Limited Partnership Act provisions prohibit that. She also has no fraudulent transfer claim to cling to in an attempt to undo the FLPs because the FLPs were created in advance of her claim. She can get a charging order on Woody's 39 percent share of the FLPs, but Woody and Marge would still control the FLPs. Maribel would probably not receive any distributed profits, only a tax bill on dividends paid out by the stocks that Woody and Marge never distributed. The charging order will not sound too inviting to Maribel, will it?

Maribel could look only to Woody's assets not owned by the FLPs. Because Woody had an incomplete asset protection plan and retained personal ownership of copyrights and business interests in a film company worth about $75,000, Woody settled the judgment for just that—$75,000 cash. Woody and Marge's FLPs helped them avoid financial disaster and settle the claim for pennies on the dollar. Moreover, they never lost control of their assets.

You may wonder why we have such protective laws for limited partnerships and limited liability companies. The charging order law, which can be traced back to the English Partnership Act of 1890, is aimed at achieving a particular public policy objective, which is that business activities of a partnership should not be disrupted because of nonpartnership-related debts of the individual partners. The rationale for this objective is that if nondebtor partners and the partnership were not at fault, why should the entire partnership suffer? U.S. law has adopted this policy for more than 100 years, culminating in the charging order law of the Uniform Limited Partnership Act and Uniform Limited Liability Company Act.

Three Tactics for Maximizing FLP/LLC Protection

You now understand the basic strategy for using FLPs/LLCs; that is, if you put your assets into the FLP/LLC they will be protected from personal creditors. This is basic outside asset protection. Assets inside the FLP/LLC are also protected against outside threats to you. Beyond this, consider these three basic rules:

1. **Don't put all your eggs in one basket.** One never knows when a court of law is going to make a surprise departure or deviation from the accepted legal norms or precedents. One never knows when an asset within a single FLP/LLC could cause a lawsuit. Life is full of uncertainties. Because the Savvy Affluent understand that they cannot control court decisions or the litigious nature of society, they protect their assets by using multiple FLP/LLC arrangements (among other tools discussed in this Key) in different states to title their assets. Titling your assets in different legal entities makes it more difficult for any creditor to come after your entire wealth because that creditor may have to conduct more investigations, file more motions with the court, and perhaps even travel to different states. The more entities used, the more difficult it will be for your creditors to attack your wealth. As a result, creditors will be more likely to negotiate more favorable settlements.

2. **Segregate the dangerous eggs from the safe ones.** Separating safe assets from dangerous assets increases the inside asset protection for the safe assets. In other words, since no dangerous assets are within the same entity as the safe assets,

a lawsuit arising from a dangerous asset will not threaten the safe assets if the safe assets are in their own LLC. As we explained in the beginning of the chapter, dangerous assets should be owned by an LLC rather than by an FLP because LLCs give better inside protection. The general partner of an FLP can be personally liable for acts within an FLP but the managing member of an LLC cannot be held personally liable for the acts within the LLC.

3. **If possible, use LLCs or FLPs in the most protective states.** Not all LLCs and FLPs are created equal. LLCs and FLPs vary greatly in their asset protection, estate, and tax benefits, based on the experience and expertise of the attorney drafting the operating agreement. However, the point here is that some states have much more protective language in their LLC or FLP statutes. Some statutes are much more creditor friendly, while others are more debtor friendly. In addition, many states have adopted uniform language. However, the examples in those states have illustrated the fact that each state's courts can interpret the statute differently. Further, over time, courts in the same state may have a change of opinion. Thus, the Savvy Affluent use legal entities domiciled in jurisdictions that offer the best law, and they make sure that a member of their team is an asset protection expert keeping an eye on developments in the field so they can switch state domiciles if necessary.

Putting It Together: An FLP/LLC Case Study

Let's take a look at a case study that uses FLPs and LLCs. Harry Gump, a 53-year-old co-owner of a retail company, and his wife Wilma, a day school teacher, have two teenaged children and have the following assets:

Safe Assets

Asset	Equity
Home (depends on state)	$550,000
Cash	$50,000
Mutual Funds	$550,000
Interest in Business	$600,000
Antiques	$20,000
Total Safe Equity	$1,770,000

Dangerous Assets

Asset	Equity
Rental Condo #1	$275,000
Rental Condo #2	$255,000
Cars	$20,000
Powerboat	$30,000
Total Dangerous Equity	$580,000

TOTAL EQUITY $2,350,000

To provide the Gump's with maximum financial security using FLPs/LLCs, we use two to four entities. Let us examine each.

Tool #1: "Gump Safe Asset FLP"

Owns:	Cash, mutual funds, business interest, and antiques
Total value:	$1,220,000
Interests:	Mr. and Mrs. Gump, 2% as general partners
	Mr. and Mrs. Gump, 96% as limited partners
	Each child 1% limited partner

Strategy: The family home is not included because of the special tax consequences afforded homes in their state. By isolating safe assets from dangerous assets, we ensure their security. Further, because Mr. and Mrs. Gump are general partners, they have 100 percent control of the FLP and all FLP assets. They are more comfortable with this ownership arrangement.

Result: All $1,220,000 is now safe from creditors or lawsuits. The Gumps may decide to gift their interests in the FLP to their children for estate and income tax reduction (read the chapters in the Fifth Key—Always Consider Taxes—to learn how to accomplish this).

Tool #2: "Gump Dangerous Asset LLC"

Owns:	Condo #1 and Condo #2
Total value:	$530,000
Interests:	Mr. Gump 1% owner as managing member; 49% as member
	Mrs. Gump 1% owner as managing member; 49% as member

Strategy: These assets are dangerous because of the likelihood of lawsuits from tenants, guests, or neighbors. While in this example one LLC owns both condominiums, a strong argument can be made to set up separate LLCs for each condo.

Result: Any lawsuit arising from the condos is isolated to the condos. All other wealth is shielded.

Tool #3: "Gump Dangerous Asset LLC 2"

Owns:	Cars and the powerboat
Total value:	$50,000
Interests:	Mr. Gump 1% owner as managing member; 49% as member
	Mrs. Gump 1% owner as managing member; 49% as member

Strategy: These assets are extremely dangerous, especially because the children drive both cars and the boat regularly. With an LLC, we protect the Gump's personal wealth from liability caused by the cars or boat. Yet, Mr. and Mrs. Gump still completely control the boat and cars.

Result: All other wealth is shielded from lawsuits arising from car and powerboat ownership. Also, Mr. and Mrs. Gump achieve personal protection through the LLC.

Without the FLPs and LLCs, the Gump family had more than $2.3 million exposed to lawsuits. Now, Mr. Gump has shielded more than 75 percent worth of that wealth . . . and we haven't even addressed the home yet. Further, they have the tools now to reduce income taxes and perhaps even eliminate estate taxes. Perhaps most importantly, they have not relinquished control over any of their assets in the process.

Consider This

FLPs and LLCs are two of the most utilized and most powerful asset protection tools we use to manage the wealth of the Affluent. We would be astounded if you did not use at least one as part of your new comprehensive financial plan. These tools not only protect assets, they can also offer income and estate tax benefits as well. Taxes and the preservation of one's estate will be discussed in depth in the Fifth and Sixth Keys. Trusts are another set of tools that offer asset protection as well as tax and estate planning benefits. These asset protection secrets are discussed in the next chapter.

CHAPTER 20

Using Trusts to Shield Wealth

Another secret tool that the Affluent use to protect their assets and maintain their wealth is the trust. A trust is a legal entity, often misunderstood by Average Americans but routinely used by the Affluent and Super Affluent. In this chapter, we will explain what a trust is and the asset protection role trusts play in the planning of the Savvy Affluent.

A Trust

A trust is a legal arrangement in which one person holds property for the benefit of another. The person who holds the property is the trustee. The trustee holds the property for the benefit of one or more beneficiaries. A trust is created by a trust document that specifies that the trustee holds property owned by the trust for the benefit of the beneficiary of the trust. The trust document also establishes the terms of how the trust should be administered and how the trust assets should be distributed during the lifetime of the trust as well as when the trust is terminated.

The following definitions and classifications should help you understand a trust and how it functions.

Definitions

1. **Grantor:** The grantor is the person who sets up the trust. He is usually the person who transfers property into the trust. A grantor may also be called the trustor or settlor.

2. **Trustee:** The trustee(s) are the legal owners of the trust property. The trustee(s) are responsible for administering and carrying out the terms of the trust. They owe a fiduciary duty to the beneficiaries—an utmost duty of care that they will follow the terms of the trust document and manage the trust property properly. A trustee may be a person, such as a family member or trusted friend. The trustee can also be an institution such as a professional trust company or the trust department of a bank. When there is more than one trustee, they are called cotrustees.

   The trustee is the legal owner of any assets owned by the trust and has legal title to the assets owned by the trust. For example, assume that Dad wants to set up a trust for his children, Son and Daughter. Dad wants his brother, Uncle, to serve as trustee. If Dad transfers his house into the trust, the title to that house will be with Uncle, as trustee of the Dad trust.

3. **Beneficiary:** The beneficiary (or beneficiaries) is the person for whom the trust was set up. In the example discussed above, the beneficiaries would be Son and Daughter. While the trustee has legal title to assets owned by the trust, the beneficiary has equitable title or the rights to the trust property. The beneficiary can sue the trustee if the trustee mismanages the trust property or disobeys specific instructions in the trust. The beneficiary may be the same person as the grantor, and can possibly be the same person as the trustee. For asset protection purposes, the trustee, beneficiary, and grantor cannot all be the same person.

4. **Funding:** Funding the trust means transferring assets to the trust. A trust that is unfunded has no property transferred to it. It is completely ineffective. You must title assets to the trust if you want trust protection as with any other legal entity or asset protection tool discussed previously. To title real estate to the trust, you must execute and record a deed to the property to the trust. Bank and brokerage accounts can be transferred by simply changing the name on the accounts. Registered stocks and bonds are changed by notifying the transfer agent or issuing company and requesting that the certificates be reissued to the trust. Other assets, such as household items, furniture, jewelry, artwork, and so forth, are transferred by a simple legal document called an assignment

or bill of sale. Your asset protection specialist can transfer assets simply and quickly.

Trust Classifications

There are four classifications of trusts. They are:

1. **Revocable trust:** A revocable trust is one that the grantor can revoke and undo at any time.
2. **Irrevocable trust:** An irrevocable trust is one that the grantor cannot revoke or undo once established.
3. **Inter vivos trust:** An inter vivos trust takes effect during the grantor's lifetime.
4. **Testamentary trust:** A testamentary trust takes effect at the time of the grantor's death. Testamentary trusts are usually created in wills, living trusts, or other documents taking effect at death. All testamentary trusts are irrevocable once the grantor dies, but are generally revocable until then.

Every trust will be either be a revocable trust or an irrevocable trust (Classification 1 or 2); and either an inter vivos trust or a testamentary trust (Classification 3 or 4). A trust either has terms that can be changed (revocable) or terms that cannot be changed (irrevocable). Further, the trust takes effect either during the grantor's lifetime (inter vivos) or takes effect at the time of the grantor's death (testamentary). For asset protection purposes, it is important to understand the differences between revocable and irrevocable trusts. In the sections following, we will discuss the differences between these two classifications.

Living Trusts: Illusory Asset Protection

Living trusts allow the grantor of the living trust the flexibility to make changes to an estate plan and to avoid unnecessary probate expenses. Probate is an unnecessary expense and hassle for the Affluent and is discussed in detail in the Sixth Key. Living trusts also effectively sidestep the hidden dangers of joint tenancy, which is discussed in the Sixth Key. Living trusts are an important piece of the comprehensive planning puzzle for the Affluent. However, many people mistakenly assume that these trusts provide asset protection benefits.

Living Trusts Do Not Protect Assets during Your Lifetime

During your lifetime, living trusts provide absolutely no asset protection. This is because living trusts are revocable. While revocability and flexibility are valuable characteristics for almost all financial planning tools, these characteristics render the living trust useless for asset protection purposes. Remember this simple rule: Revocable trusts are vulnerable to creditors and living trusts are revocable trusts. Let's explore the main reason why revocable trusts offer no protection.

Creditors can "Step Into Your Shoes," Revoke the Living Trust and Seize Trust Assets Revocable trusts, such as living trusts, are useless for asset protection because revocable trusts allow the grantor to undo the trust. If you, as the grantor, wanted to unwind a revocable trust and use the funds for yourself, you could do so. A creditor can essentially force the grantor of the trust to do this. If the grantor's creditors want to seize assets owned by a revocable trust, they need only petition the court to "step into the shoes" of the grantor and direct the funds of the trust back to the debtor. The trust assets will no longer be owned by the trust, but by the creditor personally. The creditors then have all the rights and privileges to seize these assets they now own.

Irrevocable Trusts: The Asset Protectors

While revocable trusts, such as living trusts, offer no asset protection, irrevocable trusts are outstanding for asset protection. Once you establish an irrevocable trust, you forever abandon the ability to undo the trust and reclaim property transferred to the trust. With an irrevocable trust, you lose both control of the trust assets and ownership.

Of course, this discussion assumes that in transferring assets to an irrevocable trust, you do not run afoul of fraudulent transfer laws. We introduced the concept of these laws in the introduction to this Key. Now, let's discuss why and how irrevocable trusts can protect assets.

Why Irrevocable Trusts Protect Your Assets

Irrevocable trusts protect assets for the same reason that revocable trusts do not. As mentioned earlier, revocable living trusts do not provide asset protection because creditors can step into your shoes and undo such a trust. The logic here is that if you have the power to undo your trust, so do your creditors.

An irrevocable trust results in the opposite. Because an established irrevocable trust cannot be altered or undone, your creditors cannot step into your shoes and undo the trust any more than you can. Assets in an irrevocable trust are immune from creditor attack, lawsuits, and other threats. An irrevocable trust carries a heavy price—you must give up control and ownership of the asset to gain protection.

When does such a heavy price make sense? When you (1) would inevitably gift the assets to the beneficiaries, and (2) do not foresee needing the assets for your own financial security. When both factors are satisfied, your price is not particularly heavy—as is often the case for the Super Affluent. You do not personally need the assets and the trust will accomplish what you would do yourself—distribute the assets to your beneficiaries (usually children) at some future time.

Three Pitfalls to Avoid with Irrevocable Trusts

1. You cannot reserve any power to revoke, rescind, or amend the trust or retain any rights, either directly or indirectly, to reclaim property transferred to the trust. Simply, there can be no strings attached.
2. Gifts to trusts are given the most scrutiny under fraudulent transfer laws, because there is no "for value" exchange as there is with LLCs or FLPs. Often, for asset protection purposes, these tools are superior.
3. You, as the trust's grantor, cannot be the trustee. Nor can you appoint a trustee the courts would not consider "at arm's length." Those who do not qualify for arm's length include your spouse or any close relative. Even appointment of a close personal friend will invite scrutiny, and it will be necessary to show that the close personal friend was serving independently and not subservient to the interests of the grantor. Courts closely examine the relationship between the grantor and the trustee to determine whether the trustee is only the grantor's alter ego. If there is such a relationship, courts will ignore the trust and allow creditors to reach the trust assets.

Important Note

A corporate trustee, such as a bank or a trust company, is much less likely to be judged as an alter ego, thereby giving your trust an added layer of security.

Two Clauses Your Irrevocable Trust Should Have

There are two clauses that are extremely important for an irrevocable trust to contain so that you can properly protect your assets. These clauses are not necessarily important to protect the trust creator but for shielding the beneficiaries from their creditors.

1. **Spendthrift Clause:** The spendthrift clause allows the trustee to withhold income and principal, which would ordinarily be paid to the beneficiary, if the trustee feels the money could or would be wasted or seized by the beneficiary's creditors. This clause accomplishes two goals. First, it prevents a wasteful beneficiary from spending trust funds or wasting trust assets. This is especially important to many affluent grantors who set up trusts with their children as beneficiaries. If you worry that money in trust for your children would be wasted if not controlled, then use a spendthrift clause. The trustee can then stop payments if your child spends too quickly or unwisely.

   Secondly, the spendthrift clause protects trust assets from creditors of the beneficiaries. Beneficiaries may now be young, but as adults they will face the same risks we all face: lawsuits, debt problems, divorce, a failing business, and the like. The spendthrift clause protects trust assets from your children's creditors by granting the trustee the authority to withhold payments to a beneficiary who has an outstanding creditor. If the beneficiary and trustee are at arm's length, the creditor has no power to force the trustee to pay the beneficiary. The creditor only has a right to payments actually paid by the trustee. He cannot force the trustee to make disbursements.

2. **Anti-alienation Clause:** The anti-alienation clause also protects trust assets from the beneficiary's creditors. Specifically, the anti-alienation clause prohibits the trustee from transferring trust assets to anyone other than the beneficiary. This,

of course, includes creditors of the trust beneficiary. Thus, while the spendthrift clause allows the trustee to withhold payments if a creditor lurks, the anti-alienation clause goes one step further—it prohibits the trustee from paying trust income or principal to anyone but the named beneficiaries.

Case Study: Jerry and His Kids

Jerry, from an Affluent Family, had a sizable investment portfolio, including $200,000 in mutual funds that he planned on leaving to his two children, Steve and Stephanie. Jerry knew that he and his wife could live quite comfortably without these mutual funds, and he wanted to save estate taxes and provide security to his children. Jerry, however, was concerned that his kids would spend the funds unwisely.

We established an irrevocable trust for Jerry and named his local bank's trust department as trustee. Jerry told the trust officer about his concerns for the funds. Jerry's wishes were incorporated into the trust document.

Although Steve and Stephanie were only 12 at the time, Jerry and his wife funded the trust with $20,000 worth of mutual fund interests each year—so the gifts to the trust were completely tax free. The trust was made irrevocable so that if Jerry or his wife were sued, their creditors could not seize these funds. The trust also had anti-alienation and spendthrift clauses so the funds would be protected from his children's possible poor spending habits as well as from their potential future creditors.

Jerry realized that the trust would eventually be substantial in value. He also recognized the possibility that his children would someday have creditor or divorce problems. With this irrevocable trust, Jerry protected these funds from his creditors, gifted them tax free to the trust, provided for his children's future (which he intended to do through his will or living trust), and did so in a way that fully protects the funds from his children's creditors, as well.

Other Benefits of Living Trusts

Despite its weakness for asset protection planning, the living trust is still commonly used in comprehensive financial plans and must be integrated into asset protection elements of the plan. The living trust is the ideal way to own FLP partnership interests, LLC membership interests, or other interests in entities that will provide protection.

With these legal entities owned by your living trusts, rather than in your own name, you save estate taxes and expensive probate fees down the road. You get the best of both worlds: protection of your assets while you are alive and saving your family estate taxes and probate fees when you die. This is discussed in great detail in the Sixth Key.

Consider This

As you have seen, irrevocable trusts play an important role in an asset protection plan. Trusts also offer income tax and estate planning benefits. Please take time to read the Fifth and Sixth Keys and then work with your team of advisors to see how to best integrate trusts into your financial plan. You will also see that both LLCs and trusts can be created domestically or internationally. For those of you seeking a higher level of protection for your wealth, you should read the next chapter on international planning. The benefits can be very significant for the right type of client and are definitely secrets of the Super Affluent.

CHAPTER

21

International Planning

Over the last decade, an increasing number of the Affluent have looked internationally in their wealth planning—typically, for investment opportunities, but also in the area of asset protection. In this chapter, you'll learn what to do—and what to avoid—in international planning. You'll also learn about specific tools the Affluent use in their international planning. In addition, we will discuss the major setbacks some Affluent clients endure as a result of inadequate international planning and advisors who lack international financial experience. We conclude the chapter by discussing how international trusts and LLCs are effective financial tools for protecting assets.

International Planning: A Favorite of the Affluent

Using foreign jurisdictions to protect wealth has been a popular strategy for estate and family wealth planning since the early days of the Roman Empire when emperors attempted to preserve their riches for their descendants by holding their wealth in fortresses in foreign lands. Nevertheless, international planning has never been as popular as it is today. For tens of thousands of Americans each year, international structures become part of their wealth protection plan. Certainly there are tremendous benefits to be gained by using opportunities outside of the 50 states . . . you just have to make sure you do it right.

Affluent Families around the world have established legal entities outside of their home countries for decades. In fact, for much of the world, the United States is an international financial center, with numerous tax benefits offered to foreigners who want to invest here. Nonetheless, only in the last 15 years have a significant number of Affluent Americans started taking advantage of international planning outside the United States.

Why Use International Planning

1. **Asset Protection:** Asset protection is the goal that we will focus on in this chapter. Note: Many Affluent Americans may initially indicate that they want to put some of their wealth outside of the U.S. for privacy concerns. While there certainly are some high-profile clients who do hold this as a true objective, we have found that, when one gets down to the truth of it, most clients use the word privacy to mean either asset protection or tax planning. Thus, we will not address privacy concerns separately here.

2. **Tax Planning:** A common—and extremely dangerous—misconception about international planning is that one can avoid U.S. taxation by going offshore. Simply put, this is dead wrong. *Americans are liable for income taxes on income, wherever it is earned.* The vast majority of solid international asset protection plans are tax neutral, although there may be significant tax advantages realized by captive insurance companies (Chapter 24) or foreign life insurance and annuities—*but those tax benefits are found in the U.S. tax code, not because the assets are being "hidden" offshore.*

3. **Investing:** Consider that the U.S. market now represents only approximately 35 percent of the world's capital market (contrast with more than 60 percent circa 1960) and that market share is declining. This means that if you only invest in the U.S., you are missing out on two-thirds of the world's investment opportunities. You are also making a 100 percent bet on the stability of U.S. currency, which has declined steadily over the past five years.

   Because the U.S. Securities and Exchange Commission (SEC) makes it almost impossible for foreign companies to sell their stock in the U.S., many clients use an international entity to purchase foreign securities. This way, the other two-thirds of the world's investments become available.

Dangerous International Pitfalls to Avoid

As you might imagine, in our business, we see too many Affluent people who use international planning for the wrong reasons. Often, people are so anxious to avoid taxes, shield assets improperly, or get rich quick that their otherwise reasonable judgment is clouded. Consequently, people engage in planning strategies that they would never undertake here in the U.S. Combine these desires with the virtually unregulated international jurisdictions (i.e., no reporting to the IRS, no Securities and Exchange Commission or National Association of Securities Dealers disclosure requirements, no state attorneys general remedying fraud, and so on), and one has an area ripe for potential abuse. Let's see how most clients get in trouble through improper international planning.

Offshore Planning Strategies

As explained in this Key, asset protection can be achieved in the United States through the use of legal entities such as family limited partnerships, trusts, and limited liability companies. The source of the asset protection features of these entities is the way the law treats them in terms of ownership, control, and the rights of creditors.

In this respect, international entities have many of the same asset protection features—most common are the LLC and the trust. Thus, the right way to protect assets internationally is to use the same structures and strategies one would use here in the States. Yet, the practical problem you encounter in doing so is that those entities are located in foreign nations. In foreign jurisdictions, U.S. attorneys are unable to practice and are generally unfamiliar with the law.

Unfortunately, while creating legitimate international asset protection plans is not difficult for experienced advisors, many Americans forego such planning and simply try to hide wealth in these international centers. Rather than use an entity such as an LLC, they simply set up bank or brokerage accounts in countries where there is little, if any, reporting. No one is the wiser, right?

The problem with this no-entity approach is that in any litigation— civil lawsuit, divorce, or even governmental case—there will eventually be some type of formal inquiry of assets. This might occur by way of a "debtor's exam" after a successful lawsuit, a bankruptcy filing, a list of assets for a divorce settlement, and so forth. For the no-entity approach to work, the client would have to omit the international assets or lie about their existence. This amounts to perjury, bankruptcy fraud, or obstruction of justice, depending upon the forum of the case. Thus, the ultimate success of many hidden offshore planning strategies relies on the clients' decision to commit perjury or some other crime. The Savvy Affluent understand this potential pitfall and have a group of advisors who ensure that this will not happen.

Going Offshore to Avoid U.S. Taxes Leads to Tax Evasion

As explained previously, Americans are liable for taxes on all income earned offshore. However, many international banks, mutual funds, and other financial institutions may not report earnings or interest to the IRS. This is the chasm where many greedy clients—or unscrupulous advisors—operate. This is also where tax evasion—a federal crime—is committed.

While the client is required under U.S. law to make the necessary tax reporting on income earned internationally (and advisors should instruct their clients to do so), many clients may keep quiet and hope that they are never caught. This "hide the ball" strategy is used not only by knowing clients, but also by shady advisors who concoct ever more sophisticated schemes like moving money from one trust to another company to a third foundation and so on in hopes of avoiding detection.

Although the pitch may seem complex and impressive, the Savvy Affluent know to always ask the following question: If the income will eventually accrue to my benefit, why don't I have to report it to the IRS? The Savvy Affluent know that they must steer clear of these schemes unless they want the cloud of a possible tax evasion indictment hanging over them for years to come.

Going Offshore to Get Rich Quick Leads to Scams and Frauds

The desire to get rich quick leads many clients into problems most pervasive in the investment arena. Here, scam artists and fraudsters abound, poised to take advantage of the next client who wants to get rich offshore. The Savvy Affluent understand that any investment that offers truly outstanding returns is on the radar screen of the world's most sophisticated financial institutions and their Super Affluent clientele. Then, the investment is reserved for the financial institution's billionaire clients. The Savvy Affluent know that the only thing that can be achieved from chasing fantastic returns in international markets is a significant, if not complete, loss of principal. Let's explore how some of these mistakes happen.

Working with Advisors Who Are Not International Experts

Improper international planning is not always the fault of the client. Oftentimes, it is the fault of the client's advisors, as well. Below is a list of the mistakes clients make by simply working with certain types of advisors.

As common as the situation in which a client's own motivations get him into trouble, is the scenario in which a client with good intentions gets into trouble because of the advisors. Creating a viable international plan requires expertise in international and domestic taxation, conflicts of laws, asset protection, the law of corporations and partnerships, estate planning, and others. While there are thousands of advisors in the U.S. representing themselves as experts in international planning, probably only 1 in 50 is truly knowledgeable and experienced. The Savvy Affluent are very willing to explore international planning options. However, they realize that this area can be very risky, so they require the inclusion of advisors who specialize in this area and include their other advisors in the analysis of potential planning strategies.

Advisors Can Be In over Their Heads Offshore

What are the most common shortcomings of advisors involved in international planning? The following two are always at the top of the list:

1. The advisor is not experienced in international planning.
2. The advisor is not an expert in international taxation.

The Advisor Is Not Experienced in International Planning So Clients Get Caught in Scams   A top international advisor should have experience in dealing with international havens and have contacts in those where he practices. The advisor should keep abreast of up-to-the-minute developments in the field, which, for those in the field, is easily accomplished through informal professional contacts, professional journals, and web sites.

Further, advisors should have existing relationships with top fiduciary firms in the country where their structures are established, including trust companies or bank officers, insurance managers, actuaries, money managers, attorneys, and accountants, among others. These contacts can buttress the advisor's analysis of any international opportunities.

Advisors who are new to the field, or who have not put in the years of due diligence required to be competent in offshore planning, will not have these contacts and resources. Thus, when faced with tough judgment calls regarding whether or not to use a particular trustee firm or local accountant or trust investment, they cannot accurately evaluate the risks and rewards. Too often, these advisors put clients in structures or investments that a more resourceful advisor would have avoided.

The Advisor Is Not an Expert in International Taxation   If you go offshore, you will need to use an attorney or CPA who is an expert in international taxation; that is, unless you want to risk committing tax fraud.

This is the most common failing of otherwise competent attorneys involved in offshore planning. They simply don't know all of the rules regarding U.S. taxpayers with investments and structures abroad. They may know most rules, but unless they are familiar with them all, clients will pay a hefty price—either tax penalties for not reporting correctly or by paying too high a tax rate because of a lack of tax planning.

We see this all the time with clients who have used another advisor and have created an international structure that purchased international mutual funds. Often, these are very stable, recommended mutual funds from large European financial institutions so there is no scam risk. Nonetheless, in many cases, the client is looking at a tax nightmare, paying income taxes at effective rates ranging from 46 percent to 84 percent depending on how long the client holds the investments! Investment returns become almost irrelevant when tax rates are this high.

How many advisors have heard of the PFIC QEF rules regarding the taxation of foreign mutual funds? Not many. These rules may allow investors in qualified electing funds to use U.S. income tax rates on their income from the fund, including the most favorable long-term capital gains rates. In our experience, fewer than

5 percent of international funds qualify under these rules, so most clients end up paying the horrid rates of 46 percent to 84 percent, for no reason other than the incompetence of their advisors.

International LLCs and Trusts: Most Effective Tools

By using international elements as part of your financial plan, you will have the most powerful nonexempt asset protection tools at your disposal. Done right, these tools can be used to achieve the +5 level of protection. Compared with exempt assets, which do not have professional, government, or accounting fees, these tools are expensive, but they may be the best nonexempt options for Affluent clients. One example of a tool that offers excellent flexibility, control, and protection is the Nevis LLC.

Nevis: An Important Jurisdiction for LLCs

When Nevis—a small Caribbean nation that is part of a federation with St. Kitts—began to compete for the multibillion U.S. asset protection business in the 1990s, it revised its trust and business entity laws. As part of this process, the lawmakers studied U.S. LLC statutes and improved upon them, in terms of providing asset protection for U.S. citizens. Today, Nevis has the oldest and most stable LLC legislation outside of the U.S., specifically modeled on the well-drafted Delaware legislation. The result is a superior asset protection tool—the Nevis LLC—that is used by many attorneys specializing in the field.

The Nevis LLC

As we explained in Chapter 19, domestic LLCs (those in the United States) protect your assets because a creditor of yours can only obtain a charging order against your LLC interest. This charging order entitles the creditor only to your share of any distributions actually made from the LLC (which you, as the managing member of the LLC, control). The charging order does not allow the creditor to seize your interest in the LLC or vote your interest. In this way, the assets within the LLC are shielded. Only when you decide to make distributions does the creditor get anything of value.

The Nevis LLC has these same charging order protections drafted in its legislation, paralleling the Delaware LLC law. However, it adds a number of significant benefits that the domestic LLCs cannot afford—the deterrence factors of the Nevis LLC law. These include the following:

1. **No contingency fee attorneys/local attorneys only.** This means that any creditor attacking transfers to a Nevis entity (LLC or trust) must hire a lawyer in that country who cannot work on contingency.

2. **Bond required.** Certain havens require a bond to be posted when filing a lawsuit because, in these countries, the losing party pays the prevailing party's legal fees. This is the British or Commonwealth Rule. The bond is often required to cover tens of thousands of dollars in legal fees, making the prospect of suing even more expensive. Nevis may now have this rule in place.

3. **Tough burden of proof.** In many countries, a plaintiff must prove beyond a reasonable doubt that you fraudulently transferred assets, an extremely difficult standard. In our legal system, this standard only applies in criminal cases. In your offshore havens like Nevis, however, civil suits filed to get at your entity's assets may have to satisfy this difficult burden of proof.

The Nevis LLC law is the ideal jurisdiction for an international asset protection tool because it makes it more difficult and costly to bring a lawsuit to court, more difficult to win a case and more difficult to collect on a judgment.

International Trusts: The Classic International Tool

While many U.S. asset protection experts are using Nevis LLCs in place of international trusts, there are still instances where the trust may be preferable. In the following instances, the international trust (IT) may make sense:

1. **Owning foreign insurance policies.** One of the leading international financial planning strategies today is purchasing a permanent (cash value) life insurance policy offshore. In terms of tax planning, if the policy is U.S. tax-compliant, then all of the growth within the policy will accumulate tax-free. Further, the proceeds will pay out to the beneficiary income-tax–free,

and the client can take tax-free loans against the accumulated cash values during his lifetime. This is similar to the benefits of a domestic cash value life insurance policy, which you can read more about later in this book.

2. **Multigenerational planning.** Let's say the goal of an Affluent client is to create a nest egg for future generations of children, grandchildren, and beyond. And let's say it is important that the nest egg be asset-protected in an ironclad way. In this circumstance, an international trust would be an ideal tool. This would be especially appropriate if the trust was created in a country where the law does not limit the duration of trusts under the law against perpetuities found in many U.S. states. By using an IT, the Savvy Affluent client could literally secure the family's ability to enjoy the fruits of the gift for hundreds of years as long as other estate planning tax issues were addressed.

Consider This

The benefits of international planning can be significant. However, the international tax and reporting laws are highly complex. There are many areas where an individual or advisor could make a mistake. Though all areas of planning require the assistance of advisors, no area of planning requires greater expertise than international planning. Make sure your team of advisors has an asset protection expert who can help you navigate the tricky waters of international planning. With the right planning, international planning can help protect liquid assets, real estate, and possibly your home. For both domestic and international solutions to protecting your home, read the next chapter.

CHAPTER

22

Protecting Your Home

Along with retirement accounts, the family home is often the most valuable asset of the Affluent. Even beyond its pure financial value, the home has great psychic value, as well. In fact, we find that most of our clients who engage in asset protection planning often begin with the question: "How can I protect my home?" That is why we thought it important to dedicate an entire chapter to discussing this asset and how to protect it from outside threats. This chapter will look at the pros and cons of state homestead laws, tenancy by the entirety, LLCs/FLPs, and the debt shield. You may be surprised to find out that something you always feared could actually be your ally in your quest to protect your most valuable asset. This will be another example of a secret of the Affluent that completely contradicts conventional wisdom for Average Americans.

State Homestead Law

As you learned in Chapter 18, every state has some type of homestead protection law. In most states, such as New Jersey, New York, and California, the level of protection is very low when compared with what real estate is worth (New Jersey $0, New York $100,000, California $50 to $100,000). On average, state homestead law protection is about $30,000 to $50,000 of equity—much less than the typical home value of the Affluent. (For more information on state homestead law, please revisit Chapter 18.)

Tenancy by the Entirety

Tenancy by the entirety (TBE), a form of joint ownership available in a number of states, is a decent option for clients of those states. According to Nolo, those states are: Alaska, Arkansas, Delaware, Florida, Hawaii, Illinois, Indiana, Kentucky, Maryland, Massachusetts, Michigan, Mississippi, Missouri, New Jersey, New York, North Carolina, Oklahoma, Oregon, Pennsylvania, Rhode Island, Tennessee, Vermont, Virginia, Wyoming, and the District of Columbia. The protection falls between +1 and +3, depending on the state and its court interpretations.

Inherent in TBE, are a number of risks, including the following:

1. **Joint risk:** TBE provides no shield whatsoever against joint risks; that is, lawsuits that arise from your jointly owned real estate and even, potentially, car accidents.
2. **Divorce risk:** If you rely on TBE for protection and you get divorced before or during the lawsuit, you lose all protections from TBE.
3. **Liability risk:** If you rely on TBE for protection and one spouse dies before or during the lawsuit, you lose all protections from TBE.
4. **Death risk:** TBE is a poor ownership form for estate planning purposes because, at the death of the first spouse, the entire value of the home will automatically be entered into the surviving spouse's taxable estate.

For these reasons, we do not generally recommend TBE alone as a protective tool. The Savvy Affluent generally combine tenancy by the entirety with the debt shield technique that is discussed later in the chapter.

LLCs and FLPs

LLCs and FLPs are two tools that could potentially protect a primary residence. In fact, many advisors regularly recommend these techniques to their clients who want to protect their homes. The drawbacks of these methods are perfect examples of why multidisciplinary planning is a necessity for the Affluent. Let's look at some of the problems with doing asset protection planning in a vacuum with respect to the home.

Drawbacks of LLCs and FLPs for the Home

In Chapter 19, we discussed LLCs and FLPs in detail. We will assume that this is fresh in your mind so you can see why owning real estate in an FLP or LLC would be attractive. However, when it comes to the primary residence, these entities are not very common choices of the Savvy Affluent.

Unlike other assets, the family home has unique tax attributes—most notably, the deductibility of mortgage interest and the $250,000 per person ($500,000 per couple) capital gains tax exemption. By owning the home within an LLC or a FLP, both of these tax benefits may be lost, unless only one spouse owns 100 percent of the interests in the LLC or FLP. However, in a very recent case, the court set aside the protections of an LLC when only the debtor owned 100 percent of the interests in the LLC. For these reasons, we no longer recommend single-owner LLCs and FLPs to protect the family home.

Qualified Personal Residence Trusts

When using a Qualified Personal Residence Trust (QPRT), the owner transfers ownership of the home to the QPRT irrevocably. While this is certainly effective for both asset protection and estate planning purposes, it comes with a significant cost: You no longer own your home. In fact, when the term of years is up (typically 10 years), you have to pay rent to the trust just to live in the home. Homes with mortgages on them present further tax difficulties, as well. For these reasons, while the QPRT is a strong asset protection tool, we typically do not advise using it for most younger clients whose main concern is asset protection not estate planning. Nonetheless, if it can be implemented correctly, a QPRT receives a rating of +4 or +5 protection.

The Unlikely Solution Most Advisors Can't Even Mention

Oddly enough, the best way to protect a home is probably the same way we all started owning our homes—with someone else's money. By not having any, or very little, equity in your home, the bank owns the home. A creditor has very little to gain from trying to attack the home when there is little to no equity—especially when that small amount of equity is partially or completely protected through homestead exemptions in many states.

Since we can't go back in time and stop paying down our mortgages, we have to find a way to address this issue now. Unfortunately, most advisors can't even tell you how to do this. That's right! Here is a perfect example of what was discussed in the First Key. Affluent Americans have to live in a society that is focused on Average Americans. Consider this example:

Individuals and firms in the securities and insurance industries have been the subject of a rising number of complaints and lawsuits over the last 10 years. As a result, the regulatory agencies and compliance departments of these companies have forbade their representatives from recommending that their clients remove equity from real estate and invest it into either securities or insurance products. These advisors cannot even accept loan proceeds from a refinanced property. These companies adopted this policy because they feared that less financially sophisticated homeowners wouldn't understand the risk of this maneuver and might lose their homes if the investments they made with the loan proceeds didn't perform well.

We approve of the protection of less sophisticated investors and the protection from unscrupulous salespeople (and there are many of both). However, to threaten to terminate advisors who want to help Affluent clients whose asset protection concerns outweigh the investment risks that they and their teams understand is ridiculous. In this situation, the Affluent can't even get the advice they deserve. Let's discuss that technique that most advisors can't even share but the Savvy Affluent know and implement on a regular basis: the debt shield.

The Debt Shield

The debt shield can be the most effective way to shield the equity of the home. Essentially, using a debt shield means getting a loan against most of the equity in your home. For many clients, this is counterintuitive; they want to pay down the mortgage as much as possible. While this may have an emotional appeal, for asset protection purposes, it is the exact opposite of what you want to do.

For example, to help people protect their home equity, one financial institution we examined for a client designed an interesting debt shield program. The bank loaned the client funds equal to up to 90 percent of the value of the home and then filed a mortgage—first, second, or even third—to eat up any available equity. Now the home was protected.

The loan funds were placed in an asset-protected trust, one drafted for the client by an asset protection attorney. Those funds were owned by the trust and, under the loan documents, required to be placed in the bank's CD account. Further, the bank contractually guaranteed that its loan rate would be only 1 percent more than its CD rate, meaning that this structure will only cost participants 1 percent of the home equity to implement (plus legal fees). When the client retires or feels that the threat to the home has diminished, the CD account pays off the loan and the mortgage is released.

The Enhanced Debt Shield

In the basic debt shield above, there is a real cost to the loan versus the investment—a shortfall of 1 percent per year. What if the funds you gain by shielding your home could be invested in a way that you had an opportunity to earn more within the investment than the loan interest would cost? In this way, you would make money by shielding the home through the concept of leverage we discussed in the Second Key. Certainly, this is possible in many states.

In some states, certain investment classes are asset-protected under state law—the exempt assets noted in an earlier chapter. The most common are annuities and cash value life insurance policies, which are protected in many states such as New York, Florida, Texas, and Ohio, among many others. In states such as these, you may take a loan for 6 percent to 8 percent (partially or totally tax-deductible) and be able to invest in an annuity or insurance policy that credits 5 percent to 8 percent or more (tax-deferred). When you consider that the mortgage interest may be tax deductible, the true after-tax cost to you may be as little as 3.5 percent to 5 percent. If your asset-protected investment returns approximately 6 percent (many life insurance policies have guaranteed minimum crediting rates of 3 percent or 4 percent) and you are paying only 4 percent or 5 percent (after taxes) in interest, you can actually make money while protecting your castle. Of course, this gain is not guaranteed and you could lose money in this arrangement. The Savvy Affluent understand their risks and act appropriately for their situation.

Consider This

For most Affluent clients, there is no more financially valuable and psychologically important asset than the family residence. Some states offer great homestead protection, but most states offer inadequate protection of this valued asset. If you do not enjoy unlimited homestead protection, you must make it a priority to work with your team to protect your home. If you don't protect this valuable property, there is no need to bother protecting any other assets. The only thing more valuable than your home is your future income. This is covered in the next chapter.

CHAPTER 23

Divorce Protection

O f all the risks to the Affluent, the most common threat to financial security may be divorce. According to *Divorce Magazine*'s (www.divorcemag.com) statistics from 1997, 50 percent of all first marriages in the United States end. Remarriages end in divorce 60 percent of the time. Undoubtedly an emotionally devastating experience, divorce can be a financially disastrous experience as well.

Divorce protection is not about hiding assets from a soon-to-be ex-spouse. Nor is it about cheating or lying to keep your wealth. Rather, it concerns resolving issues of property ownership and distribution before things go sour. By agreeing in advance what will be yours and what will be your spouse's, you save money, time, and emotional distress in the long run. In fact, this type of asset protection planning inevitably benefits all parties, except the divorce lawyers, of course.

Divorce planning is also about shielding family assets from the potential divorces of children and grandchildren. Given the statistics enumerated above, it is almost a certainty that either a child or grandchild of yours will get divorced. Thus, for purposes of intergenerational financial planning, this is a crucial topic unless you want to give half of your inheritance to the ex-spouses of your heirs. This is a lesson Wealthy Families have known, and addressed, for decades. Wealthy Families don't have a secret for avoiding divorce. Wealthy Families have a secret for avoiding the financial losses that can be associated with divorce. This chapter will discuss why divorce can be so financially devastating, pros and cons of prenuptial agreements, irrevocable trusts, and ways to protect your children from the financial effects of divorce.

Why Divorce Can Be a Financial Nightmare

Most Americans do not have to read newspapers to see how financially devastating a divorce can be. While high-profile divorces involving tens of millions of dollars illustrate the point dramatically, most of us need only look to family or friends to see how a divorce can create financial upheaval. The prevailing attitude toward divorce can be illustrated by a scene in the movie, *First Wives Club*. In the film, Ivana Trump explains her theory of divorce to three ex-wives, played by Goldie Hawn, Diane Keaton, and Bette Midler. "Don't get even," she says, "get everything!"

Combine this fight-for-everything attitude with the terrible odds of getting a divorce, and you have a very serious threat to financial security. In fact, a divorce threatens not only former spouses, but also their families and possibly their business partners as well. To truly understand how a divorce affects the finances of the participants, you must first understand how property is divided when the marriage is dissolved.

Community Property States

Nine states have community property laws: Arizona, California, Idaho, Louisiana, Nevada, New Mexico, Texas, Washington, and Wisconsin. Community property law stipulates that if there is no valid pre- or postmarital agreement, the court will equally divide any property acquired during the marriage other than inheritances or gifts to one spouse. Even the appreciation of one spouse's separate property can be divided if the other spouse expended effort on that property during the marriage, and the property actually appreciated concurrent or subsequent to the effort so expended. Based on these facts, it is obvious that *how* the asset is titled is not the controlling factor. Instead, *when* the asset was acquired and *how* it was treated are far more important factors in determining how the asset will be treated.

Equitable Distribution States

Noncommunity property states are called equitable distribution states, because courts in these states have total discretion to divide the property equitably or fairly. The court will normally consider a number of factors in deciding what is equitable, including the length of the marriage, the age and conduct of the parties, and the current earnings and future earning potential of each former spouse. The danger of equitable divorces is that courts often distribute both nonmarital assets (those acquired before the marriage) as well as marital assets (those acquired during marriage), in order to create a fair arrangement. In this way, courts often split up property in ways that the ex-spouses never wanted or expected.

Examples of "Disaster Divorces"

The following are examples of disastrous divorces involving the Affluent to help you consider whether you and your family are adequately prepared for divorce.

Example 1. A couple marries. This is the second marriage for each and they both have adult children from their first marriages. Without any pre- or postmarital agreement, they title many of the wife's previously separate income-producing properties (such as her rental apartment units) into the name of the new husband to save income taxes. Within two years of the marriage, they divorce. The husband gets half the rental units (in addition to alimony and other property) even though both spouses understood that the wife intended them to go to her children. The court simply ignored their understanding, giving half the properties to each spouse.

Example 2. A couple marries, each for the first time. Over the next 20 years, the husband acquires more ownership in his family's bakery business. His father, the founder, gradually transfers shares to him. At 42, he is the majority owner. He and his wife then undergo a bitter divorce, and the ex-wife is granted half the husband's bakery business as community property. She then forces high dividends and a sale of the company to a competitor.

Example 3. An internal medicine resident gets married. She and her husband discuss the cost of her medical education and agree that she should not have to compensate him for his greater financial contribution in the early years of their marriage. However, they file for divorce eight years later. The husband considers the wife's professional degree as marital property, so he claims a share in her earning potential. The court agrees, even though the couple verbally agreed to the contrary.

Can a Prenup Protect You?

A premarital agreement, or prenuptial agreement, premarital contract, or antenuptial agreement, is the foundation of any protection against a divorce. The premarital agreement is a written contract between the spouses. It specifies the division of property and income upon divorce, including disposition of specific personal property, such as family heirlooms. It also states the responsibilities of each party with regard to their children after divorce. Finally, these agreements lay out the respective responsibilities of each partner during marriage, such as the financial support each spouse can expect, and which religious faith children will be brought up in. The agreement cannot limit child support because the right to child support lies with the child and not the parent.

Requirements for a Premarital Agreement

Each state differs slightly on what is required for an enforceable premarital agreement. The following are fairly common requirements:

1. **The agreement must be in writing and signed.** Every state requires that a premarital agreement be written and signed. Many also require that it be notarized or witnessed.
   Tip: Notarize your agreement, even if your state does not require it. This adds protection against claims of duress or forgery.
2. **There must be a fair, accurate, and reasonable disclosure of each party's financial condition.**
   Tip: Attach financial statements to the agreement and have each spouse affirm knowledge of the other's financial condition.
3. **Each party must be advised by a separate attorney.** Many states either require separate legal advice explicitly or use it as a factor in determining whether or not the agreement is fair.
   Tip: Hire separate lawyers and allow enough time between the agreement and the wedding date to avoid any appearance of duress. Courts frown on last-second premarital agreements.
4. **The agreement must not be unconscionable.** Courts will not enforce a one-sided agreement. Also, the contract must not be structured to encourage divorce. For example, by stating that one spouse has no rights to property except upon divorce.
   Tip: Avoid extremely one-sided agreements. It need not be a 50/50 split, but it should provide a fair balance.

5. **The couple must follow the agreement during the marriage.** Courts disregard premarital agreements when the spouses blatantly disregard it during their marriage, such as when property designated as the husband's separate property is retitled to the wife.

> **Tip:** *Treat designated separate property as separate. If loans are made from one spouse's separate property to the marital unit, then those funds should not be commingled when repaid.*

Irrevocable Spendthrift Trusts: Ideal Tools to Keep Assets in the Family

As mentioned in Chapter 20, irrevocable trusts are very effective asset protection tools because the grantor no longer owns the assets owned by the trust. In other words, the grantor has transferred the property with no strings attached. Because the grantor neither owns nor controls the property, future creditors, including an ex-spouse, cannot claim the property. Moreover, the grantor can make children, grandchildren, and even future great grandchildren beneficiaries of an irrevocable trust. However, even though they can benefit from trust assets, the trust can be drafted so that their creditors, including divorcing ex-spouses, cannot get to trust assets.

Nonetheless, using an irrevocable trust should not be done lightly. Giving away assets forever with no strings attached can prove to be a serious consequence when protecting against divorce, lawsuit, or other threat. When would such a strategy make sense? It would make sense in circumstances where you would have inevitably given away the assets to certain beneficiaries anyway. For example, the trust might be used for assets that (1) you will leave to your children or grandchildren when you die; and (2) you do not need for your financial security. For a more detailed example, consider the Irving's case study.

Case Study: Irving's Trust Protects His Summer Home

Irving, a plastic surgeon, bought a summer home on Massachusetts' Cape Cod. He and his first wife had three small children. Unfortunately, they divorced about six years into their marriage. In the settlement, he received the summer home.

Fifteen years later, Irving was ready to marry again, now in Santa Fe. Both he and his prospective spouse had been married previously and understood divorce. Irving considered a premarital agreement to keep the summer home as his separate property. He had planned to give it to his three children but wondered whether working on the home would jeopardize this plan if he later divorced.

After speaking with Irving, we noted three important points:

1. Irving's handiwork on the home might make it marital property.
2. Irving's children and their families used the home throughout the year.
3. Irving had a lawsuit pending against him from a failed real estate venture.

Given these points, it was clear that the best strategy for Irving was to have an Irrevocable trust own the summer home, which would give beneficial interests of the home to all three children equally (which already occurred).

By using an irrevocable trust to own the summer home, Irving protected the home against possible future divorce judgments and also shielded it from other creditors and lawsuits. By including spendthrift provisions, Irving protected the home from his children's creditors as well. This will insure that the Cape house stays in the family for generations.

Protect Your Children from Divorce

When your children or grandchildren come to you, giddy with exciting news about their recent engagements, the last thing they want to hear you ask is, "Are you going to sign a prenuptial agreement?" In fact, if you weren't paying for the wedding, you might lose your invitation for asking such a question.

As you learned earlier, the secret to protecting assets from divorce is keeping the assets as separate property and not commingling them with community or marital property. You can't trust your children to do this, so you are going to do it for them . . . without requiring the consent of your child or the future (or existing) spouse.

By leaving assets to your children's irrevocable trusts, with the appropriate spendthrift provisions, rather than to them personally, you can achieve this goal. Of course, if the children take money out of the trust and use it to buy a home or other property, that property will be subject to the rules of their state. To illustrate this point, let's look at the example of Rob and Janelle.

Rob and Janelle were college sweethearts who got married right after graduation. Within a few years, their romance quickly turned sour and Rob could no longer handle the physical and emotional abuse. However, during their three-year marriage, Janelle received a sizeable inheritance and used it to pay off the couple's home. When they filed for divorce, Rob's attorney successfully argued that his time and labor on the house, and the fact that he lived in it except when Janelle occasionally kicked him out and he had to stay at his mother's, made half of the equity in the home, or $100,000, Rob's fair share. Though Rob and all of his friends will argue the $100,000 was a small consolation for what he endured, Janelle's grandparents certainly didn't intend for Rob to receive their inheritance.

What could Janelle have done differently to ensure that she protected her assets? Her grandparents could have left her the inheritance through an irrevocable trust that only allowed her to take out so much money per year. In that case, she would have used the interest from the inheritance to pay the mortgage down each month. If she did so, the corpus of the inheritance would have remained separate property and would not have been part of the divorce settlement. In the three short years of their marriage, they would have had next to no equity in their home and Rob would have left the marriage with what he brought into it and his wounded pride . . . but none of Janelle's grandparents' life savings. It is left to the reader to determine what is equitable. We aren't marriage counselors; we are only trying to help you reach your desired objectives.

In a nutshell, a little proactive financial planning can go a long way to making sure that a divorce doesn't completely disrupt a family's financial situation.

Consider This

It should be easy to understand why so few people are wealthy. So far, this Key has showed you how family wealth can be lost to personal and professional lawsuits, disability, and divorce. Luckily, you also learned in the last Key that there are many ways to protect wealth from all of those threats. There is one threat that we failed to address in this Key. That is the largest threat of all: taxes. The entire Fifth Key focuses on ways to address tax liabilities. Taxes, in fact, are so substantial a threat to family wealth that there is an additional key, the Sixth Key, solely dedicated to estate taxes. If you do not own a business, you can continue to the Fifth Key. If you do own a business and would like to learn the most efficient tool for maximizing asset protection, tax, and estate planning, you should read Chapter 24. The captive insurance company is a secret of Super Affluent business owners that may benefit you as well.

24

Using Captive Insurance Companies to Protect Businesses

Many of the Savvy and Super Affluent clients we work with have built their wealth by building a private business or professional practice. Typically, the business is not only the vehicle that allows the client to use leverage, but it is also the vehicle that creates the bulk of the client's annual income and long-term wealth accumulation. Given this fundamental importance, it is essential that a Savvy Affluent client do everything possible to protect the business and to maximize its leverage potential. The best tool for achieving such protection and leverage is the one we will discuss in this chapter—the captive insurance company (CIC). In this chapter, we will discuss what a CIC is, what benefits it offers, and how the Savvy Affluent use it to maximize the benefits they get from their planning.

The CIC

Early in the book, we stressed the importance of using tools that have multiple benefits. By using tools that offer multiple benefits, the Savvy Affluent can compound leverage and achieve a number of planning goals very efficiently. Of all the tools discussed in this book, the CIC can be the most efficient. For clients who own successful business or professional practices, the CIC often becomes the cornerstone of their ascent to Super Affluence. This is because the CIC affords the following benefits:

- Superior risk management for the business.
- Reduction in the business' insurance expenses to third-party insurers.
- The ability to capture profits on insurance business.
- Creation of a potential buyout mechanism for older owners of the business upon retirement.
- High level (+4 or +5) asset protection for CIC assets.
- Superior income tax treatment for CIC income (when the CIC is properly structured and maintained).
- Significant estate planning benefits (when the CIC is properly integrated with estate planning tools).

The CIC we will discuss here is a fully licensed insurance company domiciled either in one of the states that has special legislation for small captive companies or in an offshore jurisdiction that has similar captive legislation. Whenever a CIC is established offshore, it is critical that the CIC be compliant with all U.S. tax rules. With small CICs, this may not be difficult but still must be handled by a tax attorney or CPA experienced in these matters.

CIC as a Risk Management Tool

The CIC must always be established with a real insurance purpose; that is, as a facility for transferring risk and protecting assets. The transaction must make economic sense. Beyond this general rule, there is a great deal of flexibility in how the CIC can benefit a client.

First, clients can use the CIC to supplement their existing insurance policies. Such excess protection gives the client the security of knowing that the company and its owners will not be wiped out by a lawsuit award in excess of traditional coverage limits. As the Savvy Affluent who own businesses are concerned about all types of lawsuits—from product liability to environmental claims to employee lawsuits—this protection can be significant. Further, the CIC may even allow the client to reduce existing insurance, as the CIC policy will step in to provide additional coverage if needed.

Also, using one's own CIC gives the client flexibility in using customized policies that one would not easily find when using large third-party insurers. For example, many clients would like a liability policy that would pay the client's legal fees and allow full choice of attorney, but would not be available to pay creditors or claimants (what we call "Shallow Pockets" policies). This prevents the client from appearing as a Deep Pocket (a prime lawsuit target). Avoiding this appearance is a necessary asset protection strategy today.

In addition, the CIC has the flexibility to add coverage for liabilities excluded by traditional general liability policies such as wrongful termination, harassment, or even Americans with Disabilities Act violations. Given that the awards in these areas can be more than $1 million per case, the Savvy Affluent understand the value of the CIC for this benefit alone. Let's see how two such clients used a CIC by looking at the case study of Tom and Dick.

Case Study: Tom and Dick Use CICs

Tom and Dick are Savvy Affluent clients who each own medical surgery centers with similar revenues and each has about 100 employees. Tom feels like he is paying too much for his group's medical malpractice and commercial liability insurance policies. After our firm introduced Tom to an attorney and an actuary who specialize in CICs, he created one to issue policies that cover the least significant, most common medical malpractice and commercial liability claims (under $100,000 per occurrence). This significantly reduced his existing insurance premiums because he then had much higher deductibles for his third-party insurance policies.

Tom believed he could reduce his insurance premiums to commercial insurance companies, implement successful risk management programs, reduce the claims of the center, and reduce his overall payments and costs. Ultimately, he hoped that the CIC would help him increase the profits of the center. He was right. While a significant portion of the $1.5 million in total payments was paid out to cover claims, there was still more than $1 million in his CIC reserves after five years.

Tom also had the CIC owned by a trust for his family, so he was able to build the wealth created by the CIC out of his taxable estate.

Dick had a different approach. He established a CIC to insure lesser risks that were not covered under commercial insurance. These policies included Medicare fraud defense, HIPAA litigation expense, and malpractice defense policies, which are available only to pay for the company's legal fees but not to pay claimants.

After five years, Dick's CIC did not pay any claims. At this point, the premiums are still growing as reserves of the CIC to be used to pay future claims.

Dick was also considering bringing younger partners into his business. He plans on using the CIC as part of an exit strategy for his business as well, with each new partner responsible for paying some of his buyout—from both the business and the CIC.

In addition to business owners, two other categories of the Affluent that can use CICs are entertainers and professional athletes. Let's examine how a CIC might work for these types of clients by looking at the case study of Mike.

Case Study: Mike the Professional Athlete Uses a CIC

Mike is a professional basketball player, making more than $8 million per year in salary and endorsements. As with any athlete, the risk of an injury interrupting or ending his career is significant. Mike would like to insure against this risk. While many of Mike's fellow players are advised to simply get an insurance policy from a specialty lines carrier such as Lloyd's of London, Mike gets better advice.

Mike is most concerned about a career-ending injury, not a relatively minor or even average injury. Mike decides to create a CIC that writes policies covering loss of income from all types of injuries (knees, ankles, wrists, hands, and so on). A reasonable premium for Mike is about $1 million per year, given his age and preexisting conditions. Mike gets to deduct the full $1 million he pays to his CIC, which, in turn, reinsures the risk of the most serious injuries to Lloyd's for a premium of about $500,000. This way, Mike is covered for all injuries; he self-insures for minor injuries and gets the same coverage as his teammates for serious injuries. All of his dollars are treated in a tax favored way and are asset-protected from his creditors.

The case study about Mike demonstrates that clients can sometimes purchase policies, like CICs, from traditional third-party insurers. However, they would not enjoy the powerful asset protection, tax, retirement, and estate planning advantages described here. In essence, the question for the client becomes:

> If I am going to use insurance to protect against risk, why give away the potential profits, asset protection, tax, business, and estate planning benefits when I do not have to?

Let's examine a few of the benefits of having a CIC more closely.

CIC: Compared to self-insuring—the rainy day fund. Because our society has become so litigious, many nonSavvy Affluent clients have been self-insuring against potential losses like the ones named above. These clients have simply saved funds, which will be used to pay any expenses that arise if a risk comes to fruition. This is the proverbial rainy day fund. While a rainy day fund may prove wise, the client would be better off using a CIC to insure against any risks. That is because, as discussed above, once the premiums are paid to the CIC, the funds enjoy the highest levels of asset protection (+4 or +5), can be structured to grow outside the taxable estate, can be structured to layer into a business exit strategy, and can enjoy extreme income tax advantages as well. None of these benefits are found with the rainy day fund.

No loss of control. When investigating the merits of a CIC, many clients are concerned with losing control of the funds paid to the CIC. While the clients' concerns are certainly justified, the proper CIC structure allows for complete control by the client. Typically, the bank and investment accounts of the CIC are handled much the same way as any other business account. The account is in the name of the business, but all the decisions about the account are made by the owner (who would be the Savvy Affluent business owner). In many instances, the same advisors who helped us write the Eighth Key—Invest Wisely—are the ones who are managing the investments of our clients' CICs. The CIC does not require a client to trust any other person or entity with control of the CIC assets.

Avoiding land mines. As previously mentioned, the CIC structure must be properly created and maintained. If not, all risk management, asset protection, estate, business, and tax benefits may be lost. For these reasons, using professionals who have expertise in establishing CICs for clients is critical—especially so for the attorneys and insurance managers involved. While using such experts and a real CIC structure may be more expensive than some of the cheaper alternatives being touted on the Internet or at fly-by-night seminars, this is one area where doing it right is the only way to enjoy the CIC's benefits and be 100 percent compliant.

Who can afford a CIC? Setting up a CIC requires particular expertise as explained above. Thus, as might be expected, the professionals most experienced in these matters charge significant fees for both the creation and maintenance of CICs. Setup costs are typically around $100,000 and annual maintenance costs another $50,000 per year. While these fees are significant and often fully tax-deductible as a reasonable business expense, the CIC's potential risk management, tax, business, estate planning, and asset protection benefits often combine to make it a very attractive option for the Savvy Affluent. There is no better way for successful business owners to leverage their advisors than to work with them to create such a flexible and efficient planning tool as a captive insurance company. To see if a CIC is a good idea for you and your business, a comprehensive feasibility study can be done for about $7,500.

Consider This

The Affluent face various financial threats that range from operational problems to exit strategy challenges and from lawsuit threats to taxes. The Savvy Affluent not only want to mitigate these risks, they also want to do so in an efficient manner. For these reasons, the Savvy Affluent who own successful businesses use captive insurance companies. A CIC can be a valuable tool that helps address many of the Savvy Affluent business owner's planning challenges at one time. In fact, perhaps no other tool described in this book can impact a client's overall wealth protection and long-term wealth accumulation as much as a CIC. There is no other asset protection tool that offers such significant income tax and estate planning benefits as the CIC. To learn more secrets the Savvy Affluent have used to manage their taxes and estate planning, you should continue reading the Fifth and Sixth Keys.

THE FIFTH KEY

ALWAYS CONSIDER TAXES

You don't have to be Affluent or make a lot of money to want to legally pay less in taxes. The famous judge Learned Hand once said: "No American is required to pay any more tax than the law would allow . . . there is not even a patriotic duty to do so." The difference between Average Americans and the Savvy Affluent is that the latter group always considers the tax impact of anything they do.

The Savvy Affluent understand that every additional dollar earned will be decimated by federal, state, and local taxes that may approach 50 cents. They also know that up to 50 percent of the family's after-tax net worth will be subject to federal estate and state inheritance taxes every time wealth transfers from one generation to the next. The Internal Revenue Code (IRC) is structured in a way that makes it almost impossible to accumulate wealth and pass it to future generations without significant friction. This is why the secret to building and maintaining a family fortune—building Wealthy Families—can be directly related to a family's ability to manage taxes.

You can't possibly expect to manage taxes unless you understand taxes first. Everyone should read the next chapter, "Uncle Sam's Pieces of Your Pie," to learn exactly what taxes threaten wealth accumulation. This will help you better understand the motivation for, and benefits of, the strategies in the subsequent chapters. These are tools that may help you reduce, defer, or even eliminate some of these taxes while providing you, your family, or your business additional financial benefits. By learning and implementing the techniques in this Key, you will be able to reduce unnecessary taxes and build a fortune much more quickly. This is a key to achieving greater levels of Affluence.

CHAPTER

25

Uncle Sam's Pieces of Your Pie

Y ou can't expect to successfully overcome any challenge until you fully understand the challenge itself. In this chapter, we will explain how great an impact taxes have on your finances. We will also share techniques Wealthy Families have used to successfully reduce unnecessary taxes for decades. If you need any additional motivation to save on taxes, we know dozens of families that have been able to save tens of thousands to hundreds of thousands of dollars per year during their lifetimes, and millions of dollars in taxes at the time of death by integrating these strategies into their comprehensive financial plans. Let's get started by examining where and how all of this tax revenue is generated by looking at four types of taxes:

- Incomes taxes
- Taxes on investments or capital gain tax rates
- Estate taxes
- Income in respect of a decedent (IRD)

Income Taxes

Everyone pays income taxes on salaries and other income. Do you know exactly how income taxes are computed? Most people believe that they move from income tax bracket to income tax bracket—increasing the percentage they pay on each dollar earned as they move forward. The truth is that every individual (in the same filing category) pays the same tax rate on the first $15,100 of income. As a taxpayer's income crosses a threshold into the next tax bracket,

Table 25.1   2006 Federal Income Tax Table—Married Couples Filing Jointly

If taxable income is over:	But not over:	The tax is:
$0	$15,100	10% of the amount over $0
$15,100	$61,300	$1,510.00 plus 15% of the amount over $15,100
$61,300	$123,700	$8,440.00 plus 25% of the amount over $61,300
$123,700	$188,450	$24,040.00 plus 28% of the amount over $123,700
$188,450	$336,550	$42,170.00 plus 33% of the amount over $188,450
$336,550	no limit	$91,043.00 plus 35% of the amount over $336,550

only the dollars earned within that bracket are taxed at the higher rate. Table 25.1 illustrates how income tax is determined for married couples who filed jointly in 2006.

In order to better understand, how income tax is tabulated for families, let's look at an example of Stewart and Coco.

Stewart and Coco are married and file jointly. Stewart makes $90,000 per year, while Coco runs an in-home business that generates $10,000 per year. For simplicity, let's assume they have no deductions and they live in a state with 0 percent state income tax. Based on their salaries, they have $100,000 of total adjusted gross income.

On the first $15,100 of income they pay 10%	$1,510
On the next $46,200 (up to $61,300) they pay 15%	$6,930
On the next $38,700 (up to $100,000) they pay 25%	$9,675
Total tax	**$18,115**
Marginal tax bracket	25%
Effective tax rate ($18,620/$100,000)	18.12%

Let's also assume that Stewart and Coco spend $6,000 a month on their expenses and they save the rest.

Gross income	$100,000
Income tax	$18,115
After-tax income	$81,885
Expenses	$72,000
Savings	$9,885 for retirement

Beware: Present Income Tax Rates Are Very Low and May Rise

As we write this book, federal income tax rates are at one of the lowest points in the history of the U.S. income tax. See Table 25.2.

Table 25.2   Federal Income Tax Rates

Year	Top Marginal Federal Income Tax Rate
1920	73.0%
1930	25.0%
1940	81.0%
1950	91.0%
1960	91.0%
1970	71.0%
1980	70.0%
1990	28.0%
2000	39.6%
2008	35.0%
2011 on	39.6%

Source: Citizens for Tax Justice, May 2004.

The Savvy Affluent understand the information presented in Table 25.2 and what it means; that is, tax rates are currently at a historical low and will likely rise, possibly significantly, in the future. They remember when the highest marginal federal income tax rates were well over 50 percent. Could the largest U.S. deficit in history and a potential shift in power in Washington lead to higher rates sooner rather than later? Are you willing to bet your hard earned money that rates will not increase again?

If Stewart and Coco put away 10 percent of his salary into a tax-deductible vehicle like a retirement plan, it would look like this:

Gross income	$100,000
Deduction	$10,000
Taxable income	$90,000
Taxes	$15,615
Net income	$74,385
Expenses	$72,000
Savings	$2,385

Coco and Stewart have $10,000 in pretax retirement savings to add to the $2,385 of after-tax savings for a total of $12,385 in total savings instead of the $9,885 they had before!

Taxes on Investments

Once you earn money and pay income taxes, you aren't done with tax payments. This is only the tip of the tax iceberg. You may spend the money you earn (after taxes) on small items and pay sales tax, or you may buy real estate and pay annual property taxes. Another possibility is that you save the money and invest it in some type of investment. Common investment choices of Average Americans include savings accounts, certificates of deposit (CDs), money market funds, stocks, bonds, mutual funds, cash value insurance policies, and real estate. A general discussion of investments is offered in the Eighth Key. The investment choices of the Savvy Affluent will be described in detail in the Ninth Key.

Most investments can generally be classified as either income or growth vehicles. In some cases, an investment may offer both. Income investments are those that offer some type of regular return (income) to the investor. Your bank accounts, CDs, and money markets give you an interest payment each year. If you own traditional bonds, you receive a coupon every six months or year. If you own rental real estate, you may collect rental income. All of these interest payments, bond coupon payments, and rent checks are added to your income for the purpose of calculating taxable income discussed above. If you are in a 25 percent marginal income tax bracket like Stewart and Coco, then you will have to pay tax of 25 percent on those payments. If you are in a 35 percent marginal tax bracket, then you will pay 35 percent of the investment gain in taxes on that investment income. Of course, if you are not in an income-tax-free state (most are not), you could pay up to 10 percent in additional state income taxes as well.

Not all investors require immediate income from investments. Because the Affluent don't need current income from investments, they can afford to invest in riskier investments while looking for greater long-term appreciation. The Affluent are looking for growth vehicles like stocks (usually small cap or technology types), hedge funds, certain mutual funds, individually managed accounts, and life insurance contracts that may have any of these vehicles as underlying investments. These investments and growth vehicles are further discussed in the Eighth and Ninth Keys.

When you invest with a particular company, your money is used to help grow that firm. The company that receives your investment will reinvest the proceeds to potentially increase the net worth (value) of the company. As the value of the company increases, the value of your shares in the company will also increase. You do not receive a regular check from the company. Rather, you have the right to sell your shares of the company. If you realize this type of profit on your investment, you are responsible for taxes on your capital gains.

For tax purposes, capital gains can be categorized as long-term or short-term. Short-term is defined as realized (sold) appreciation of an asset that you owned for less than one year. If you have a short-term gain, it is treated exactly the same way (for tax purposes) as the interest, coupons, and rental income above. In Rob and Janelle's case, their short-term capital gains would be taxed at 25 percent (plus any applicable state income taxes). Of course, if their combined earned income and investment income reach $123,700, then each additional dollar will be taxed at 28 percent.

If you hold an asset for more than one year, the government gives you a benefit. You can pay long-term capital gains tax rates on your realized appreciation. Currently, these rates are 10 percent of the growth (for individuals who are in the lowest tax bracket) and 15 percent for all other taxpayers (plus applicable state taxes). This benefit gives an incentive to investors to keep their funds in one place. This stability is much better than the constant buying and selling, which could significantly disrupt business. This tax incentive also acts as a deterrent to potentially unethical short-term trading.

Back to the example of our happily married couple who filed jointly, Stewart and Coco. Let's say that Stewart and Coco invest

$7,000 of savings in a 5 percent money market. This generates a $350 interest payment annually. They must add this $350 to their $100,000. Because they are in a 25 percent marginal tax bracket, the additional federal income tax liability will be $87.50. The $350 growth will only really be worth $262.50 (3.75 percent, instead of the 5 percent they thought they were getting) to them after taxes.

Beware: Current Capital Gains Tax Rates Are Very Low and May Rise

As we write this book, capital gains tax rates, like ordinary income tax rates, are at the lowest point in the history of the U.S. capital gains tax. See Table 25.3.

Table 25.3   Top Federal Capital Gains Tax Rate

Year	Top Federal Capital Gains Tax Rate
1940	30.0%
1942–1967	25.0%
1970	32.3%
1977	39.9%
1980	28.0%
1990	28.0%
2000	20.0%
2008	15.0%
2011 on	20.0%

Source: Citizens for Tax Justice, May 2004.

The Savvy Affluent understand the information presented in Table 25.3 and how it impacts their wealth and assets. Tax rates are low now and could easily become much higher in the relatively near future. Because their planning is long-term, the Savvy Affluent take the probability of an increased capital gains tax rate into account in their planning. There is more discussion of this dilemma as it pertains to real estate and 1031 exchanges in the Ninth Key.

Is Uncle Sam's triple dip enough? No, it isn't. After you pay your income taxes, sales taxes for your purchases, property taxes on real estate, and taxes on all of your investment gains, there is still more tax to be paid.

Estate Taxes

When you pass away, Uncle Sam has an estate tax for those of you who might be worth more than $1 million at the time of your death (assuming you live until at least 2011). That $1 million may include the combined value of your home, retirement plans, real estate, brokerage accounts, and insurance policies. While the rates might be between 40 percent and 55 percent, for estimation purposes we will assume the estate tax rate to be about 50 percent for ease of calculations throughout the book. That means that half of what you think you will leave your children could go to taxes. For a complete description of the estate tax, how it works, why the supposed repeal is a fairy tale, and how to avoid the unnecessary costs associated with it, please read the Sixth Key, which focuses on estate planning.

IRD: The Only 70 Percent Tax Trap

Lastly, there is a combination of taxes that severely threatens those of you who hope to be worth more than $1 million and who might die with a retirement plan or an IRA you would like to leave your children. There is something called income in respect of a decedent.

No tax discussion is complete without mentioning IRD. IRD refers to the taxation of income earned by a deceased person who didn't pay tax on the income before passing away or hadn't received the money before passing away. This is income that would have been taxable had the decedent lived long enough to receive it. These income items include unpaid salaries, bonuses and commissions, as well as qualified retirement plans (such as pensions and 401(k)s), roll-over IRAs, and variable annuity appreciation. Statistically, the qualified retirement plan and IRA balances are by far the most significant IRD assets.

Figure 25.1 shows an example of how a retirement plan might be distributed at the time of death.

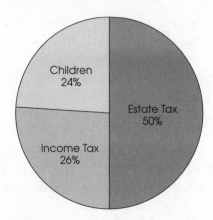

Figure 25.1   Distribution of IRD

Based on this figure, you should be aware that it is possible for less than $250,000 of a $1,000,000 retirement plan or IRA to reach your children after all taxes are paid.

Consider This

It may seem crazy that there are so many ways that you can lose your wealth to taxes. Our tax laws are the most complex system of rules created by mankind. We will never master them all. The best we can hope to do is attempt to manage the system. Hopefully, you understand how much money is at stake and will take this section very seriously. Managing taxes may prove to be the most important Secret of the Affluent you will need to master. In the next chapter, we will learn practical ways to legally reduce taxes.

CHAPTER 26

Use Retirement Plans

If you see a long history of tax benefits being afforded to a particular behavior or asset, this is generally because Congress believes that the behavior or asset provides some economic benefit to society as a whole. We will revisit these types of tax benefits for home ownership, real estate, and cash value life insurance later in this section and in the Ninth Key. In the case of retirement vehicles, the theory is that by encouraging people to fund their own retirement, the government—and the rest of us taxpayers—will not have to support them in retirement.

Two retirement tactics of the Affluent are:

1. Maximizing available qualified retirement plan contributions for all members of the family.
2. Maximizing investments in vehicles that are similar to qualified plans for all members of the family.

To succeed, the Affluent must leverage assets, capital, and advisors.

By creating separate business entities to manage real estate and liquid assets, the Affluent are able to create employment opportunities for members of their families. By creating income opportunities for family members, the Affluent accomplish two things:

1. They generate effective wealth transfers to junior generations.
2. They create opportunities for such family members to make tax-deductible contributions to their own retirement plans.

Maximizing the Use of Qualified Plans

Because tax-deductible retirement plan contributions are limited for each person, having additional family members earning income within a family business offers a Wealthy Family multiple tax-deductible contributions. This technique reduces the total tax liability for the family. In the Fourth Key—Asset Protection—you learned that qualified retirement plans are generally afforded the highest level of protection from creditors (+5). The use of multiple contributions also affords Wealthy Families a greater level of asset protection for their total wealth as more money will be invested into this exempt asset class. In addition to the reduced taxes and increased family savings, this strategy helps protect those savings from lawsuits. All of these benefits are integral for long-term, sustainable affluence.

There are many types of tax-deductible retirement vehicles. They fall into one of two categories: defined contribution plans or defined benefit plans.

> **Defined contribution plans** restrict the amount you can contribute to the plans on an annual basis. These include all forms of IRAs (individual retirement accounts), profit sharing plans, money purchase plans, 401(k) plans, and others.
> **Defined benefit plans** restrict how much can be in the plan at any time. The broader category, defined benefit plans, includes fully insured defined benefit plans, which are also known as 412(i) plans. Typically, defined benefit plans are used to help older individuals catch up on lost contributions.

The choice and implementation of the right plan for the situation will be determined by your planning team. The benefits of that planning will vary widely depending on each family's circumstances and the ages and salaries of the employees.

Maximize the Use of Vehicles Similar to Qualified Plans

Another tactic of the Savvy Affluent is to use tools and techniques that mirror many of the benefits of retirement plans. Since retirement plan contributions are limited and the annual contribution amounts are based on the retirement needs of Average Americans, the Affluent need to utilize alternative saving and investment methods to meet their significantly higher long-term retirement needs. A common strategy to enhance long-term retirement income and reduce taxes on investment gains is to invest in cash value life insurance. This will be explained in detail in the Ninth Key where we discuss the Secret Investments of the Affluent. If you want to maximize long-term, tax-efficient retirement income, you should definitely take time to review the Ninth Key.

Consider This

Retirement plans are a great way to achieve a high level of asset protection, while reducing current tax liabilities. In addition, the use of vehicles like cash value life insurance policies can help the Affluent avoid taxes on investment gains and enhance their retirement incomes. Other vehicles, like FLPs and LLCs can offer tax benefits as well. These are discussed in the next chapter.

CHAPTER

27

Borrowing Lower Tax Rates

In Chapter 26, you learned that by creating income opportunities for family members the Savvy Affluent increase the family's total capacity for tax-deductible retirement contributions. By shifting the ownership of income-producing assets to family members in lower marginal income tax brackets, Wealthy Families have been able to reduce total family income taxes even further.

How FLPs and LLCs Help Reduce Taxes

In the asset protection Key, you learned that family limited partnerships (FLPs) and limited liability companies (LLCs) are effective asset protection tools when exempt (+5) assets will not suffice. In addition, if used properly in the right situations, FLPs and LLCs can also save tens of thousands of dollars in income taxes each year. By gifting interests of the FLP or LLC to family members who are in lower marginal income tax brackets, the donors are effectively income sharing. A percentage of the income generated within the FLP will be taxed at the lower rates of the partners in lower marginal tax brackets. Typically, these are children or grandchildren. While the exact rules are more complex, generally, as long as the child is over 18 years old (or over 24, if a full-time student and a dependent), the child's share of the income will be taxed at a rate that is presumably lower than that of the working parents. (For more detailed information on this topic, please contact us.) Let's see how this works by reading the case study of Danny and Rina.

Case Study: Danny and Rina's LLC Reduces Income Taxes

Danny and Rina had annual taxable income of $100,000 from their rental real estate, which was worth $1 million. In a 40 percent combined state and federal tax bracket, their total income tax on this income came to $40,000. To reduce their taxes, they set up an LLC.

The LLC was funded with the real estate. Danny and Rina appointed themselves as managing members, so they have 100 percent control. They gifted a 3 percent membership interest to each of their four children (Zach, Elgin, Earvin, and Jerry) for a total of 12 percent removed from their estate. Because each child's interest would be valued at about $20,000 (3 percent of $1 million, less the minority valuation discount), no gift tax applied to the transfers to the children. Danny and Rina made these 12 percent transfers to their children annually for five years.

Under the LLC agreement, the children were taxed on their share of the LLC's income; which, after five years, became 60 percent. Thus, in year five, 60 percent of the FLP's taxable income would be taxed at the children's lower tax rates. So, when the LLC assets earn $100,000 in income, 60 percent of that income was taxed at the children's rate—15 percent. Thus, their tax bill for operation of the LLC was $16,000 (40 percent on $40,000, the parents' share) plus $9,000 (15 percent on $60,000, the children's share). Danny's family tax savings would therefore be as follows:

Total tax with the LLC, year five:	$25,000
Total tax without the LLC, year five:	$40,000
Year five family income tax savings with the FLP:	**$15,000**

It must be remembered that there were also savings in years one through four. What's more, under the LLC agreement, the managing members did not have to distribute any LLC income to the members. This was totally within the discretion of Danny and Rina as managing members. Thus, Danny and Rina could pay all LLC taxes with the income and reinvest the remaining proceeds.

Use Tax-Efficient Investments

Tax-efficient investments are used by the Affluent in order to build wealth and protect assets. In the beginning of this Key, you learned that taxes on investment gains could significantly stunt long-term appreciation. You also learned that taxes on investment gains in states with state income taxes could be as high as 40 percent to 44 percent of the short-term growth and 20 percent to 24 percent of the long-term growth. To explain how a small differential in after-tax returns can have a significant impact over a long period of time, we would also like to add a simple law of finance to help you.

> "The Law of 72" states that 72 divided by the annual after-tax rate of return of an investment will give you the number of years it takes an investment to double in value.

Under the Law of 72, an investment that returns 9 percent per year doubles in value every eight years. In 24 years, a $100,000 investment that grew by 9 percent per year would be worth $800,000. What would happen if this investor paid less attention to taxes? Would it make that much of a difference? Let's see. A $100,000 investment at 6 percent (because 33 percent of the 9 percent pre-tax gain was decimated by taxes) would take 12 years to double in value. At the end of 24 years, this investment would only be worth $400,000. If your investments lose 33 percent of the return to taxes, you could end up with half as much money in your investment account at the end of 24 years. Half? That is a significant reduction indeed! Is the possibility of doubling your savings reason enough to pay attention to taxes on your investments now?

The Savvy Affluent have always focused on after-tax investment returns. This is why they have so much money. Sometimes, tax management means investing in vehicles that are tax-exempt. Other times, it means hiring advisors who take a more active role in managing taxes. It can also mean investing to generate losses to offset gains.

Consider This

In Chapter 19, you learned that limited partnerships and limited liability companies are favorite asset protection tools of the Affluent. In this chapter, you learned how the Savvy Affluent use these same tools to share income with family members in lower tax brackets. In the Sixth Key, you will learn how these tools can be valuable estate planning tools as well. This is an example of how one tool can offer numerous benefits to a Wealthy Family. You will learn more about this philosophy in the Ninth Key. For now, let's focus on more ways to save unnecessary taxes by getting the government to pay for some of your health insurance costs. This is the topic of discussion in the next chapter.

CHAPTER

28

Long-Term Care Insurance

In this chapter, you'll learn how to reduce taxes while providing an important financial planning tool for your family—long-term care insurance (LTCI).

Conventional financial planning wisdom tells us that the reasons for buying long-term care are twofold:

1. To make sure you have enough money to pay for potentially devastating medical costs later in life and still have enough money to support your retirement (covered in the Seventh Key).
2. To protect your inheritance from high medical costs, so you can leave what you had planned to your children and grandchildren (covered in the Sixth and Seventh Keys).

What's more, you can also deduct your long-term care insurance premiums and reduce your taxable income. As an individual taxpayer, you can deduct up to the eligible amount of the LTCI premium. Table 28.1 shows the eligible tax deductible premium in 2007.

If you have your own corporation, are a sole proprietor, or own an LLC or partnership, you can possibly take much larger deductions for LTCI than indicated in Table 28.1. A C-corporation can deduct all LTCI premiums for owners and employees. If you do not have a C-corporation (you have an S-corporation, LLC, or partnership), you can only deduct additional LTCI expenses by covering employees and their spouses. Theoretically, you could employ your

Table 28.1   Eligible Tax Deductible LTCI Premium in 2007

Attained Age	Limitation on Premiums
Age 40 or less	$290
Age 41–50	$550
Age 51–60	$1,110
Age 61–70	$2,950
Age 71 and older	$3,680

Source: Internal Revenue Code §§213(d)(1)(D), 213(d)(10).

spouse and achieve the maximal tax deduction you desire. The basic guidelines regarding LTCI paid through a business by the employer are:

- Employer-provided LTCI treated as accident and health plan. Source: IRC §7702B(a)(3)
- Deductible by employer (subject to reasonable compensation). IRC §162(a)
- Total premium excluded from employee's income (not limited to eligible premium). IRC §106(a)

The reason why deductions for long-term care are allowed is because LTCI is considered to be a form of health insurance that pays for a variety of health costs, which may or may not be covered by Social Security, Medicare, Medicaid, or your state plan. The details of long-term insurance and our recommendations on what to look for in an LTCI contract are covered in Chapter 44. (You should read the chapter on LTCI in the Seventh Key to get a full understanding of how LTCI will help you and your family.)

You may wonder, "Doesn't my state or Medicare pay these expenses?" The answer is, "Yes . . . and no." As an example, the State of California will not pay for a senior's medical bills until that individual has depleted all but $2,500 to $3,000 of his net worth. In lay terms, this means that if a retirement plan, home, or any investments are titled to an individual, or have been titled in the individual's name in the last five years, the state will require those assets to be sold to pay for medical costs. In addition, the state will then take all but $30 per month of the individual's income as reimbursement for the coverage.

It isn't hard to see how this so-called "Medicare spend-down" could deplete someone's assets very quickly. We don't know about you, but we could not live on $30 per day—let alone $30 per month—and we certainly wouldn't subject our parents to that poor of an allowance. As a result, we have purchased long-term care insurance for our parents.

Caution

The numbers above refer only to the state (Medi-Cal) or Medicare paying for some of your LTCI. You should also keep in mind that Medicare only pays after you spend three days in a hospital, for nursing home care only (not in-home care), for needs that are "medically necessary" (custodial needs are the most common and are not covered), and for only 20 days. Thereafter, Medicare only pays a daily benefit of $105 that ceases if the patient is not improving. For more detailed information on Medicare, please visit www.medicare.gov.

Consider This

Advances in medicine allow us to live longer. The longer we live, the more likely we are to develop a condition that may require sustained, costly, medical attention. Unfortunately, government programs like Medicaid will not adequately protect us. As a result, we have to protect ourselves with long-term care insurance. If we structure our business affairs properly, we can get a tax deduction for helping ourselves. The tax code also allows us to use deductions for helping others. This is covered in the next chapter on charitable planning.

29

Charitable Planning

The will to give is strong in many people. As a society, we cherish the right to give to the charitable institutions of our choice. The will to give is what we refer to as "charitable intent." We want to give. Often, the biggest hurdles to giving are that we do not know how to give or we assume that our family will suffer as a result of our giving. Our goal here in this chapter, and in the chapter on charitable planning in the Sixth Key, is to show you a few ways the Affluent make charitable gifts that benefit the charity and their families at the same time. This is possible because of the tremendous tax benefits the IRS grants for charitable gifts. Before we examine the ways to use charitable giving to reduce income taxes, let's take a look at the basic tax rules regarding charitable giving.

Direct Gifts

Direct gifts are gifts that are made to a charitable organization for their immediate use. The federal tax code provides for current income tax deductions for gifts to charities that have qualified under 501(c)(3) as a charitable organization. The tax rules governing charitable giving are rather complex. Our explanation will be rather simplistic but should give you a basic understanding.

The IRS distinguishes between "public charities" (universities, hospitals, churches, and so forth) and "private charities" (private family foundations are the most common). What's the difference? If the gift is given to a public charity, you can deduct the amount of the gift from your adjusted gross income (AGI) up to a maximum of 50 percent of your AGI. If the gift exceeds this amount, you can apply the excess as deductions against future years' income for five years.

If the gift is to a private charity, then you can only deduct a maximum of 30 percent of your AGI, but this also can be applied forward five years. Let's see how public and private charities differ in the case study of Charitable Chris.

Charitable Chris: Give to the Foundation or to the Alma Mater

Chris is a retired entrepreneur who created a small private family foundation a few years ago to give something back to the community. He involved his children in the foundation and realized some significant tax benefits. Now Chris has $50,000 worth of highly appreciated stock he doesn't need to support his retirement needs. As a result, he would like to make a gift to charity. His annual AGI is only $30,000 per year from the consulting work he does. Chris is considering giving the stock to his family foundation or to his alma mater, where he sits on the board.

If he gifts the stock to the foundation, he will only be able to deduct $9,000 per year from his tax return (30 percent of AGI). If he gifts to the university, he will be able to deduct $15,000 (50 percent of AGI). Because he can only carry the deduction forward five years, he'll only be able to apply $45,000 worth of deductions using the family foundation, but he'll be able to use all $50,000 of deductions if he gifts to the university.

Indirect Gifts

Indirect gifts are often called split interest or planned gifts because some of the benefit from the gift is for the benefit of the charitable organization and some of the benefit of the assets being gifted will be retained by the grantor (or donor) and his family. The real beauty of charitable giving from the family perspective is that the IRS also allows tremendous tax benefits for indirect gifts—those left to charity through a trust or annuity. In fact, the IRS also allows deductions for indirect gifts through irrevocable charitable remainder or lead trusts, and through charitable gift annuities, which provide lifetime income to the donor as guaranteed by the charity and monitored by the state. By using an indirect gift, charitable planning can truly be a win-win-win situation: You win, your family wins, and your favorite charities win.

Common Charitable Giving Scenarios

The following are the most common charitable giving scenarios, where it makes financial sense for a family to consider charitable planning because of the tax benefit.

Sale of a highly appreciated asset. Many Affluent people, especially those over 50, hold highly appreciated assets—usually real estate or stocks that have grown enormously in value over time. Even more problematic is when there are few assets making up the bulk of someone's net worth. This is often the case when there is a closely held family business or a family farm. Regardless of the asset, you may want to sell the asset but don't want to pay the capital gains tax, thus reducing the after-tax value of the asset by up to 24 percent. Through the use of charitable planning strategies, you may be able to unlock some of the appreciation and significantly reduce the capital gains tax while benefiting a favorite charity as well.

Need to generate family income from investment assets. The past 10 years have seen unprecedented growth of personal wealth in the form of portfolio appreciation. However, when clients seek to reshuffle their asset allocation to produce more income and diversify their portfolios, they will be hit with a substantial tax on their gains. By giving to a charity, you have the chance to be creative in your approach to convert paper gains to cash flow, save taxes, and turn nondeductible items into tax-deductible ones while addressing charitable objectives at the same time.

Estate Planning. The most powerful benefits of charitable planning can be enjoyed when used as part of a multidisciplinary financial plan. As you'll learn in the Sixth Key—Preserve Your Estate—when you die, your family could pay as much as 40 to 60 percent in federal and state estate taxes, plus income tax on IRD assets such as pensions and IRAs. Charitable giving mediates many of these taxes. In the Sixth

Key, we'll address charitable planning as it pertains to estate planning in more detail.

The Most Common Charitable Tool: The Charitable Remainder Trust

Let's assume you have one highly appreciated asset you would like to sell but are reluctant to do so because of the significant capital gains taxes you would owe. At the same time, you are looking for ways to reduce your current year's taxable income and would like to receive an ongoing income stream. Moreover, you would like to diversify your overall investment portfolio. Usually, this would mean selling that highly appreciated asset, paying the high taxes and reinvesting with a substantially reduced amount. In this situation, the charitable remainder trust (CRT) may be an ideal option for you.

Used properly, a CRT can potentially:

- Reduce current income taxes with a sizable income tax deduction.
- Eliminate immediate capital gains taxes on the sale of appreciated assets, such as stocks, bonds, real estate, and just about any other asset.
- Increase your disposable income throughout the remainder of your life.
- Create a significant charitable gift.
- Reduce estate taxes that your estate might have to pay upon your death, thus leaving more for your heirs after your lifetime.
- Avoid probate and maximize the assets your family will receive after your death.
- Protect your highly appreciated property from future creditors.

Think of a CRT as a tax-exempt trust that provides benefits to two different parties. The two different parties are the individuals receiving income and the chosen charity or charities. The "income beneficiaries" (usually you or your family members), typically receive income from the trust for either their lifetimes or a specified number of years (20 years or fewer). At the end of the trust term, the chosen charity will receive the remaining principal to use for its charitable purposes.

How a CRT Works

A CRT is an irrevocable trust that makes annual or more frequent payments to you—typically until you die. What remains in the trust then passes to a qualified charity of your choice.

A number of tax-saving advantages may flow from the CRT. First, you will obtain a current income tax deduction for the value of the charity's interest in the trust. The deduction is permitted when the trust is created even though the charity may have to wait until your death to receive anything. Second, the CRT is a vehicle that can enhance your investment return. Because the CRT pays no income taxes, the CRT can generally sell an appreciated asset without recognizing any gain and paying any tax on the sale. This enables the trustee to reinvest the full amount of the proceeds from a sale and thus generate larger payments to you for the rest of your life.

Using Life Insurance for Wealth Replacement

Many people would be more motivated to make gifts to charities, but they are afraid that they won't leave an adequate inheritance to their heirs. The Savvy Affluent understand that they can make donations during their lifetimes, save income taxes, and find a way to leverage the tax deduction to achieve a similar, or sometimes larger, inheritance for their heirs than if they hadn't utilized charitable planning. This concept of using life insurance for "wealth replacement" will be discussed below.

A trust is eligible for the estate tax deduction if it passes assets to one or more qualified charities at the time of one's death. If you wish to replace the value of the contributed property for heirs who might otherwise have received it, you can use some of your cash savings from the charitable income tax deduction to purchase a life insurance policy on your life held in an irrevocable life insurance trust for the benefit of your heirs. This is called a "wealth replacement trust."

Often, through the leveraging effect of life insurance, it is possible to pass on assets of greater value than those contributed to the trust. In this way, your heirs are not deprived of property they had expected to inherit. In fact, your heirs may find it advantageous to receive cash, in the form of proceeds from a death benefit, as opposed to an asset that they did not wish or know how to manage. Let's see how this works:

1. You gift a highly appreciated asset to the charitable remainder trust. You receive a current income tax deduction that you can use to reduce your income tax liability for up to five years.
2. The CRT sells the asset. Neither you, nor the CRT, pay any taxes on the sale. One hundred percent of the value of the asset is preserved and invested in a tax-free environment.
3. You receive a larger annual distribution from the CRT than you would have received if you had paid taxes on the sale of the asset and invested the proceeds in a taxable environment.
4. Although the annual distribution is taxable, it is taxed in accordance with how it was earned in the trust. This form of taxation is beneficial given the lower dividend and capital gains tax rates. The income beneficiary will save a significant amount in taxes each year.
5. After the death of all income beneficiaries, the remaining assets from the CRT go to your selected charity.
6. A wealth replacement trust can be funded with insurance to replace those assets given to charity and give the family even more than they would have received had no charitable planning been done.

The CRT's Cousin—The Charitable Lead Trust

When it comes to charitable trusts, CRTs seem to get all the attention. But the cousin of the CRT, the charitable lead trust (CLT), also can provide significant charitable and tax benefits, particularly in an environment of lower interest rates.

With a CLT, sometimes called a charitable income trust, you transfer cash or income-producing assets to the trust. The trust then pays out income earned by the assets to a designated charity or charities. The payout may be an annual fixed dollar amount set at the time of the transfer—called an annuity trust—or an amount based on a percentage of the assets in the trust at the time of each annual payout—called a unitrust.

At the end of a specified number of years, the remaining assets in the trust are distributed to the noncharitable beneficiary, usually someone other than you or your spouse. It could be your children, grandchildren, other family members, or a trust for the benefit and protection of any of these heirs. This timing is, in effect, the opposite of the CRT, in which the donor receives current income from the trust assets and the assets go to the charity at the end of the designated time.

Gift tax may be due at the time the assets are transferred to the trust, because noncharitable beneficiaries (your family) will ultimately receive the assets. However, this can often be planned so that no gift tax will be due. This is because (1) the gift is discounted, as the beneficiaries won't receive the gift for some time; and (2) you receive a gift-tax deduction because a charity is receiving the income from the assets (the deduction is based on the amount transferred into the trust and the amount of time the assets are to remain in the trust). Furthermore, the gift won't be taxed at all if its discounted value is less than your remaining applicable gift tax exclusion.

Consider This

If you have a charitable intent and want to reduce current income taxes, capital gains taxes, or even estate taxes, then you should seriously consider charitable planning techniques. Often, you and your family will stand to benefit as much as the charity itself. The right team of advisors can help you understand the costs and benefits of charitable planning and manage all of the complex issues. If you want to find out ways to more efficiently invest for those other people you take care of—your children—you should read the next chapter on tax-efficient educational funding.

CHAPTER 30

Educational Planning

In the Second Key, you learned that many Affluent Americans first used leverage when they leveraged their education to increase their learning potential. Almost all children of the Super Affluent attend college and many attend graduate school. The Savvy Affluent know that keeping wealth in their family for multiple generations will ultimately depend on their children and their ability to continue to utilize advisors efficiently.

The Savvy Affluent not only want their children to be well educated, but they also want to pay for this costly expense in as efficient a manner as possible. The average cost of a four-year education at a private college for a student graduating in 2000 was $85,356. With a 6 percent inflation estimate, the estimated cost of a four-year private education for the graduating class of 2020 will be more than $273,000. Of course, if your child goes to an Ivy League school, like many children of the Affluent do, the total cost of the under-graduate degree could be well over $500,000. If you consider that the Working Affluent may pay almost 44 percent in income taxes *and* between 15 percent and 44 percent in taxes on capital gains and dividends, it may seem almost impossible to save for a child or grandchild's education while also putting away funds for retirement. In this chapter, we will discuss five types of tax efficient college investment options that you should consider in order to preserve your wealth.

Tax-Efficient College Investment Options

If you have children or grandchildren who might go to college, graduate school, medical school, or law school, there are tax-efficient ways to save for this future expense. The short list of potential tax-efficient investment options includes:

1. 529 College Savings Plans
2. 529 Prepaid Tuition Plans
3. Uniform Gift to Minors Act (UGMA) and Uniform Transfers to Minors Act (UTMA) Trusts
4. Cash Value Life Insurance
5. Coverdell Plans (formerly education IRAs)

Because the Coverdell plan contribution limits are $2,000 per year and that amount is completely inadequate for Affluent Americans, we will exclude it from our analysis. To compare and contrast the first four plans, we want to consider each of them across a number of metrics. Then, we will offer qualitative discussion about the contribution limits, tax benefits, access, and flexibility of each plan to help you understand why the Affluent use some plans more than others.

In order to do so, let's consider Table 30.1 (see pages 184–185).

Reducing the Comparison from Four to Three Plans

The first thing we want to make clear is that we don't like prepaid tuition plans. Though these plans allow parents to lock in tuition rates at state universities and colleges when they make contributions, we see the inflexibility of the plans to be too much to overcome. Given how difficult it can be to get children to clean their rooms or take out the trash, we find it ludicrous to base the success of a plan with hundreds of thousands of dollars in it on our ability to convince our children to attend one of a few colleges we chose for them when they were two years old. Practically speaking, we can't make that assumption. Practically speaking, we want to compare 529 plans (not prepaid tuition plans) to UGMA/UTMA plans or trusts. Then, we want to compare 529 plans to cash value life insurance.

Basics of 529 Plans

A 529 plan allows an individual to make annual tax-free gifts of $12,000 to any person. It also allows a couple to make gifts of up to $24,000 per year to each child. With the 529 College Savings Plan, an individual can make five years worth of gifts in advance. Total benefits include:

- Contributions over $24,000 are allowed—gift-tax-free.
- You, the donor, control the withdrawals.
- You may change the beneficiaries.
- You receive any tax benefits.
- You direct the type of investments (from a short list of choices).
- The money grows tax free.

Contributions Greater than $24,000 May Be Allowed—Gift-Tax-Free

You may already know that an individual can make annual tax-free gifts of $12,000 to any person and that a couple can make such gifts of up to $24,000. With the 529 College Savings Plan, an individual can make five years worth of gifts in one year without paying a gift tax. The 529 Plan allows you to allocate those gifts over the next five years. Thus, a couple can gift $120,000 tax free in one year to a 529 plan for each child or grandchild.

Total proceeds in a 529 plan are capped. The amount differs from plan to plan but many caps range from $220,000 to $260,000. This means that a set of parents could gift $120,000 to a 529 plan and a set of grandparents could gift an additional $120,000 to the same child's 529 plan and no gift taxes would be paid. Larger amounts could be gifted, but gift taxes would apply.

When you compare the 529 plan to the educational IRA (now called a Coverdell Plan), whose annual contribution limit is $2,000, there is no debate about which is the better choice.

You, the Donor, Control the Withdrawals and the Beneficiaries

Unlike a UGMA account or education IRA, you control the withdrawals and may change the beneficiaries of a 529 plan. If one child doesn't go to college or receives a scholarship, you may change the

Table 30.1 Comparison of Tax-Efficient Educational Funding Options

	529 Savings Plan	529 Prepaid Plan	UGMA/UTMA	Cash Value Insurance
Income Limitations	None	None	None	None
Maximum yearly contribution per beneficiary (all numbers double when gifts come from two parents or grandparents)	Annual federal gift tax exclusion (up to 5 years in advance)	Annual federal gift tax exclusion (up to 5 years in advance)	Annual federal gift tax exclusion	Unlimited as policy is owned by parents
Account earnings	Tax-free, if used for qualified expenses	Tax-free, if used for qualified expenses	Taxable	Tax-free
Ability to change beneficiaries	Yes	Yes	No	Yes
Control of withdrawals	Owner of account	Owner of account	Transfers to child when child reaches legal age	Owner of policy

Investment options	Ready-made portfolios of mutual funds	Tuition units guaranteed to match tuition inflation	Wide range of securities	Various, depends on policy chosen
State tax deductible contributions	Varies by state	Varies by state	No	No
Qualified use of proceeds	Any accredited post-secondary school in the U.S.	Varies by state	Unlimited	Unlimited
Penalties for nonqualified withdrawals	10% penalty withheld on earnings	10% penalty withheld on earnings	No	No
Taxation of qualified withdrawals	Tax-free	Tax-free	A portion may be exempt; income may be taxed at child's rate	Tax-free
Ownership of assets for financial aid purposes (may vary by institution)	Account owner	Student	Student	Exempt for student aid

terms of the plan to benefit someone else. You can also make these changes as often as you like as long as the beneficiaries are related. In fact, you can even name yourself the beneficiary if you plan to go back to school.

If you change your mind and want to withdraw the funds and use them yourself, you may do so. The only drawback is that you must pay a 10 percent penalty in addition to ordinary income taxes on any growth of the funds in the plan.

You Receive the Tax Benefits

The funds in a 529 plan grow on a tax-free basis. Because annual capital gains and dividends are not taxed in the 529 plan, the account balance has the potential to grow faster than if invested in comparable taxable investments. If you consider that dividends and short-term capital gains are taxed at rates that may be as high as 44 percent in some states, the 529 plan could grow twice as quickly as a UGMA or UTMA that offers no real tax deferral benefit.

You may also be able to reduce estate taxes by using a 529 plan. The plan's high contribution limit provides a convenient way to effectively lower the taxable value of your estate. As you'll learn in the Sixth Key, federal estate taxes can be as high as 55 percent for Wealthy Families who may not pass wealth to the next generation until after 2011. In light of this fact, the ability to reduce your taxable estate while providing educational funding for family members should be very attractive.

Important Note

Tax-deductible contributions can be enjoyed in some states. That's right! Some states actually allow an income tax deduction for contributions. That's a tax deduction to go along with the tax deferral that accompanies the plan. If you're not sure if your state offers a deduction, visit the very informative web site: www.savingforcollege.com.

You Direct the Type of Investments

Some 529 plans allow you to invest in a variety of stock, bond, and money market funds. You may have a choice of a growth portfolio or a balanced portfolio. There's even a company that offers an

"Age-Based Portfolio" that focuses on growth in the early years of the child and automatically rebalances every few years to focus more on capital preservation as college approaches. There is no extra fee for this added service.

Those of You with UGMA Accounts

If you already have a Uniform Gift to Minors Account, there's no need to fret. Congress has allowed for UGMA funds to be placed into 529 plans and those funds will be treated with the same tax benefits as all other 529 plans.

Shortfall of the 529 Plan

If you make your scheduled contributions, don't mind the risk of the stock market, and don't die, the 529 plan is a much better alternative than just saving money in your brokerage account with the intention of cashing it in to pay the bills later. However, we can't guarantee that you will live to see all of your children go to college or graduate school, and you can't invest in a 529 plan without subjecting your funds to market risk. For these reasons, you may want to consider some type of life insurance as part of your college savings plan. There are two plans to consider. If you are going to invest in a 529 plan, you should also invest in a decreasing term life insurance policy. If you need $1 million because your two young children will someday attend Ivy League schools, then you should buy a $1 million decreasing term policy that reduces by your annual contribution amounts. To illustrate this point, let's refer to the following:

Year	Child's Ages	Amount in 529 Plans	Amount of Term Insurance
1	2 & 4	$40,000	$1,000,000
2	3 & 5	$84,000	$950,000
3	4 & 6	$132,400	$900,000
5	6 & 8	$244,200	$800,000
10	11 & 13	$637,500	$500,000
15	16 & 19	$1,279,000	$0

If you are very concerned about the stock market's volatility and don't want it to have a significant impact on your children's educational funds, you should consider a whole life policy with a AAA-rated insurance company. This is a very stable investment and will grow at a steady rate. Even in 2001, one of the worst years in recent stock market history, one AAA insurance company paid more than 7.5 percent on its whole life policies. In addition to the tax-free cash accumulation inside such a policy, there is also a minimum death benefit to protect against an early death. When your children eventually attend college, you can then use tax-free loans to withdraw money from the policy and keep the death benefit intact.

Unconventional Wisdom—Life Insurance as an Investment

The last few pages focused on the benefits of 529 plans versus UGMA and UTMA plans. Now, let's compare the 529 plan to cash value life insurance. The only benefit the 529 plan has over the insurance policy is that, in some states, the 529 plan offers a state income tax deduction. Generally speaking, this could give the 529 plan a grade of an A+. Practically, this benefit may be very limited. First, some states don't have state income taxes. Second, the few states that offer a state income tax deduction also have either a phaseout of the deduction for high income earners or they limit the state tax deduction to a couple thousand dollars per year. An 8 percent state income tax rate for a $2,000 deduction is only worth $160 per year. That isn't significant for Affluent Americans.

The tax pendulum could swing back the other way when using a 529 plan if your children earn academic or athletic scholarships, choose to attend a less expensive school, or don't attend college at all. Let's look at an example of how this could create a tax problem for the parents.

If the parents invest $100,000 into a 529 plan that grows to $200,000 and they don't want to spend the funds for a child's education, they could be subject to income taxes and penalties that total $50,000 or more. The flexibility of a 529 plan is excellent if you are talking about transferring funds from one child's plan to another child's plan. However, the flexibility of using the funds for other things is quite poor.

Let's look closely at how life insurance fares in a comparison to the 529 plan. First, let's look at contribution amounts. Unlike all of the other college funding options, there is no practical maximum on how much a parent can invest in a life insurance contract. We have seen affluent clients invest more than one million dollars per year in insurance policies. There are financial underwriting guidelines, but there should be very little problem contributing much more than the $12,000 or $24,000 per year limit of the 529 plan.

Second, let's look at the tax benefits of the life insurance policy. Like the 529 plan, the funds grow without taxation. Also, if you compare withdrawals from the 529 that are used for educational expenses to policy withdrawals and loans, those are equal. The big difference arises when you want to use the 529 values for something other than qualified college costs. Where the 529 plan is fully taxable plus a 10 percent tax penalty, there is no tax on any withdrawals from an insurance policy if you don't violate modified endowment contract (MEC) guidelines or lapse the policy (which the insurance professional on your team should be able to help you easily avoid). This tax benefit leads to a discussion of flexibility.

Third, the life insurance policy offers you much more access and flexibility. Not only can you use the funds for anything you like, but you can also protect your children at the same time. If you contribute $100,000 to a 529 plan and die, your children will get no more than $100,000. If you contribute $100,000 of premiums to a life insurance policy and die, your heirs may get $2 million or more. When you finish reading this book, you will see at least a handful of uses for life insurance. When you compare this to the sole tax-penalty-free use of 529 plans, it is obvious how life insurance can be a much more valuable component of your financial plan.

To look at a review of the different options, please consider the following:

	529 Savings Plan	529 Prepaid Plan	UGMA/ UTMA	Cash Value Insurance
Contribution Limits	B+	B+	B−	A+
Tax Benefits	B− to A+	B− to A+	B−	A−
Access (reversibility)	B−	C−	F	A
Flexibility of Plan	B−	C−	F	A+

Consider This

If you have children, grandchildren, nieces, or nephews whom you would like to assist in their educational funding, or if you or your spouse might go back to school, you may consider a 529 College Savings Plan. If you are looking to build an efficient, flexible financial plan that can easily be altered to manage different issues as they arise, you should consider funding cash value life insurance as a funding vehicle for college savings planning. There is much more detailed discussion of insurance policies for this and other purposes in the Ninth Key—Use the Secret Investments of the Affluent.

31

Is Your Tax Advisor Helping or Hurting You?

Recall the example we described in Chapter 12 regarding a client of David's former law firm. As you remember, that client's self-imposed audit showed that he could legally file amended tax returns and claim a multimillion-dollar refund.

Lessons to Be Learned

While the above case is extreme, it is not unusual. It demonstrates the two ways millions of taxpayers get in trouble with tax planning by relying on tax professionals who (1) incompetently cause unjustified underpayments of tax; or (2) are so conservative or close-minded that they actually cost the client through gross overpayments of tax.

When you add the federal, state, and even municipal taxes, the Affluent pay marginal income taxes at the rate of 40 percent to 45 percent. At these rates, the following question becomes very important: Does your tax advisor—CPA, attorney, or other professional— suffer from one of the drawbacks below?

Incompetence: Not admitting when an area is beyond their expertise. This is the most obvious issue for any advisor. While it may be obvious to avoid the incompetent advisor, the signs of incompetence are not so apparent. If you do realize it, it is often too late.

Lack of Multidisciplinary Skills: Skilled in one area and not the other. More common than incompetence is the situation where the client's advisor is skilled in one area of practice but not knowledgeable about another tax area. This is understandable. Tax planning is like medicine. Each area has become so complex that one can only hope to become an expert in one discipline. In the medical arena, most patients and physicians realize this and readily accept the idea that patients are regularly referred to other specialists. A gastro-enterologist would no sooner make diagnoses of skin conditions than a dermatologist would handle a digestive disorder. Yet this is what happens all the time in the tax area. Note: this happens in all disciplines of financial planning.

When an advisor is faced with an issue beyond his expertise, he tends to do one of the following:

1. Admit his lack of knowledge and refer the client to another expert.
2. Try to quickly get up to speed on the issue (on the client's dime).
3. Simply reject any recommendations that he does not understand.

    Too often, we see tax advisors resort to this option, rejecting a potentially beneficial strategy for their client because it is out of the advisor's area of expertise.
4. Feign overprotectiveness: "Don't listen to anyone else but me."

We see accountants and attorneys who refuse to work as part of a multidisciplinary team. Often, this is because they fear losing the client to another advisor if they admit that what another advisor recommends actually makes sense. While these advisors will never actually tell the client not to listen to another professional, their behavior speaks for them when they reject another professional's suggestions with arcane arguments and references that they know the client will not be able to evaluate on his own.

Consider This

Certainly, there is no easy answer to the dilemma of how to choose a competent tax advisor who has a great deal of experience working with Affluent clients, can handle complex planning, and is comfortably between overly aggressive and overly conservative. We are not suggesting that you abandon your current CPA or tax attorney. We are merely suggesting that you take an active role in your tax and estate planning, bring new solutions to your advisor or bring in other professionals to assist your advisor in a coordinated team approach. Since you are the client who will ultimately pay for the planning (or lack of it) that is put into place by your advisors, it behooves you to make sure that your planning fits your needs and tax goals.

THE SIXTH KEY

PRESERVE YOUR ESTATE

For the Savvy Affluent, estate planning is an important part of the overall financial plan. They know that working hard, using leverage, protecting assets and investing wisely can all be undone by estate and inheritance taxes. By making estate planning a priority early on, the Savvy Affluent avoid unnecessary taxes and ensure that the wealth they have built benefits their families for generations to come.

It is not just estate and inheritance taxes one must avoid in estate planning. Consider also the following:

- Accidentally disinheriting family members. Each year, millions of Americans title property in joint ownership without realizing that this form of ownership supersedes our wills, leaving the property to our joint owner rather than to those we named in our wills. This disinheritance risk might be lurking in your estate plan right now.
- The costs and delays of probate. These can be significant if not planned for in advance.
- Future generations losing funds through irresponsibility, lawsuits, or divorce. All of these can be prevented by savvy estate planning today.

In this Key, you will learn about tools you can use to reduce and even eliminate estate taxes, avoid disinheritance risk, avoid probate, and even deal with problem assets such as pensions, IRAs, and family businesses. Specifically, you will learn the secret of how to preserve your estate through such tools as wills and living trusts, the AB living trust, estate planning life insurance policies, family limited partnerships, limited liability companies, and charitable donations.

CHAPTER 32

The Truth about the Estate Tax Repeal

It is true that in a limited sense Congress repealed the estate tax as part of the 2001 Tax Relief Act. If you die in the year 2010—and only in 2010—the estate tax will indeed be repealed for you. Beyond this simple statement, however, there is much uncertainty. There is a strong likelihood that estates will be taxed heavily in the foreseeable future. Let's look at the facts surrounding the supposed repeal so we can understand what challenges we face.

The Estate Tax Repeal

The temporary Estate Tax Repeal has begun and is scheduled to be fully phased in by 2010. Before that time, the law reduces the estate tax on the estates of those who die during the intervening transitional period. It does this in two ways. First, in a provision that benefits all estates, it steadily increases the individual exemption amount. The original exemption amount was set at $675,000 per person in 2001; then it rose to $1 million per person in 2002 and 2003; $1.5 million per person in 2004 and 2005; and $2 million per person in 2006, 2007, and 2008. The exemption amount is scheduled to rise to $3.5 million per person in 2009 before being repealed completely in 2010. Married couples, with proper planning, are able to take advantage of two exemptions in their estates. Thus, in 2008, a couple with a $4 million estate could die and avoid all estate taxes with relatively simple planning.

The second tax-saving feature during the transitional period is a reduction in the top estate and gift tax rates, both of which were 55 percent in 2001. Effective January 1, 2002, the top rates of 53 percent and 55 percent were temporarily eliminated and replaced with a rate of 50 percent on taxable estates in excess of $2.5 million. The top rate is then further reduced by 1 percent per year until 2007. During that year it will be lowered to 45 percent, and will remain at that level until the tax is repealed at the end of 2009. These changes will only help wealthier taxpayers because these top rates affect only estates of more than $2.5 million.

The Evaporation of the Repeal

In the previous section, we used the term "temporary" in a few places. This was not an accident. The current repeal is only a temporary repeal. If you live another few years, there is likely to be no repeal or even tax rate reduction whatsoever. This begs the question, "Is this repeal real or simply a fairy tale?"

In the fairy tale of Cinderella, when she did not return to her home by the time the clock struck midnight, her fine clothes turned to rags and her carriage turned into a pumpkin. Similarly, the estate tax repeal becomes fully effective January 1, 2010. However, unless the entire estate tax repeal is reapproved by Congress prior to 2011, the clock strikes midnight for the repeal and the tax law returns to where it was before the 2001 change was enacted. Of course, a Democratic-controlled Congress and White House could change the tax law long before 2010. While the likelihood of there being a Republican-controlled Congress and White House can be cause for speculation, no one truly knows whether or not the repeal will be reapproved before 2011. One certainly should not gamble the family's entire estate plan on this uncertainty.

It is important to understand that, in the absence of a reapproval of the repeal, the estate tax is not simply reinstated at the lower tax rates and larger exemption amounts enjoyed in 2009. Rather, the exemption amount is returned to the level allowed by the law we had in 2001 (a relatively minor $1 million per person exemption) and the marginal tax rates are again raised to a top rate of 55 percent. In this regard, if the repeal is not reapproved in the next two years, most of the estate tax reduction gained over the 10-year period will be lost.

According to many experts, it is possible that the repeal will itself be repealed before we even get to 2009. When Congress passed this legislation, the budget office was projecting multitrillion dollar surpluses in the federal government. This was back in the spring of 2001, before the economy began to falter, before the destruction of September 11, 2001, and before the prolonged military battle with terrorism at home and abroad. In 2007, the United States had the largest budget deficit in the history of the country. In addition, the dollar had depreciated approximately 40 percent against the Euro since the tax law change. The federal government can no longer afford to give away predicted future surpluses. In fact, it may have to take back some of the funds it has already given away just to balance a budget without the expenses of war. To support a continued effort in the Middle East, new sources of tax income will be a necessity.

Experts predict that the estate tax arena will be the first one targeted in this way, as the 2001 repeal only helped the richest 1 percent of taxpayers . . . a small enough minority that politicians won't be overly concerned about a public relations nightmare. Certainly, a rescission of the estate tax repeal would be easier to pass than a further reduction of Social Security benefits (which most people over age 65 utilize).

Even if the fairy tale does become reality and the estate tax repeal continues past 2010, the gift tax will still remain. The 2001 act did not repeal the gift tax. Even after the potential estate tax repeal, the gift tax will continue to be imposed on gifts in excess of the lifetime gift exemption. This exemption increased to $1 million in 2002 with no further increases slated. This may seem strange, but it does make some sense. You have to die to trigger estate taxes. We don't think many people would die to take advantage of low estate tax rates in a given year. However, gifts are made during one's lifetime. If you had an ability to make unlimited lifetime gifts without being taxed, there would be a serious threat to the tax system. People could play a big economic shell game, moving money to lower taxpayers and taking back the funds when it suits them. This could basically eliminate all state income tax revenue and make tracking funds almost impossible.

What did happen in 2001 was that the gift tax rates were scheduled to be reduced to the same tax rates that applied to estate taxes until 2010. Then, in the year where there may not be any estate taxes, gift tax rates will be capped at 35 percent. Incidentally, 35 percent was the top marginal income tax rate when the 2001 law was passed. There was good reason for linking the top gift tax and income tax rates. Congress decided to retain the gift tax to discourage taxpayers from making tax-free gifts of income-producing property to family members in lower income tax brackets. Such transfers would be an easy way to reduce the overall income tax burden on the family. Although it will still be possible to make such transfers after the potential estate tax repeal, the continuation of the gift tax will act as a "toll charge" for taxpayers engaging in this type of planning.

Hidden Tax Hikes within the Repeal

Another problem with the supposed repeal is that one new tax appeared and another tax exemption will be eliminated. In other words, some families are already paying higher taxes at death under the new law and many other families will pay substantially more tax if the repeal stays in effect. Let's review some of the implications of the repeal so you can see how this repeal may actually cost most families more in taxes.

State estate taxes have reappeared, so total taxes are higher. Prior to the repeal, the estate of a Wealthy Family was entitled to a dollar-for-dollar federal estate tax credit for any state death taxes paid by the estate. What this means is that the estate tax rate was capped at 55 percent, but some of that money went to the federal government and some went to the state. Under this old scheme, individual states shared heavily in the tax revenue of the IRS. Thus, they had no need to impose their own estate tax other than the amount they would get from the federal return (this was called a "sponge tax" as the states soaked up their piece of the total tax). This scheme was repealed by the 2001 Act, effective for those dying after 2004.

The estate tax reduction eliminated the states' pieces of the estate taxes as of 2004. Now, the states receive 0 percent of the estate taxes. Basically, the government reduced taxes by 10 percent, but took away up to 16 percent from the states. The federal government actually collects more taxes now than it did before the repeal. Taxpayers thought they would pay less, but that didn't last very long.

The states were not happy losing out on tax revenue. Except for states like Nevada, which has more money than it needs as a result of the gambling-fueled tourist industry, practically every state runs at a deficit. To fight this tax loss, many states instituted their own version of estate taxes called state inheritance taxes. The states charge a tax on the assets that are left as an inheritance in their state. An estate planning attorney recently told us that approximately 15 states currently impose their own state estate tax, in addition to the federal estate tax, at rates up to 16 percent of the value of the estate. As a result, Wealthy Families can actually pay combined federal and state taxes of more than 60 percent of the value of the estate at death. Obviously, the only winners in this poorly planned scenario were the federal tax agencies. Taxpayers are worse off under the repeal than before it! Do most people understand this? No. Most Affluent Americans think it was a good thing for them. The Savvy Affluent know better. The Savvy Affluent also know that every taxpayer will suffer from the repeal when it comes to selling appreciated assets.

Any repeal means a loss of basis step-up at death. Currently, the second generation does not pay capital gains taxes on the sale of appreciated assets when they sell them. Rather, they pay only the estate tax on the total value of the asset (which is a much higher rate). The *quid pro quo* for repeal of the estate tax was the loss of step-up in income tax basis at death. Currently, for estate tax purposes, most property owned by a decedent receives a tax basis equal to its value at the date of death. Under the Repeal Act, property acquired from a decedent will generally retain the decedent's tax basis after December 31, 2009. This practice is known as the "carryover basis." When the recipient of the property eventually sells it, he will be compelled to compute the gain using the decedent's cost basis. In most cases, the decedent's basis will be less than the date-of-death value, resulting in an increased capital gains tax.

The legislation contains two major exceptions to carryover basis. The first exception is for estates valued at less than $1.3 million; the second exception is for property worth up to $3 million passing to surviving spouses. Nonetheless, for larger estates, the additional capital gains taxes will take a large bite out of any potential estate tax savings. Moreover, there will certainly be an increase in administrative difficulty and an increased cost in determining the cost basis of assets purchased 20, 30, 50 or more years ago by now-deceased relatives.

The repeal fails to address IRD. In addition to the estate tax, income tax must be paid on certain assets left in a decedent's estate at death. This tax is levied on what is called income in respect of a decedent (IRD). Because combined federal and state income taxes—including those characterized as IRD taxes—can be as high as 45 percent, and estate taxes range from 45 percent to 49 percent during the transitional period, the combined tax rate can escalate to 75 percent or more on IRD. This means less than 25 percent of certain assets will go to your heirs at death unless you make a plan to avoid this serious problem. Which is the most common property subject to the high tax burden of IRD? Amounts left in pensions, profit-sharing plans, and IRAs.

Consider This

There has been a lot of talk about the estate tax repeal, yet the tax law change is only temporary. Even if it becomes permanent, which is unlikely today, new taxes have emerged at the state level and for capital gains that fill the tax void left by a repeal. Thus, if you truly want to see that your estate passes on to your family, you must implement an estate plan and not rely on the government tax agencies to make changes that will help you. The following chapters in this Key will help you do this.

CHAPTER 33

Wills and Living Trusts

A will and a living trust are the foundation to any estate plan and are the "secret" that the Affluent use to protect their assets. Without them, your family's wealth will become public information, and the government will decide who gets what assets when you die. In this chapter, we will discuss the importance of wills and living trusts and how to avoid unnecessary pitfalls of living trusts that trap many less savvy families.

The Government's Will

Are you surprised to know that you already have a will even if you have never written one or had an attorney draft one? It is true. If you die without any will, then you get the universal will that your state government has written for all of its citizens. This is what is known as dying "intestate." While this may seem like a good thing, it probably is not because there is no guarantee that the way the government will split up your estate is the way you would want your property to be divided.

There are various negative consequences of a government will. While the precise rules vary among the 50 states, typically the laws are very rigid and formulaic. Usually, all of your nearest relatives get a piece of your property but no one else does . . . not friends, cousins, charities, and so on. Furthermore, no one gets more than the state-allotted share, even if it's seemingly unfair. Often, this ends up hurting the surviving spouse. In this all-too-common scenario, the decedent's grown children may get some of the money meant for the surviving spouse, even if it means the surviving spouse then has too little to live on.

Moreover, the absence of a will often leads to expensive and lengthy court battles by family members contesting the division of assets. Sometimes family members produce a questionable will in court, trying to establish a rightful claim to a portion of the estate. Once again, this can be avoided by having a valid will in place.

Finally, if you have minor children and you and your spouse die without a will, the courts will decide who becomes the legal guardian of your children. What parent would want to have an unknown judge make the decision of who will care for their children if they die? Avoid this tragedy and create a valid will including an Appointment of Guardian sooner rather than later.

The Need for a Will and a Living Trust

Having a will is certainly better than not having a will. However, your entire estate will be stuck in the probate process if you only have a will. Probate is a process by which the state administers your will. Probate is time-consuming, public, and quite costly in many states. The Savvy Affluent always combine a living trust with a short will called a "pour-over will." This combination ensures the vast majority of the estate will avoid probate and keeps the estate plan private. Before we examine how a living trust works, we must first see why it is so important to avoid probate.

The Pitfalls of Probate

Delays: Probate often takes between one and two years to complete in many states. During that time, your beneficiaries must wait for their inheritance. Perhaps worse, the representatives of your estate may have to petition the court for permission to conduct any transactions involving your estate assets during this time. This process could make it difficult to sell estate property or invest estate assets during the probate process.

Costs: Probate can cost between 3 percent and 8 percent of your "probate estate" or the value of your entire property passing under the will. This pays the courts, the lawyers, appraisers, and your executor (the person in charge of handling your affairs during this process), among others. In some states, these probate fees are paid on your gross estate—not taking into account any mortgages on your assets. In these states, if you die owning $1 million worth of assets that have mortgages of $800,000, your estate will pay probate fees based on the $1 million market value of your estate, or approximately $50,000. This is money that could have gone to your beneficiaries rather than to the courts and lawyers.

Privacy: Probate is a public process in all states. Anyone interested in your estate can find out who inherits under your will, how much he or she inherits, the beneficiaries' addresses, and more. While you may not be famous or worry about the newspapers exploiting this information, think of your beneficiaries—your surviving family members. They certainly will not appreciate the many financial advisors calling them with hot tips on investments. These salespeople find beneficiaries by examining probate records. They know who they are and how much found money they have to invest.

What seems fair to some may seem completely unfair to others. This is definitely the case with privacy and probate. Probate is designed to make sure that all potential beneficiaries are given an opportunity to review the will and make objections. For this reason, the will has to be public. When you die, it could take a very long time just to track down all potential beneficiaries (especially if they live abroad) to give them notice. Not only will your intended heirs have to wait a very long time, but they may also lose a significant part of an inheritance to people you haven't spoken to in decades. Even if the probate process does distribute your assets to the people you intended, they still have to pay the costs of administering this process.

Control: In probate, the courts control the timing and final say-so on whether your will—and the wishes expressed in your will—are followed. Your family must follow the court orders and pay for the process as well. This can be extremely frustrating.

Double Probate: If you own real estate outside of your state of residence, your will must be probated *again* (in an ancillary proceeding) in each state where real property is located.

You are probably thinking, "Why would anyone choose to use a will as the estate planning document of choice when probate is this unappealing?" It is hard to believe. We are continually astonished by how many families endure the time and expense of probate when it is completely avoidable by simply having a living trust.

The Problem-Solver: A Living Trust

As mentioned earlier, a living trust is a legal document that provides direction for the use of your assets (and body) at the time of your death. A living trust is a revocable trust, meaning you can change it at any time. During your life, the assets transferred to the trust are managed and controlled by you, the trustee, just as if you owned them in your own name. When you die, these trust assets pass to whomever you designated in the trust, automatically, outside of the probate process. Other benefits of the living trust include:

- Avoiding the unintentional disinheritance caused by joint tenancy or joint ownership (this happens in most second marriages).
- Preventing court control of assets if you become incapacitated.
- Protecting dependents with special needs.
- Providing for guardians of children if you are incapacitated (but still alive).

Funding the Trust

The transfer of assets to the living trust is also known as "funding the trust." If you create a trust and don't fund the trust with assets, it is just a useless piece of paper. This is like building a car and not putting an engine in it. If you want to get any benefit from your trust, you must fund it.

Funding the trust is a secret that the Affluent know well. When you transfer your assets to your living trust while you are alive, you maintain 100 percent control over these assets as though you still own them in your own name. For your car, stocks, bonds, bank accounts, home, or any other asset, the process of transferring an asset to your living trust is the same. If the asset has a registration or deed, change the name on such a document. If the asset is jewelry or artwork that has no official ownership record, use an assignment document to officially transfer ownership to your living trust.

These ownership changes will transfer the name of the registration or deed to the "John Doe Revocable Living Trust" or "John Doe, Trustee of John Doe Revocable Living Trust," rather than "John Doe" as it now reads. As sole trustee of the trust, you have the same power to buy, sell, mortgage, invest, and so on, as you did before. Further, because the trust is revocable, you can always change beneficiaries, remove or add assets, or even cancel your trust entirely.

It must be remembered that the transfer of assets to the living trust is a necessary activity. While it has no income tax ramifications at all (you are still treated as the owner for income tax purposes), it is crucial to gain the probate-saving benefits afforded to you at the time of your death. Below is a list of some of the valuable benefits of a trust that allow you to achieve important estate planning goals without sacrificing your quality of life. The benefits of a trust include the following:

You may name yourself or someone else as trustee. You need not name yourself as the trustee of your living trust, although most people do. You could name an adult child, another relative or close friend, or even a corporate trustee, like a local bank or trust company. However, if you do not like the way the outside trustee is handling the trust, you always have the power to remove him.

When you die or become disabled, your successor trustee will take over. If you are the trustee while you are alive, you will name, in your living trust, someone (or possibly a corporate trustee) as the successor trustee. That person or entity will take over the trustee duties when you die or become disabled. If you have a co-trustee while you are alive, that person will have complete trustee duties after you have died. These duties involve collecting income or benefits due your estate, paying your remaining debts, making sure the proper tax returns are filed, and distributing your assets according to the trust instructions. This person or entity acts like an executor for a will. However, unlike a will, actions under a living trust's directions are not generally subject to court interference.

You decide when your beneficiaries receive their inheritances. Another significant advantage of a living trust over a will is that you, rather than the courts, decide when and how your beneficiaries get their inheritances. Because the court is not involved, the successor trustee can distribute assets immediately after concluding your final affairs. This can take as little time as weeks or even days.

If you choose, assets need not be distributed right away. Instead, you may direct that they stay in your trust, managed by your individual or corporate trustee, until your beneficiaries reach the ages at which you want them to inherit. One of the advantages to distributing assets in this manner is that while the assets remain in the trust prior to distribution, they are protected from creditors—a feature that may interest you if you have concerns about your heir's creditors or possible divorce.

The successor trustee must follow your trust instructions. Your successor trustee (as well as your primary trustee if it is not you) is a fiduciary—a legal term meaning that the trustee has a legal duty to follow the living trust instructions and to act in a reasonably prudent manner. The trustee must treat the living trust as a binding legal contract, and must use his best efforts to live up to the obligations of the contract. If your successor trustee mismanages the trust by ignoring the instructions in your living trust, the trustee could be legally liable.

Consider This

As you have seen, wills and living trusts are a must for any estate plan. They are truly the building blocks of a quality estate plan. As you will see in the upcoming chapters, they are merely a small piece of a comprehensive estate plan. The next chapter on Living Trusts will explain why every Affluent family must use this tool.

34

The A-B Living Trust

For many Affluent American couples, there is a financial blunder hidden in their estate plans. It lurks because many Affluent couples plan to provide for the surviving spouse by having the first spouse simply leave everything to the surviving spouse. Most Americans, in fact, don't know any other way to leave money to support the survivor. *This mistake may cause your family to pay hundreds of thousands of dollars in unnecessary estate taxes.* Savvy Affluent clients know of a tool that helps them preserve their estate: the A-B living trust.

In this chapter we will discuss how you can take advantage of tax breaks offered by the government in the context of the A-B living trust. The tax breaks are the unified tax credit (UTC) and the unlimited marital deduction (UMD).

UTC and UMD

To understand why one should not simply leave everything to the surviving spouse, you must first realize the two fundamental creatures of our estate tax system: the unified estate tax credit and the unlimited marital deduction.

> **The unified tax credit (UTC):** The UTC translates into a dollar amount that can be left by a decedent estate tax free (commonly called the "estate tax exemption"). As explained in the opening chapter of this Key, after the 2001 changes, this exemption grew to $1.5 million in 2004 and 2005, $2 million in years 2006 through 2008, and will rise to $3.5 million in 2009.

We often explain the UTC as a "get-out-of-estate-taxes-free" card, like in the board game Monopoly. Every one of us gets one of these cards to use either during our lives or at the time of our deaths. However, the card is nontransferable and, if not used at death, is lost forever.

The unlimited marital deduction (UMD): The UMD rule means that a decedent can leave an unlimited amount to a surviving spouse without any estate tax—provided both spouses are U.S. citizens.

Unfortunately, when thinking about their estate plans, too many married couples look at the UMD as their solution. They simply leave everything to their spouse, using the UMD to avoid all estate taxes. While this effectively eliminates all estate taxes at the first death, it is a penny-wise and pound-foolish mistake. That's because the first spouse did not use his UTC, or get-out-of-estate-taxes-free card. Because he didn't use it, it is gone forever.

While this seems innocuous when the first spouse dies, the IRS gets you back when the second spouse dies. At that point, the surviving spouse's estate can only make use of one exemption. That means everything over the exemption amount will be subject to estate taxes—at rates above 40 percent.

To illustrate this point, let's take a look at the case study of Tina and Mike.

Case Study: Tina and Mike

Tina and Mike owned a home with $500,000 of equity, had life insurance policies with combined death benefits of $2,000,000, had another $500,000 in a retirement plan, a business worth $500,000, and general investments totaling $500,000. They might not think of themselves as "Affluent," but to the federal estate tax authorities they are "estate taxable."

When Mike died in 2007 and left everything to Tina, there was no federal estate tax, because of the unlimited marital deduction. Tina inherited the entire estate and lived off of the earnings until she died the next year in 2008.

As per Tina's will, the entire estate went to her children when she died. In 2008, the children were not taxed on the first $2,000,000 worth of property they inherited from their mother because of the UTC. The children must, however, pay federal estate taxes on the amount in excess of $2,000,000, or in our example $2,000,000. The tax rate maxes out in 2008 at 45 percent. This means the children will be paying almost $900,000 in federal estate taxes.

The terrible fact about the case of Tina and Mike's children is that the entire $900,000 of taxes could have been avoided rather easily. Moreover, Tina still would have been able to live on the earnings of what Mike left her during her last year. This could have been achieved by implementing an A-B living trust.

The A-B Living Trust

The A-B living trust is a revocable, testamentary trust that is also referred to as a loving trust, family trust, A-B trust, or living trust. The A-B living trust is the building block of estate planning as it helps maximize the exemptions and provide other benefits. When using an A-B living trust, the property is divided into two buckets, bucket A (or Trust A) and bucket B (or Trust B), at the death of the first spouse. Most people transfer assets that are the equivalent of the UTC amount into bucket B, which ultimately goes to the heirs. The balance of the property is then transferred to Trust A, which becomes the trust for the surviving spouse. During his or her lifetime, the surviving spouse can be full legal owner of Trust A. As trustee, the surviving spouse can do virtually anything with the assets of the trust. This trust can be made completely revocable during the lifetime of the surviving spouse.

The concept of Trust B is different. The surviving spouse does not technically own Trust B. But he or she will have the ability to draw income and interest from the trust; may be able to use the property (for example, live in the home); use the principal for health, education, maintenance, and support; and typically use up to either 5 percent of the principal or $5,000 a year for any reason whatsoever.

After the death of the second spouse, the Trust B assets go directly to the heirs without any estate taxes. This is true even if the value of the assets has grown to equal more than the UTC amount.

Trust A, which belonged to the surviving spouse, will also be distributed to the named beneficiaries. First, all existing debts and liabilities will be paid off. Then, depending on the year of the death, the wealth that is equivalent to the UTC amount will be transferred estate tax free to the beneficiaries. If the value of the Trust A assets exceed the UTC amount, then that portion of the estate will be subject to estate taxes. After paying the federal and state estate taxes, the assets will be transferred to the heirs.

Case Study Revisited: Tina and Mike

Let's now assume that during their lives Tina and Mike hired an attorney to create a joint A-B living trust and they funded it properly. When Mike died, the trust created Trust B and funded it with the UTC amount in 2007, which was $2 million. During the rest of her life, Tina had access to the principal for support, maintenance, health, and lifestyle maintenance . . . nearly anything she needed. She lived in the home as well. The remainder of the property—$2 million—funded Trust A, which Tina accessed and spent for whatever she needed.

When Tina died in 2008, Trust B paid out directly to the beneficiaries of that trust—their kids. Because Trust B qualified for Mike's UTC when it was funded, there is no estate tax on what is left in the trust; whether it has grown past $2 million or been spent down to less than $2 million.

Any property left in Trust A will qualify for Tina's UTC. Thus, if there was less than $2 million in this trust when she died (and likely there was because she had been living on the interest and a portion of the principal of the $2 million), there would be no estate tax on this portion either. In this way, the A-B living trust would have saved Mike and Tina's family $900,000 in estate taxes.

Consider This

Under our estate tax rules, any married Affluent couple whose total assets might put them above the estate tax exemption amount by the time they pass away (in 10, 20, or 50 years) should use A-B trusts. It is really that simple. Without such a trust, one spouse is throwing out his get-out-of-estate-taxes-free card for no good reason. The next chapter is going to explain a very common and significant mistake that many couples make. In this chapter, you will learn why a couple should never own any assets in their own names or jointly.

CHAPTER 35

Joint Ownership and Disinheritance Risk

The most common way for married couples to own any property is to own it jointly. Though this is very common, it is very inappropriate for the Affluent. Not only does this form of titling assets leave you unprotected from lawsuits, but this form of ownership actually creates estate planning problems. By owning assets jointly, you can negate all of the work you may have done with your living trust. This is a serious problem that the Savvy Affluent know to avoid and you should, too. In this chapter, we will discuss the dangers of joint ownership.

The Dangers of Joint Ownership

Joint ownership is the most popular form of ownership for Average Americans' real estate holdings and bank accounts. This is not so for the Savvy Affluent. With joint property, when one owner dies, the property automatically passes to the surviving joint owner(s). In this way, jointly owned property passes outside of a will and avoids the expense of probate. Because it avoids probate, common sense would seem to recommend joint ownership. But the Savvy Affluent know better.

As you have seen and will see again here, joint ownership is almost always a big mistake. Because joint ownership overrides living trusts and other estate planning, it can render your hard work useless and ruin your estate plan.

Joint ownership threatens your estate plan because any property you own jointly will pass automatically by right of survivorship to the surviving joint owner(s). In the eyes of the law, this automatic transfer takes effect the instant you die, before any will or living trust can dispose of your property. In this way, your will or living trust will have no effect on jointly held property. If you designated certain beneficiaries in a will or trust to receive your share of jointly held property, they will be disinherited and the surviving joint owner(s) will take it. This avoidable tragedy occurs every day in this country because people do not realize the dangers of joint ownership and because their advisors are not giving them adequate information.

The Negative Side Effects of Joint Ownership

In order to fully understand the negative consequences of joint ownership, consider these stories:

1. William, a man in his late 60s, marries for the second time. Shortly after the wedding, he puts all of his significant property—his home, his winter vacation condominium, and his stock portfolio—into joint ownership with his new wife. Within six months, William dies. The home, the condo, and the stocks all go to William's new wife. His three children and eight grandchildren inherit virtually nothing, even though William had made ample provisions for them in his will.

2. Susan's will bequeathed her property equally to her son and daughter. Because her son lives near her and he pays her bills, Susan put her house, her safe deposit box, and her bank account in joint ownership with him. When she dies, Susan's son will get all of the money in the bank account and safe deposit box, as well as the house, regardless of the provisions of the will. Unless the son is extremely generous, the daughter will get close to nothing. Do you want to rely on your children's generosity to carry out your estate plan?

3. Assume the same situation as in example 2, but add to the facts that the son has serious creditor problems. He is $15,000 overdue on credit card debt and has defaulted on a loan. His creditors can come after the bank account, the safe deposit box contents, and likely the house the moment Susan dies.

The only real beneficiaries of Susan's estate may be banks and finance companies.

4. Cecilia, a single mother in her 30s, is trying to build a college fund for her eight-year-old daughter, Debbie. Cecilia has invested some of her excess income in buying old multi-family homes, which she and her partner fix up and rent to owners. While her relationship with her partner has been strained at times, Cecilia nevertheless takes title to the investment properties in joint ownership with her partner without realizing that if she dies before they resell the properties, her partner will take them all and leave nothing for Debbie's daughter.

Many well-intentioned people get stuck in these predicaments because they do not know any better and their advisors are not doing their jobs. Sometimes, owners may not even realize what type of ownership they have chosen. In other cases, people consciously decide to use joint ownership because they know it will avoid probate. Avoidance of probate is never a reason to use joint ownership.

Never Use Joint Ownership to Avoid Probate—Use a Living Trust

Assets titled in joint ownership and assets titled in a living trust both avoid probate. As described in the previous chapter, your interest in these assets will pass outside the probate process at your death if you use a living trust. Thus, if your goal is to avoid probate, use a living trust rather than joint ownership. You will get many more benefits without any of joint ownership's pitfalls.

Consider This

After reading this chapter, you should now understand the dangers of joint ownership and should see the value of using a living trust. Another common estate planning mistake results in wasting 50 percent of life insurance proceeds. This is covered in the next chapter.

36

Estate Planning Life Insurance Policies

Every Savvy Affluent client's financial plan should involve cash value life insurance because of its asset protection exemption value, tax-free growth, and ability to access cash values tax free. This was discussed in the Fourth and Fifth Key and will be discussed throughout the Ninth Key as well.

This chapter is not going to discuss how the cash value of life insurance can be a tax-efficient wealth accumulation vehicle as that is covered in the Ninth Key. This chapter focuses on the death benefit proceeds of life insurance. Many Affluent clients maximize their investments in cash value insurance policies for tax-efficient wealth accumulation and asset-protected cash values. Older Affluent clients often purchase second-to-die (or survivorship) insurance policies for the pure death benefit. That will be the focus of this chapter. We will call such policies estate planning life policies or EPLPs.

Strategies for Maximizing Insurance Proceeds

Estate planning life policies are life insurance policies that are purchased for the primary purpose of transferring wealth and creating liquidity for future generations. This is in sharp contrast to the insurance policies that were discussed in the Fourth and Fifth Keys and will be heavily stressed throughout the Ninth Key. The life insurance policies discussed in those chapters were created primarily for wealth accumulation, not estate planning, reasons.

For estate planning purposes, it is important to remove the EPLPs from your taxable estate to maximize the after-tax proceeds you leave your heirs. The following are two popular strategies for removing the EPLP proceeds. Both have distinct drawbacks and pitfalls.

1. **Having the spouse own the policy or be its beneficiary.** One popular method of sheltering EPLP proceeds from estate tax is to name your spouse as owner or beneficiary of the policy. This works as long as the surviving spouse will spend down the policy proceeds before dying. As you learned previously, the IRS is happy to have you pass everything to the surviving spouse, so that you throw away one get-out-of-estate-taxes-free card (unified tax credit) without using it. That's because when the surviving spouse dies, the IRS gets a piece of everything above only one exemption amount rather than only the amount above two combined exemptions.

   A second pitfall of this approach is that you lose all control of the proceeds when you die. They will pass to your surviving spouse outright. If your spouse spends them down foolishly, gets remarried and divorced, or is sued, then your planning will benefit someone other than your family members. As you'll see below, you can control the funds even after you're dead and keep them in the family for generations by using a special life insurance trust that dictates exactly how the funds can be used.

2. **Having the children own the policy.** A different approach for removing EPLP proceeds from your estate is to have your children own your EPLP and indicate that they will receive the proceeds at your death. They can apply for the policy, pay the premiums (with money you may gift to them), and receive the proceeds at your death. If the policy and the proceeds are outside your estate, no estate tax will be due.

   However, there are some drawbacks to this strategy, such as:

   ◆ If the EPLP proceeds are paid to children, your surviving spouse may run short of funds to pay bills. This can be a very big problem in the situation of second or third marriages, as children may not agree to support a stepparent.

   ◆ If the EPLP policy is a cash-value policy (typical in estate-planning situations because it is permanent, and not term, life insurance) your kids may be tempted to borrow against the policy, thus reducing the payable death benefits.

♦ If there's a divorce, the EPLP policy may be considered a marital or community property asset of your children, and some of the cash value could end up going to an ex-son-in-law or ex-daughter-in-law.

♦ If your children are still minors, the policy would have to be owned by a custodian or a guardian.

The Irrevocable Life Insurance Trust

The Affluent know that they can avoid many of the pitfalls discussed above by creating an irrevocable life insurance trust (ILIT) to be the owner and beneficiary of their life insurance policies. An ILIT is an irrevocable trust designed to purchase life insurance for the benefit of your children and grandchildren.

There are many benefits of having an ILIT. First, if the ILIT owns the policy, it's out of your taxable estate. Moreover, a properly structured ILIT can keep the proceeds from spendthrift children and their disgruntled spouses or creditors. The funds can be used to cover estate taxes; provide an income stream; pay off debts, mortgages, or notes; and keep other valuable and needed assets intact for the family.

In many cases, the ILIT will use the insurance proceeds to buy illiquid assets, such as shares of a closely held business, real estate, or other assets from your estate, to keep them in the family. A purchase of this type is considered a tax-neutral exchange, so no tax will be due on the asset itself. Alternatively, the trust can lend money to your estate, with the loan secured by the estate's assets. This is sometimes done to use the money to pay the estate taxes that are due on the other assets. Because estate taxes are due within nine months from the date of death, this ability to have liquid cash available is crucial to avoid selling assets in a quick sale in which the family may not get the best price.

In either case, the estate will receive cash that can be used in a variety of ways. Later, the trustee can distribute the assets to the trust beneficiaries, the surviving spouse and/or children. This can be done in a lump sum, or, if desirable, the assets can be maintained in trust for the beneficiaries' later benefit and use. If kept in trust, these funds can be structured so that creditors of the surviving spouse, children, and even grandchildren will have no access to them—even in the case of lawsuits, bankruptcy, and divorces. In this way, the ILIT can be an asset-protecting tool for many generations.

If the trust is structured for the long term, it often makes sense to have its assets grow in a tax-efficient manner. This can easily be accomplished by having the trust purchase a variable annuity. The bottom line: All the insurance proceeds are available to help pay estate taxes and provide cash for whatever needs might arise. Your family keeps control over the assets. No distress sale of family assets will be necessary to raise money to meet the estate tax obligations when you have properly structured life insurance outside your taxable estate to provide liquidity.

Accessing Irrevocable Gifts: A Valuable Secret

Quite often a client will ask us if there is a way to use an ILIT to own life insurance and still have access to the policy's cash values during retirement. Though many advisors unfamiliar with planning for the Affluent would say no, we work with our estate planning attorney partners around the country to do this on a regular basis for our clients.

Essentially, the only persons who could access the cash values during your life would be the ILIT beneficiaries. However, if the policy insures your life, then you cannot be the trustee—or the beneficiary—of the ILIT. Thus, you personally could not have access to the cash values. However, if the policy insures only your life, then your spouse could have access to the cash values if she were a trust beneficiary. Further, if the policy was on your joint lives, often called a "survivorship" or "second-to-die" policy, then the children or grandchildren could access the cash values to the extent they were trust beneficiaries, or the trustee could utilize cash values to benefit them. This could include paying their college tuitions. There are also more advanced combinations of legal entities and insurance policies that are outside the scope of this book.

Consider This

Life insurance is a very important piece of any financial plan. How you own life insurance can have a very different impact on how that insurance will benefit you, your family, or your business. It is very important that you work with your team of advisors to determine how to utilize an insurance trust in your planning. Another way to own life insurance, and other assets, is in either an FLP or an LLC. These tools will be discussed in the next chapter.

37

Family Limited Partnerships and Limited Liability Companies

In the Fourth Key, we explained how the Affluent use family limited partnerships (FLPs) and limited liability companies (LLCs) to shield assets from risks. In this chapter, you will learn how FLPs and LLCs—in addition to being excellent asset protectors and income tax reducers—are superior estate planning tools as well.

The Three Benefits of FLPs and LLCs for Estate Planning

FLPs and LLCs have three major benefits for estate planning. Let us examine each separately.

1. **FLP/LLC assets avoid probate and continue.** Assets owned by your FLP/LLC do not go through probate. Only your interest in the FLP/LLC will. However, if you structure your LLC so that your intended beneficiaries eventually own most of the FLP/LLC shares when you die, these beneficiaries will control the FLP/LLC and its assets when you die. Your beneficiaries can effectively control the FLP/LLC assets or business while the probate process continues its deliberation over distribution of your remaining membership interests. Because probate can last several years, this continued control can be crucial for operating a business or real estate interests.

2. **FLPs/LLCs allow you to get property out of your estate without giving up control.** Because your estate only pays taxes on property you own at death, a common tax-saving strategy is to gift your property away during your lifetime. The property goes to people you wish to inherit your assets at the time of your death and the government gets a smaller share. The main objection you might have to this type of planning is that you will have to give up control of the property while you are still alive. That's where the FLP/LLC can be of particular value.

   If the FLP/LLC owns the asset(s) and you are made the FLP general partner or LLC managing member, you get the best of both worlds. You can gift FLP/LLC interests to intended beneficiaries and remove the value of those interests from your estate yet you still control the FLP/LLC and all of its assets while you are alive. Let's see how this works by referring to the case study of Stewart's Mutual Funds.

Case Study: Stewart's Mutual Funds

Stewart, a 63-year-old psychotherapist, owned almost $1.1 million in mutual funds. He set up an FLP to own the mutual funds, naming himself as the sole general partner. At the outset, he owned 2 percent of the FLP as general partner and 93 percent as limited partner, gifting 1 percent each to his five grandchildren. Since this 1 percent was worth approximately $11,000, the gifts to each grandchild were tax-free.

Stewart can continue to gift each grandchild $11,000 in FLP interests each year, completely tax-free. If Stewart lives to age 75, he will give $660,000 worth of FLP interests to his grandchildren ($132,000 each), tax-free. This equates to 60 percent of the FLP.

This $660,000 will no longer be in his estate and will not be subject to estate tax. Moreover, any future growth of the gifted portion of the FLP will also be out of the estate.

Because Stewart's other assets put him in the 48 percent state and federal estate tax bracket, his tax savings using the FLP will be $316,800 (48 percent of $660,000). Because he is the FLP's sole general partner, Stewart retains control over the mutual fund investments while alive and can determine the amount of distributions. In this way, Stewart maintains significant control of his assets for his lifetime, pays less estate tax, and also provides more for his grandchildren.

Note that the FLP agreement and the gift structuring must be carefully crafted or Stewart's retained control could be grounds for the gifted FLP interests being brought back into his estate for tax purposes.

3. **FLPs/LLCs lower estate taxes on assets they hold.** You may not want to gift your entire FLP/LLC interests during your lifetime or may start such a gifting program too late to give away much of your wealth. In either case, you will die owning FLP/LLC interests, which are then subject to the estate tax. The issue thus becomes what valuation will the IRS attach to your remaining FLP/LLC interests? It may not be:

Your percentage ownership in the FLP or LLC	*times*	The fair market value of the FLP or LLC assets

This is because of powerful tax rules applying to FLPs and LLCs regarding valuation discounting.

Valuation Discounting Using FLPs/LLCs

An important estate tax benefit of the FLP/LLC is that FLP/LLC interests often enjoy discounted values by the IRS. The IRS recognizes that owning a percentage ownership of an FLP/LLC that owns an asset is generally worth less than owning the asset outright. If you own a $20 bill and hold it at death, then the IRS would assign an estate taxable value to that bill of $20. However, if you died owning a 20 percent interest in an LLC with four other family members—all with equal management rights and the LLC owned $100—the IRS would allow a valuation of your 20 percent interest at a number well below $20. Here's why:

The IRS would first allow a "lack of marketability discount" to that interest, recognizing that your LLC interest is not really marketable so its value should be reduced for tax purposes. There is likely not much of a market for your 20 percent LLC interest when the other LLC members are all family members. Who would want to own part of an LLC worth $100 when the other owners are members of one family? What would an outsider pay for such an interest? This discount is available even if you retain all the management rights in the LLC.

Second, because you own less than 50 percent of the LLC, the IRS will also apply the minority ownership discount to your interest unless you have retained most or all of the management rights. Again, the IRS recognizes that there is very little market interest for shares of an LLC that others control.

Both of the aforementioned tax valuation discounts can be maximized by the proper drafting of the FLP/LLC agreement. Any provisions that restrict the transferability of any FLP/LLC interests will weigh toward a higher lack of marketability discount. Likewise, clauses that limit the control of minority interest holders will substantiate greater minority ownership discounts. In this way, with proper drafting, FLPs and LLCs can often enjoy valuation discounts of 20 to 30 percent or more. This can translate into an estate tax savings of millions of dollars in larger estates.

Case Study Revisited: Stewart's Mutual Funds

Assume that when Stewart dies, he still owns 40 percent of his FLP interests—having gifted 60 percent to his grandchildren during his lifetime. This 40 percent partnership interest, as part of his estate, is subject to estate taxes. Assume also that the mutual funds in his FLP have a value of $2 million when he dies. His 40 percent interest in the FLP is then economically worth $800,000 (40 percent of $2 million).

For estate tax valuation, however, the IRS may agree that Stewart's FLP interest is worth only around $500,000. The IRS will allow both the lack of marketability discount and the minority ownership discount. The lack of marketability discount exists because Stewart's five grandchildren own the other FLP interests, so nonfamily members would not be interested in buying his interests. Also, under the

FLP agreement, the FLP interests are not freely transferable. The minority ownership discount may be applied because Stewart owns only 40 percent of the FLP when he dies, if he has gifted a majority of general as well as limited partnership interests. Even in this situation, he will retain de facto control if the other general partnership interests are split 12 percent to each grandchild—only one needs to side with him in a vote for him to control a majority!

These valuation discounts translate into an estate tax savings of about $144,000 (48 percent of $300,000). More importantly, he retains significant control over his funds while he is alive.

Consider This

The FLP and LLC are tremendous estate planning tools. These benefits are in addition to their significant asset protection benefits. It is hard to imagine how any plan for a Savvy Affluent client could be complete without at least one FLP or LLC. In most cases, multiple LLCs are used. If you review the Fourth and Fifth Keys, you will see the other benefits that these tools offer.

CHAPTER

38

Avoiding the 70 Percent Tax Trap of Pensions and IRAs

In the Fifth Key, we highlighted the fact that there is one type of asset that can generate a tax that can be as high as 70 percent—your retirement plan. This results from a combination of income and estate taxes being applied to retirement plan balances at death. By leaving less than 30 percent of your retirement plan assets to your heirs, it will be very hard to achieve a high level of affluence for the future generations of your family.

One of the common sense lessons you will hear repeated in the financial media is that you should contribute as much as you can to your retirement plans (pensions, profit-sharing plans, IRAs, 401(k) plans, and so forth). The conventional wisdom is that because they offer an income tax deduction and tax-deferred growth, these plans are a huge tax win for the client.

Once again, for the Affluent, this conventional wisdom could be terrible advice. Retirement plans are a potentially dangerous tax trap for three reasons:

1. It is likely that the participant will ultimately pay income taxes at the same or higher rates when taking distributions from the plan.
2. The client may not need most (or all) of the funds in retirement.

3. Perhaps most damaging, any funds left in these plans at death will be decimated by taxes. Quite literally, these plans act as "traps," capturing huge sums of money that are eaten up at tax rates of 70 percent to 80 percent.

If you can accumulate more in your pension, profit-sharing plan, IRA, or other retirement plan than you will use (because you have other assets, an inheritance, or die early), this chapter is a crucial one for your overall estate planning. In this chapter we will discuss how both unaware and very aware taxpayers can get caught in this tax trap as a result of things that are both in and out of their control. This is what makes this trap so dangerous. Let's examine the three dangerous traps of retirement plans.

Trap #1: You May Pay Tax at the Same—or Higher—Tax Rates

A common misconception among the Working Affluent is that when they retire, they will be in a lower income tax bracket. Though this may be true for some, there are myriad reasons why this may not be true for you. One reason is that you may become accustomed to a certain quality of life that you don't wish to scale back when you retire. You didn't work hard in your career and as a parent so you could be put out to pasture and live on tomato soup and grilled cheese sandwiches. In fact, many retirees will increase their expenses and do the things they didn't have time to do when they were working 50, 60, or 70 hours per week. Most notably, the thing they will do is travel. Nonetheless, even if you do scale back your quality of life, you still may have to pay more in living and entertainment expenses because of inflation.

For example, just 15 years ago we used to go to the movies for $3 to $5 per ticket and we could go see the Boston Red Sox play at Fenway Park for $34 (two tickets at $17 each). Last week, we paid $12 per ticket to see a movie and the same Red Sox box seats are now $125 . . . each!

Not only might your lifestyle, which you can control, increase your expenses (and taxes) in retirement but your plan itself might also contribute to increased taxes. The IRS has rules requiring what are called minimum required distributions (MRD) from retirement plan assets. This means you must start taking money out of your retirement plans at age 70½, whether you need the money or not. Of course, if you take the money out of the plan, you must pay income taxes on those withdrawals.

These minimum required distributions can be quite high—bringing a higher tax burden with them as well. You invest your funds inside the retirement plan and those assets grow on a tax-deferred basis. This means you get greater accumulation than in a taxable account. Consider this tax deferral along with the stock market returns you may realize (despite current market conditions, the 70-year average is still well more than 10 percent per year). The larger accumulation forces even higher MRDs. This can affect your tax bracket in retirement as well.

Lastly, you may have other income-producing assets like rental real estate, another business, limited partnerships, dividend-paying stocks, bonds, and money market accounts. Each of these income-producing assets adds to your income and increases your income tax bracket.

Given the amount of invested assets inside and outside of retirement plans, and the continued long-term growth of the securities markets, many Americans will enjoy retirement incomes that will put them in the same tax bracket as they are in now. For example, we have a client named Frank, a 50-year-old dermatologist with $500,000 in his profit-sharing plan. By the time he is in his late 60s and begins his planned retirement, assuming 9 percent to 10 percent annual growth, the plan funds will likely grow to $3 million. If Frank withdraws only the interest from the plan from then on without using any principal or other sources of income (like Social Security), Frank and his wife will likely still be in the top tax bracket for the rest of their lives.

What this means is that for the majority of the Working Affluent and all of the Super Affluent, the value of the tax deduction and deferral are not as great as conventional wisdom would espouse. Clients like this have no tax arbitrage; that is, they simply get the deduction at one tax rate and then pay the tax at the same rate. In fact, the plan may actually cause "reverse arbitrage" as distributions from the plan will be taxed as ordinary income (likely subject to a 35 percent-plus rate for wealthier clients), while gains outside of a plan would be subject to a federal capital gains rate capped at

15 percent. A *Wall Street Journal* columnist reviewed this comparison, concluding that for many taxpayers qualified plans were a "fool's game" (April 15, 1999).

Trap #2: You May Not Need the Funds in Retirement

The second dangerous trap of retirement plans is that some people may not need the funds while they are in retirement. Because the amounts contributed to retirement plans are relatively small for the Super Affluent, most will accumulate significant nonplan assets over their careers. If plan contributions are capped at $40,000 or less (in most cases), what happens to the rest of the after-tax earnings? Over a career, they end up in nonretirement plan brokerage accounts, ownership interests in closely held businesses, rental real estate, precious metals, cash value life insurance, or any number of other investments.

Given the compounded interest on your investments in the securities and real estate markets over 10 to 30 years, these nonplan investments can throw off significant income in retirement—so much so that the retirement plan assets are hardly even needed. Though this is a problem we should all hope to have, it is a problem nevertheless and it needs to be addressed.

We see this problem with many of our Super Affluent clients, including, by way of example, our client Charlie, a 58-year-old software executive. Charlie contributed $20,000 to his pension for each of the last 25 years. Meanwhile, he and wife Margie have also amassed $1.2 million in other investment accounts. By the time he retires, which he plans to do at age 65, he should have enough in his brokerage accounts for a very comfortable retirement.

Charlie and Margie Won't Need Pension Funds to Retire

Clients:	Charlie and Margie
Ages:	Charlie 58; Margie 57
Average Pension Contribution:	$20,000 for 25 years
Nonpension Investing:	$20,000 for 20 years
Present Pension Balance:	$2.2 million
Outside Investments:	$1.2 million
Planned Retirement Age:	65
Forecasted Pension Balance, Age 65:	$4.4 million (10% annual return)
Forecasted Outside Investments, Age 65:	$2.3 million (8% post-tax return)
Post-Tax Earnings on Outside Investments, Age 65:	$184,000/year ($15,000+/month)
Post-Tax Amount Needed for Retirement:	$10,000 post-tax per month

As you can see from the preceding list, Charlie, who earned about $275,000 per year over the first 25 years of his career, did not even maximize his pension contributions during that time ($30,000 per year was allowed). Instead, he chose to control some of his investments himself (about $20,000 per year) in a separate investment account. By the time he retires at age 65, Charlie will clearly have enough to fund his retirement (he and Margie need about $10,000 per month post-tax) just from his nonpension plan investments.

To be extremely conservative, let's advise Charlie and Margie to keep another $1.4 million of the pension funds secured for emergencies. That still leaves $3 million of the pension at age 65, which will continue to grow. Charlie and Margie think that this $3 million, plus most of this growth, will benefit their children and grandchildren as designated in their will and trust. As you'll see next, they are really benefiting the IRS and state tax agencies, because more than 70 percent of the funds will be eaten by taxes if they don't change their plan!

Any Funds Left Will Be Decimated By Taxes

The third trap of retirement plans is that any funds in the plan will be decimated by taxes if they are not used by the taxpayer and spouse during their lifetimes. Most nonSavvy Affluent clients are surprised that the vast majority of these funds end up with state and federal tax agencies. They are shocked to learn that after paying taxes for a lifetime of work, their "tax qualified" plan will be taxed at rates from between 70 percent and 80 percent. Most clients, when hearing these facts, are shocked, appalled, and want to learn how to do something about it. Let's take a look at how these taxes are levied and what you can do about it. The first thing you must review is the meaning of IRD.

Basics of IRD

As discussed in Chapter 25, IRD stands for income in respect of a decedent. IRD is income that would have been taxable to the decedent had the decedent lived long enough to receive it. Whoever receives these items of IRD must report them as gross income and pay any resulting income taxes in the year in which the items are actually received, generally, the year of death (spouses are entitled to defer IRD until payments are actually withdrawn).

The IRD is taxable income that is assessed taxation in addition to any federal estate (death) taxes and state estate or inheritance taxes. Federal and state income tax rates (including those characterized as IRD) can reach up to 45 percent in many states, and estate tax is assessed between 45 percent and 48 percent (we'll assume 48 percent here), assuming no additional state estate tax (an increasingly unlikely assumption). When you combine both taxes, you can see how quickly the combined tax rate escalates. Although the rules provide for a partial income tax deduction for estate taxes paid, the total tax on assets characterized as IRD assets can be more than 70 percent in some cases.

What types of assets qualify for the dreaded IRD treatment? Income earned by a decedent but not yet paid, such as bonuses or commissions, qualify as IRD. Once they are paid to the estate, they'll be hit with income taxes and estate taxes under the IRD rules. The most important asset hit by IRD? Retirement plans, such as pensions, 401(k)s, and IRAs (to the extent contributions were originally tax deductible).

In order to see how IRD eats up a retirement plan, let's refer to the case study of Jim.

Case Study: Jim

Jim is a single professor whose other assets exceed the current estate tax exemption. His IRA is fully taxable as it was funded entirely with tax-deductible contributions. (The same illustration could be made for a married couple, but the estate tax wouldn't be due until the second spouse dies if that individual was the plan beneficiary due to the unlimited marital deduction.)

Assuming Jim's fully taxable IRA has a value of $1 million at his death, Jim's estate (or heirs) would first pay $460,000 in estate taxes and then pay another $251,212 in state and federal income taxes (45 percent of the remaining amount after giving a deduction for federal estate taxes paid). Thus, only $283,780 is left out of the IRA for Jim's beneficiaries—less than 29 percent! More than 70 percent of the funds—built over a lifetime of working and paying income taxes—were taken by the IRD tax system. Let's see how that happened (assuming Jim lived in a state with only a "sponge" estate tax prior to the state enacting its own estate tax).

Jim's IRA: IRD Eats Up Over 70 Percent!

IRA Value—IRD Item	$1,000,000
Total Estate Taxes	($465,000) due
Balance in Estate	$535,000
Income in Respect to a Decedent	$1,000,000
IRD Deduction	($441,750)
Taxable IRD	$558,250
Income Tax (45%)	($251,212) due
Amount for Beneficiaries	$283,780
Total Taxes	$761,212 (76.1%)

How to Avoid the Tax Trap

In more than one place in this book, you will see Judge Learned Hand's quote: "No person is obligated to pay as much tax as possible—there is not even a patriotic duty to do so." This is an important philosophy the Savvy Affluent fully embrace, as they always look for ways to reduce taxes. So what can you do about the pension situation? The answer to that question depends on where you are in your retirement plan funding.

For all Average Americans, and most Working Affluent, it still makes sense to maximize participation in qualified retirement plans. In fact, this may be 100 percent true for your plan at this point. It really depends on an accurate financial analysis of what your plan balance is and what you project you will need to spend in retirement. If, after such a financial analysis, it looks like you now have more in your retirement plans than you will need in retirement, then you should consider ending participation as soon as possible. Ideally, you want to amass just enough in retirement plans to cover retirement expenses and provide a safety buffer.

What if you have already built up a large balance in a pension or IRA and now realize that you won't need some or all of the funds in retirement like our previous example of Charlie and Margie? Unless you want 70 percent or more of these funds to go to state and federal taxes, you must do something . . . and the earlier the better.

Essentially, you have three potential strategies for attempting to reduce the heavy tax burden on qualified plans:

1. Stretch IRAs
2. Liquidate and Leverage strategy
3. Pension Insurance Purchase strategy

In this section, we will examine each strategy separately.

Strategy Option #1: Stretch IRAs

Recently, stretch IRAs have been discussed as a viable tax-reduction option. Stretch IRAs lengthen the time over which distributions must be taken from retirement plans or rollover IRAs. They also allow you to leave the IRA to your heirs, who can then stretch out the distributions over their lifetimes and pay income taxes as they receive the funds. The common belief underlying this strategy is that tax-deferred growth is always a great idea. However, when you crunch the numbers you will realize that the stretch IRA is generally a bad idea for anyone who will have an estate tax liability and it may be only a minor benefit to everyone else.

There are at least two reasons why stretch IRAs are not beneficial:

1. Stretch IRAs completely ignore the estate tax problem.
2. Stretch IRAs may create additional unnecessary taxes for your heirs.

Let's consider both problems briefly.

Stretch IRAs Ignore the Estate Tax Problem   If you think your estate will be worth more than $1 million when you die, you will probably have an estate tax problem. The stretch IRA gives your heirs the benefit of deferring their withdrawals and deferring their income tax liabilities. The IRS doesn't care that the children or grandchildren have not received the money. The total value of the IRA will still be included in the estate at the time of your death. This will force your heirs to pay estate taxes right away. To illustrate this point, let's look at the case study Jeff Leaves a Business and a Stretch IRA.

Case Study: Jeff Leaves a Business and a Stretch IRA

Jeff listened to his advisor, who told him to create a stretch IRA so he would avoid the 70 percent IRD problem at death. When Jeff passed away, his three children received his family restaurant and a stretch IRA worth $800,000. The total estate tax bill was $700,000. His children didn't want to sell the restaurant, so they took the $700,000 out of the stretch IRA to pay the estate tax bill. The kids should be happy because they now have the business and an additional $100,000, right?

Wrong. The kids now owe income taxes on the $700,000 withdrawal (income taxes are never waived or avoided with a stretch IRA). Their average state and federal income tax rates were 40 percent. Therefore, they owed $280,000 in income taxes because of their $700,000 withdrawal the year before. They used the last $100,000 from the IRA and took out a $180,000 loan against the business to pay the $280,000 tax bill. Then, they owed income taxes on the $100,000 withdrawal—another $40,000 to the IRS—and they owed another $15,000 of interest on the loan. This put them in the hole on another $55,000. Eventually the children had to sell the business to pay off their debts. Jeff's plan failed because he received bad advice from his financial advisor.

Stretch IRAs Could Cost Your Heirs More Taxes   The stretch IRA may generate more taxes for your heirs for three reasons:

1. Your heirs may be in the same or higher tax bracket than you are by the time you die. If you die in your 70s, 80s, or 90s, your heirs will be in their prime earning years and will likely have another income to put them in that higher marginal tax bracket. You may be deferring 27 percent tax rates today in lieu of 35 percent tax rates later.

2. All withdrawals will be taxed as ordinary income when withdrawn from the plan by you or by your heirs. The long-term capital gains rate of 15 percent doesn't apply to appreciated investments inside retirement plans. If you'd taken the funds from the plan and paid the taxes earlier, you would've had the opportunity to invest in long-term investments, and you or your heirs could possibly realize 15 percent tax on your gains—or no taxes on gains, if you received the step-up in basis at your death.

3. You have no flexibility for intergenerational planning. You can only invest in securities inside a stretch IRA. You cannot buy life insurance. If you left the stretch IRA to your children and they didn't need it and wanted to leave it for their children, they

would have to let the income-taxable IRA appreciate. It would continue to be income and estate taxable until their children receive the money. If you'd paid the taxes and left the children after-tax dollars, the children could have invested in tax-free life insurance or a tax-free 529 plan for your grandchildren. You wouldn't be handcuffing them with a stretch IRA.

In our opinion the stretch IRA can be both shortsighted and penny-wise and pound-foolish. Of course, if you or your spouse is completely uninsurable, if your IRA is your only asset, if your estate definitely will not be worth over $1 million when you pass away, then the stretch IRA may make sense for you. If you don't meet all those conditions, you should seriously consider another alternative.

Strategy Option #2: Liquidate and Leverage

The liquidate and leverage (L&L) strategy is much superior to the stretch IRA. In fact, you can think of this strategy as allowing you to leverage your IRA, 401(k), or pension, five to twenty-five times!

Assume that you and your spouse are 60 years old and have $1 million in your qualified plan. Because you have accumulated significant assets outside of your plan, you are sure that you won't need $600,000 of the funds, or the interest on those funds, in retirement. Let's assume that other assets will account for your estate tax exemption amount. In that case, more than 80 cents of every dollar in your plan will go to the government if you don't take action. Below, we will discuss a strategy that is very popular with the Savvy Affluent and practically absent from most financial plans. A technique known as liquidate and leverage can maximize lifetime income from a pension, minimize total taxes, leverage the gift tax exclusions, and maximize the total estate to junior generations.

The L&L Method: Onetime Gift   The L&L strategy will ensure that your heirs not only get the full $600,000, but also an additional $2.9 million as well. Best of all, they will receive the $3.5 million tax-free! The L&L steps are as follows:

1. Take $600,000 out of the plan and pay the $240,000 in income taxes (assuming a tax rate of 40 percent). As we learned from Jim's case, this liquidation eliminates IRD and saves at least 6 percent of the $600,000, or $36,000.

2. Use a portion of your estate tax exemption amount and gift the remaining $360,000 to a properly drafted irrevocable life insurance trust (ILIT).
3. The ILIT then purchases a second-to-die life insurance policy on you and your spouse. Depending on your age, health, net worth, and other factors, that policy might be worth $1.5 to $3.5 million.
4. When you die, the insurance company pays up to $3.5 million, income tax-free, to the irrevocable life insurance trust. Then, all $3.5 million will be available to your heirs' estate tax-free as well.

If you consider that the $600,000 in your plan would have been worth less than $80,000 to your children and grandchildren (if you lived to age 80 and the funds grew at 8 percent), the L&L strategy leaves your heirs more than four times that amount—over $2.7 million more to your heirs after taxes!

8% growth for 20 years = 4.66 times your original investment
4.66 × $600,000 = $2,786,00

After 72 percent tax, your heirs receive approximately $783,000. Wouldn't you rather leave your heirs $3.5 million than $783,000?

Alternative L&L Method: Guaranteed Income/Annual Gifts   Many clients, even the Affluent, don't like paying for insurance in one lump sum. Others already have life insurance policies that require annual premiums. Still others aren't sure how much of their retirement plans they need. They only know how much they need each month to pay their bills. For these people, the guaranteed income/annual gifts method of L&L is ideal. The guaranteed income/annual gifts method is a combination of three techniques. First, the retirement plan assets are used to purchase a life annuity. A life annuity will pay a monthly, quarterly, or annual payment to the annuitant (you or your parents) for as long as you live. This way, you never run out of money. Second, the annuitant will gift the after-tax proceeds from the life annuity to an irrevocable trust for the benefit of the second or third generation. Third, the trust will purchase a life insurance policy on the annuitants (usually the senior generation). To illustrate this point, let's consider the case study of Marian.

Case Study: Marian's Guaranteed Income Allows Gifting

Marian, a 78-year-old woman, has $800,000 in retirement plan assets. By purchasing a life annuity with the $800,000, she receives a guaranteed monthly payment of $8,600. After taxes, she still has $5,400 per month. Because she has some income from her municipal bonds, which are outside her retirement plan, and additional income from Social Security, she only needs $2,000 of the retirement plan income to pay her family's bills and to fund the college savings plans she created for her grandchildren. This leaves Marian with $3,400 per month of excess income. She gifts this $3,400 per month to an ILIT, which pays for a $1 million life insurance policy that is guaranteed to Marian's 115th birthday!

By using these steps, Marian took $800,000 of potentially 70 percent taxable money and turned it into guaranteed supplemental income for herself and a $1 million inheritance for her son and grandchildren.

Strategy Option #3: Pension Insurance Purchase

The IRS and ERISA allow for certain types of retirement plans to purchase life insurance within the plan with pretax dollars. Typically, we use profit-sharing plans here because the rules are most generous for these types of plans. Thus, for clients with rollover IRAs, they will have to roll the IRA back into a properly drafted profit-sharing plan (PSP) before being able to take advantage of this strategy.

From this point forward, let's assume you have a retirement plan that you don't expect to completely empty before you die. What can you do? You can purchase life insurance on yourself inside your retirement plan. When you die, the insurance company will pay a death benefit to your retirement plan.

While some Affluent clients will argue that life insurance is not a good investment in their plan, consider two factors: (1) as noted elsewhere in the book, the policies can reflect almost any underlying investment you want—tied to a money manager you select (within a PPVUL or PPLI—see the Ninth Key), mutual funds you choose (within a variable insurance policy), or even a market index (like the S&P 500 within an equity indexed life insurance policy); (2) you must consider the tax consequences of the investment. Here, when considering IRD, life insurance will almost always outperform other investments.

Mutual Funds vs. Life Insurance—A Surprise Upset Winner

Let's assume that you could invest $500,000 in mutual funds inside your retirement plan. After 20 years, assuming a 7 percent return on your mutual funds, you would have approximately $2 million in your retirement plan. If you died at that point, your spouse would have access to the funds but would have to pay income taxes on any withdrawals. If you assume a combined state and federal tax rate of 40 percent, the $2 million pension is worth $1.2 million to your spouse. Then, if your children wanted the funds, there might be estate taxes to pay.

If you invested the same $500,000 into a $1.8 million life insurance policy, you might think you would be at a disadvantage versus investing in the mutual funds. You would be wrong. At the end of 20 years, after paying for mortality costs and administrative expenses of the life insurance policy, your policy only had $600,000 of cash value at the time of your passing. When the $1.8 million death benefit paid to the pension, only $600,000 of the benefit was income taxable to the spouse. A payment of $240,000 was due to the IRS and the remaining $1.56 million went to the spouse tax free! That is 30 percent more money to the survivors. The same estate tax rates would apply, but 30 percent more money escaped the pension . . . and the taxes associated with it. This is not an aggressive strategy any more than buying a home for the tax-deductible mortgage interest is. It is a benefit that is clearly spelled out in the Internal Revenue Code. It is simple, but very few people take advantage of it.

Consider This

If you are a member of the Affluent and have a sizeable pension balance, you should be concerned that your heirs may unnecessarily have to pay the 70 percent tax on IRD. What you can do is work with your advisory team members who are familiar with pension law, life insurance, and estate taxes and ask them to help you with your planning. There is one other significant threat to your retirement assets. Unlike IRD, this threat raises its ugly head while you are still alive. It is the increasing cost of long-term care. This is addressed in the next chapter.

39

Protection from Rising Medical Costs

It may seem like medical costs are a lifetime issue and estate planning is a death issue. The Savvy Affluent are familiar with the soaring costs of medical procedures and nursing home care and how they may wipe out retirement funds and an inheritance for a future generation. The Savvy Affluent realize the folly of relying on the government to provide for their medical coverage and their comfortable retirement. Thus, they recognize the role that long-term care insurance (LTCI) must play in their financial and estate plan.

Long-term care is considered a type of health insurance because it pays for a variety of health costs that may or may not be covered by Social Security, Medicare, or your state plan. The details of long-term care insurance and our recommendations on what to look for in an LTCI contract are covered in the Seventh Key. The Fifth Key offers a discussion of the income tax benefits of LTCI planning. The purpose of this brief chapter is to explain why LTCI is an important part of any estate plan. By reading *Wealth Secrets*, you will gain a full understanding of how LTCI will help you and your family in many areas—including protecting an inheritance from rising medical costs.

If you met with your advisors to discuss your estate plan under the 2001 laws, you probably didn't count on having to pay $100 to $300 per day for nursing home or in-home care. You also probably didn't factor in medical expense inflation rates of 5 percent to 10 percent per year that could make a very mediocre $100/day nursing home in year 2000 dollars cost more than $500 per day in 2020. If you need long-term care for just one year, it could use up $182,500 of funds that you had hoped would go to your children or grandchildren.

Do You Need LTCI?

According to the Center for Long Term Care Financing, Americans face approximately a one-in-ten chance of spending at least five or more years in a nursing home after age 65. Close to half—48.6 percent— of people age 65 and older may spend time in a nursing home. More startling is that 71.8 percent of people over age 65 may use some form of home health care! Do you think the developments in medicine will help or hurt this situation?

The longer people live (as a result of these advancements) the greater the likelihood that they will eventually need some significant medical assistance on a long-term basis. We may find treatments for cancer or osteoporosis, but that just increases the likelihood of eventually having Alzheimer's or some other debilitating disease that forces us to require significant, and very costly, care.

Table 39.1 lists some costs, by city, for nursing home care as compiled by the MetLife Assisted Living Market Telephone Survey 2002.

Table 39.1   The Average Annual Cost of Nursing Home Care

Anchorage, AK	$120,815	Omaha, NE	$75,555
Los Angeles, CA	$63,875	Las Vegas, NV	$72,635
San Diego, CA	$68,620	New York, NY	$100,010
San Francisco, CA	$91,250	Cleveland, OH	$83,950
Stamford, CT	$126,655	Philadelphia, PA	$68,985
Miami, FL	$70,445	Providence, RI	$66,065
Honolulu, HI	$80,300	Nashville, TN	$46,355
Chicago, IL	$51,100	Dallas, TX	$52,195
Boston, MA	$88,695	Houston, TX	$52,195
Baltimore, MD	$58,035	Arlington, VA	$74,825
Detroit, MI	$45,990	Rutland, VT	$73,365
St. Paul, MN	$72,270	Seattle, WA	$74,460
St. Louis, MO	$54,020	Milwaukee, WI	$64,970

Source: MetLife Web site.

Nursing home care costs in most cities in Table 39.1 range between $5,000 and $8,000 per month. Some are as inexpensive as $4,000 per month and some can be as expensive as $10,000 per month or more. Is there any reason to believe that nursing home care will become less expensive? Are you willing to risk losing this much of your estate to nursing home costs or would you like to plan ahead?

The important point to take from this chapter is that you will likely eventually pay for long-term care coverage. The question is: Will it be paid for in advance or will it be paid for from your intended inheritance or retirement funds?

You may wonder, "Doesn't the state or Medicare pay these expenses?" The answer is, "Yes and no." For example, the state of California will not pay for a senior's medical bills until that individual has depleted all but $3,000 of his net worth. That means that if a retirement plan, or a home, or any investments are titled to an individual, or have been titled in the individual's name in the last five years, the state will require those assets to be sold to pay for medical costs. In addition, the state will then take all but $30 per month of the individual's income to pay for their coverage.

It isn't hard to see how this could deplete someone's assets immediately. You are likely willing to buy insurance, create a living trust, and consider other estate planning strategies. Ignoring long-term care planning could be a potentially devastating mistake. Let's plan not to make it ourselves.

If you intend to leave an inheritance, then you may wish to purchase long-term care insurance now, while you have the money. You can purchase an LTCI policy in one year, over 10 years, over 20 years, or make payments every year for the rest of your life. You also have options to have all of your premiums go to your heirs at death . . . even if you collect on the policy during your lifetime. In fact, there are policies on the market today that combine a universal life insurance guaranteed death benefit for your heirs with a guaranteed daily benefit for long-term care costs. This can be an ideal tool to achieve two planning goals.

Consider This

Rising medical costs can be a significant cost for any retiree. If planning is not implemented in advance, these costs can wipe out retirement funds and any inheritance that would have otherwise gone to your heirs. By purchasing long-term care insurance, you are making sure that soaring medical costs don't take away the head start you wanted to leave your children or grandchildren or destroy the legacy you wanted to leave behind. It can be an important part of the multi-disciplinary financial plan of every Savvy Affluent client. Of course, if you aren't interested in leaving an inheritance to your heirs, you need not sit back and let medical costs and taxes take your money. You can implement charitable planning that will leave your estate to a deserving cause and give you tax benefits while you are alive. This is the focus of the next chapter.

40

Charitable Estate Planning

The Affluent and Super Affluent often want to give back to the world that provided them with success. The Savvy Affluent, however, take this charitable intent and use it to create as much benefit as possible to their families, while benefiting the charity at the same time. In this chapter, we will briefly examine only one tool often used in charitable estate planning—the charitable remainder trust (CRT). Because charitable planning is such a vast topic, we can only hope to give you a tiny hint of the types of planning we implement for our clients.

> To give away money is an easy matter and in any man's power, but to decide to whom to give it, and how large and when, and for what purpose and how, is neither in every man's power nor an easy matter.
>
> Aristotle

Rather than ramble on about a series of planning options, we think it best to be succinct and show the power of charitable planning through the story of Steve and Martha.

Steve, a 56-year-old orthopedic surgeon and his 48-year-old wife Martha, an OB/GYN doctor, have two boys, both finishing graduate school. As a result of prudent investing, good luck, and some great investments in some start-up businesses, Steve is considering early retirement so he can travel and enjoy his hobbies of flying and sailing.

In addition to his significant retirement plan account, Steve has $3 million in essentially zero-basis stock in his friend's company, which he helped finance in return for stock. He is in line with qualified stock options to acquire an additional $5 million over the next three years. Faced with planning for the disposition of an estate of $10 million (almost all of it in an undiversified portfolio), Steve and Martha decided that they'd like part of their financial plan to include a plan to eliminate estate taxes, if possible. In short, they're willing to give to charity those assets that would otherwise default to the IRS in the form of estate and capital gains taxes.

As a part of this strategy, they will also make aggressive gifts of stock to their two sons and other family heirs over the next few years through family limited partnerships. By freezing estate growth and squeezing the value of the assets, we hope to be able to eliminate all unnecessary estate taxes. Additionally, our plan will provide an excellent retirement income stream through the use of a charitable remainder trust.

Examine the following carefully, as we will refer to it next.

Steve and Martha Use a CRT to Benefit Charity and Their Family

	Sell	CRT
Net fair market value (FMV)	$3,000,000	$3,000,000
Taxable gain on sale	$3,000,000	
Capital gains tax (20%) at federal level	$600,000	
Net amount invested	$2,400,000	$3,000,000
Annual return of reinvested portfolio	10%	10%
Reinvested for 10% annual income produces annual retirement income of	$240,000	
Trust payout of 5% (averaged with 10% returns over trust term of 40 years)		$452,999
Annual average after-tax income (@ 39% tax and 20% capital gains rate for CRT payout)	$146,400	$321,622
Years—projected joint life expectancy	40	40
Taxes saved w/$616,290 deduction @ 39%		$240,358
Tax savings and cash flow over 40 years	$5,856,000	$13,105,233
Total increase in cash flow	$5,856,000	$13,105,233
Total value of asset in estate in 40 years	$2,400,000	$0
Estate taxes on this asset at 48%	$1,152,000	
Net value to family	$1,080,000	
Total insurance expense—wealth replacement	$0	($530,000)
Insurance benefit in wealth replacement trust	$0	$3,000,000
CRT remainder value to family charity	$0	$20,415,967

What is happening here? The stock that Steve owns is publicly traded, so its value is readily ascertained and is easily transferable to the family charitable trust. This CRT will take the highly appreciated stock and sell it without being taxed on its sale. It will then reposition the proceeds into a more balanced portfolio of equities designed for both growth and security.

The CRT, with Steve as co-trustee, will buy and hold stocks and mutual fund shares so that most of the portfolio will continue to appreciate while Steve and Martha, as income beneficiaries, receive quarterly payments of 5 percent of the trust's value every year. They've made the decision that leaving each son with a $5 million inheritance is part of their family's financial goals, so with some stock and life insurance held in an irrevocable life insurance trust, the two boys will be well protected for the future.

Everything else in their estate will either be spent during retirement or left to their favorite charity when they pass away. After examining the numbers, Steve and Martha felt that it made great sense to re-exert control over their social capital and follow through with their plan. Because Steve felt a need to sell in order to diversify his unbalanced portfolio, the only comparison to be made was between (1) selling the stock himself, paying tax, and reinvesting the net proceeds and (2) contributing the stock to the CRT, having the CRT sell the stock, avoiding any tax on the sale (because the CRT is a tax-exempt entity), and reinvesting inside the CRT. We have made such a comparison in the "sale" and "CRT" columns of the previous example.

You can see that the benefit to their family of the CRT is significant. Steve and Martha will enjoy $118,000 in additional annual retirement income in the CRT scenario ($264,000 post-tax versus $146,000 post-tax). Over their joint life expectancy, this difference will amount to more than $5 million!

Furthermore, because of the use of life insurance in a wealth replacement trust, their kids will get more out of that asset than in the "sale" scenario ($3 million of insurance proceeds income and estate tax-free vs. a $2.4 million asset netting $1.08 million to the family after estate taxes).

By combining a charitable remainder trust with a wealth replacement trust for their heirs, Steve and Martha will be able to enjoy a greater retirement income than they had anticipated and leave a substantial estate-tax-free legacy to their children. As if that were not enough, they are able to leave more than $21 million to charity. This is quite an accomplishment, yet it is feasible with the right financial planning and advisors.

Consider This

Although you may not have the wealth of the Super Affluent, you may still be able to benefit from charitable planning. Once you have protected your family wealth from lawsuits, taxes, and estate taxes, you have put your family in a better position. Now, the most important thing to do is to protect your family from financial catastrophes. These can include premature death, disability, and poor investments. The Seventh Key—Avoid Financial Disasters—will help you protect yourself and your family from these terrible threats.

THE SEVENTH KEY

AVOID FINANCIAL DISASTERS

Many people believe the roadmap to financial success includes focusing on a goal, putting your head down, and relentlessly pushing ahead until you reach your ultimate goal. Though hard work and perseverance are common personality traits of the Working Affluent, another key ingredient to long-term financial success exists among all of our Affluent clients. Every single Wealthy Family we encountered was able to avoid, or at least mitigate, catastrophic financial losses through a combination of luck and risk management planning. Since we do not espouse luck as a prudent strategy, we will focus on managing financial risk by planning to protect your family from financial disasters.

One common financial disaster that can result in a significant loss of assets is a civil lawsuit. The Fourth Key—Protect Assets—offered a dozen specific solutions to help mitigate litigation risks. Though lawsuits are a significant risk in today's society, they do not pose the most significant risk to one's wealth.

This Key will explore additional financial disasters and litigation risks that must be addressed if you wish to achieve and maintain wealth like the Affluent. These risks include personal and business risks as well as health and financial events. More specifically, these risks include:

- Premature death of a family member.
- Premature death of a business partner.
- Disability of the breadwinning family member or business partner.
- Long-term care needs of a family member.
- Running out of retirement assets.

41

Premature Death of a Family Member

The emotional distress caused by the premature death of a loved one can not be exaggerated. Long before the psychological scars begin to heal, financial devastation may begin for surviving family members.

There are various obstacles to successful financial planning in the case of unforeseen death because, simply put, none of us knows when our time will come. The 2003 National Safety Council's study on deaths (www.nsc.org/lrs/statinfo/odds.htm) and the 1999 U.S. Census Bureau's Statistical Abstract of the United States, which includes data from the year 1997, reported the following statistics in regard to types of unforeseen death:

- There is a 1 in 24 chance (4.17 percent) that you will ultimately die from a stroke.
- There is a 4 percent chance you will die from an accident or the adverse effects of one.

Moreover, it has been found that approximately 1 in 12 people will die from an unforeseen risk. In addition, a number of people will find out they are terminally ill and their families will not be able to purchase personal life insurance to help them manage the financial burden created when they pass away.

Another obstacle to successful financial planning in the case of unforeseen death is that most people don't enjoy contemplating, let alone discussing, the death of a family member. As a result, few families are financially or emotionally prepared for this traumatic event.

In this chapter we will discuss two financial losses that can occur at the time of death:

1. Loss of income.
2. Loss of an estate (via estate taxes and probate costs).

The Savvy Affluent use particular insurance planning strategies to efficiently manage the risks that often result from the premature death of a family member. The Savvy Affluent know the secret of how to protect their financial wealth and assets from the death of a patriarch or matriarch. Let's explore how this can be done.

Income Protection

A key to successful planning for the Savvy Affluent is an ability to put one's fear of death aside and focus on the financial impact a death may have on a family. The first financial impact of death, especially for younger families, is the lost income. Once a father or mother has passed away, they obviously will not earn any more income. If the family hasn't met all of its saving goals (most don't until the income earners are well into their 50s), there will be a significant financial strain from the death. The key to maintaining wealth is making sure that no financial catastrophe wipes out the family. To show you how significant this loss of income can be, consider the following.

The present value of 20 years of lost income for the average American family (with $45,000 of annual income) is approximately $636,000. That means that, at the time of death, the family would be in the same financial situation if they had 20 years of income or had a lump sum of $636,000.

For a Wealthy Family whose breadwinner earns $150,000 per year, the present value of 20 years of lost income is more than $2,100,000. For a Super Affluent family whose breadwinner is earning $1,000,000 per year, the present value of 20 years of lost income is $14 million. The simple estimate implies that a family needs approximately 14 times the annual income of the breadwinner to replace 20 years of lost income. If you have a younger breadwinner or a breadwinner who intends to work 30 more years, the multiple used to approximate the present value of future income is 18 times one year's income.

What these examples illustrate is that a family needs life insurance in the amount of at least 14 times the annual income of each wage earner just to keep them on track to meet their financial goals (assuming that their current earnings were keeping them on track). Also, this estimate assumes no adjustment for inflation. As such, the Savvy Affluent typically purchase life insurance in the neighborhood of 20 to 25 times income in order to avoid financial disasters and protect their future income for their families.

Estate Preservation

Although the Sixth Key focuses on the most common estate planning tools of the Affluent and Super Affluent, this section will only focus on how the unforeseen death of a family member affects the preservation of one's estate. In particular, the second most significant financial disaster that may occur after a premature death can be the loss of the estate.

For example, if the sudden death involves the loss of a husband and a wife (or the second of the two of them passes on), there could be significant estate taxes liabilities. As you may recall from the Sixth Key, the second death in a family with a net worth over $1 million could result in estate taxes of approximately 50 percent (taxes of up to 75 percent on pensions and IRAs, too). Estate taxes and unnecessary probate costs can really throw a wrench into a family business or real estate portfolio. If there is valuable family real estate or a family business, these assets may have to be sold to generate liquidity to pay the tax bill. The Savvy Affluent never let taxes or laws dictate when they sell their assets. They make sure that they have adequate liquidity so they can wait out poor sellers' markets and never are forced to have a fire sale.

The Savvy Affluent use life insurance to preserve their estates. The intelligent use of life insurance has helped Wealthy Families avoid financial disasters and maintain their level of affluence from generation to generation. Conversely, many Average Americans with less savvy financial planning strategies have lost valuable assets through the combination of poor planning, unlucky timing of deaths, and unexpected taxes. Because the Savvy Affluent know that they don't know when they will die and certainly don't know whether it will be a good time to sell assets when they do die, they see insurance policies designed to preserve an estate as very important tools in their overall financial planning.

Consider This

Since family members are unlikely to be able (and possibly unwilling) to support themselves in the event of the premature death of a breadwinner, the Affluent know that one must have a life insurance policy. Because life insurance is cheaper when the applicant is younger and healthier, and is often unavailable once the applicant develops serious health issues, we strongly suggest you secure life insurance as early as possible. You learned in the Fourth Key that many states offer complete protection of the cash values of life insurance policies. In the Sixth Key, you learned how life insurance is an important piece of the estate planning puzzle. In the Ninth Key, you will learn how life insurance is one of the two secret investments of the Super Affluent. From this chapter, you need only understand that life insurance is the only way to protect your family from the financial disaster of a premature death. For those of you who own businesses and have partners, the next chapter will explain how devastating a death can be to a business, the partners, and the partners' families.

CHAPTER

42

Premature Death of a Business Partner

Though the odds of premature death in the family and business context are nearly the same (though some would argue the self-employed suffer more stress-related injuries and die earlier), we find that businesses address this risk even less frequently than families do. This is very disturbing on two levels. First, similar probabilities of premature death in both situations should result in similar attention from both family members and business owners. Because this isn't the case, there is a statistical anomaly. Second, and much more inexcusably, a business is created for the sole purpose of generating financial benefit.

Since families are generally formed from love between two people and not from a mutual financial goal, it is more understandable for a family to spend its time addressing emotional and social issues like education and child rearing and to fail at managing its finances. However, for a business that was created with the purpose of making money, there is no excuse when owners completely ignore this potentially devastating risk.

Always Expect the Unexpected

As owners of a private business, professional practice, or other venture, the Working Affluent often spend ten hours per day, six or seven days per week getting their businesses to the point where they can provide a measure of security for their families. We know because we have been there ourselves. Nonetheless, those who ignore one fundamental legal contract jeopardize all of their hard work. This very important legal contract is the buy-sell agreement; that is, an agreement that all owners sign agreeing how the business will be valued at the time of one partner's death or disability and how the purchase of the shares will be paid.

Without a buy-sell agreement, partners and surviving family have no legally enforceable plan for how this transaction will take place. At a time when the family is grieving and possibly struggling to pay its bills, members of that family will look to the surviving partners' business for help in their time of need. At the same time, the surviving partners may be struggling to get by without the services of a valuable owner. The last thing either of these two groups need at this time is a power struggle over money. In too many cases, the absence of a buy-sell agreement at the time of death can cause bankruptcies of the families or a forced sale of the business.

The Savvy Affluent are always prepared for the unexpected. They understand that the buy-sell agreement is a must for any partner or shareholder in a private company who wants to see the business continue and succeed after he passes away. The buy-sell agreement is just as important for the families of the surviving partners as they want to have funds to buy out the deceased partner's family and continue with their business. At a seminar on entrepreneurship at UCLA, we heard a venture capitalist say: "You never should start any business before you know how you will exit that business." This is something the Savvy Affluent know. Let's consider some of the questions that Savvy Affluent business owners ask themselves.

- What happens if and when any of my partners die? How will their families fare as owners of my company? Do I want them as new partners? How will I buy them out at that time?
- What happens to my share of the business if I decide I want out of the business or I decide to retire?
- What happens if any of my partners become disabled or get into messy divorces? Will I have to take on their spouses as partners?
- What happens to my family if I die or become disabled? How will I know they get their fair share of the business?

Let's look at the case study of Fred and Bob, involving only one of the many areas where a buy-sell agreement has great utility. As you'll see, their story of a two-person firm losing one partner is a pretty typical case.

Case Study: Fred and Bob

Fred and Bob are owners of a $10 million (annual revenues) printing company. Fred has the sales expertise, while Bob runs the production side of the operation. Their overall profitability results from their joint efforts. If Fred were to die prematurely, Bob would have to either hire a new employee or promote someone to fill Fred's position. A new hire would be unlikely to duplicate Fred's results.

At the same time, Fred's widow would want to continue to take the same money out of the business that they received before Fred's death. In fact, if Fred's widow is raising a young family or has children in college, she may have to force a sale of the business at a distressed price just to meet her needs. Maybe Fred's son is also in the business and has his own ideas about how things should be run. Perhaps Fred's spouse wants to see Fred's son take over his father's place. It wouldn't matter that little Fredo is incompetent. There are so many problems that can arise. Needless to say, it may be impossible for Bob to continue a profitable business under such circumstances.

Unless you want to have to sell your business to pay your late partner's family or take on the spouse or child of your late partner as your new partner, you must plan ahead. Only by planning ahead can you and your partners answer these questions in a way that satisfies all parties, while enabling the business to be maintained. As mentioned earlier, the best tool for solving the dilemmas that arise from these questions is the buy-sell agreement in its various forms.

The Buy-Sell Agreement

A buy-sell agreement is an agreement that all owners sign that stipulates how the business will be valued at the time of one partner's death or disability and how the purchase of the deceased partner's shares will be paid. There are various ways to structure buy-sell agreements, depending on the goals and circumstances of the owners and the business itself. In all arrangements, there are some basics regarding buy-sell agreements that can apply to any type of business. Specifically, the benefits different stakeholders can gain from a buy-sell agreement are universal.

Practically speaking, buy-sells can be used for corporations, partnerships, limited partnerships, limited liability companies (LLC) and other business structures as well. To simplify the text, we will use the words "business owner" generically to mean any type of business owner, including a shareholder in a corporation, partners in a partnership, and members in a LLC. In the list below, we discuss the benefits of a buy-sell agreement for the business and remaining owners; each owner; and the family.

Benefits to the business and remaining owners: There are various benefits of the buy-sell agreement for both the business and its remaining owners. First, a properly planned buy-sell agreement will provide for the orderly continuation of the ownership and control of the business. This continuation should survive the death, disability, divorce, or bankruptcy of any owner and should provide for a seamless transition in the event any owner wants to retire and sell his ownership share.

Second, the buy-sell agreement can prevent unwanted outsiders from becoming owners and can eliminate the need for negotiation with surviving spouses and children. The agreement may also perform the role of a succession plan by providing for continuity or orderly succession of business management. Further, the buy-sell agreement is often used in conjunction with life and disability insurance policies to effectively provide liquidity for the business to purchase the outstanding ownership interests of the disabled or deceased partner.

Perhaps most important, the buy-sell agreement guarantees that the remaining owners will continue to control the business and be able to participate in the future growth of the business. This also prevents a competitor from purchasing ownership interests from a retired, disabled, or a deceased owner or surviving family member who desperately needs the money. Thus, the buy-sell guarantees continuity of management in the business, ultimately making the business more attractive to customers, creditors, and employees.

Benefits to each owner: From the standpoint of a living business owner, the buy-sell agreement can provide the individual partner with an opportunity to negotiate and obtain the fairest or best price for his share of the business. In the case of retirement or disability, the agreement can be an additional source of funds for each owner.

Benefits to family members: The buy-sell agreement also benefits the family members in the case of death and disability in various way. For a deceased owner's family, the existence of the buy-sell can assure the family or estate a liquid asset rather than an illiquid minority interest in a privately held business that would be extremely difficult to sell. As mentioned earlier, this can be extremely important as the surviving family may be burdened with estate tax payments. The agreement itself may provide a valuation of the business interest, which can be used for estate tax filing purposes. This may save the survivors the additional headache and expense of securing another valuation and fighting the IRS on that value.

If one owner becomes disabled, the buy-sell contract guarantees that the disabled owner's family does not have to become involved in the business in order to protect the family's interest. The buy-sell agreement frees the disabled owner and his family from the risk of future business losses and creates funds that may be used to pay medical bills and living costs. This creates peace of mind as the disabled owner knows that he has retrieved his investment in the business and does not have to continue to worry about its future.

The Buy-Sell Agreement Plus Disability Policies

Savvy business owners always have signed buy-sell agreements that guard against financial ruin in the event of the unexpected death or disability of a business partner. More important, they supplement the life insurance funding of the buy-sell agreement with lump sum disability policies on the partners to ensure that they can buy each other out in the event of a premature death or disability. Without the proper disability policies as part of a buy-sell agreement, a business may fail as soon as one partner becomes disabled.

Funding the Agreement

Because the buy-sell agreement contemplates a buy-sell transaction at the time of an owner's death or disability, insurance policies are generally recommended to fund the transaction. There are many reasons for this, including the following:

- Insurance policies pay a predetermined amount, with proceeds available at exactly the time when they are needed as a funding source (no liquidity concerns).
- Proceeds will be available regardless of the financial state of the business at that point (as long as premiums have been paid).
- The business leverages the cost of premiums to create the proceeds, thus, it costs the business less to buy insurance than it would cost to save money in a special buyout fund.
- The economic risks of early death or premature disability of any owner are shifted to the insurer.
- Insurance proceeds are paid to the owner or owner's family income tax free.

If the payment contemplated under the agreement is not a lump sum cash or periodic payment other than through a disability insurance policy, it is important to consider some type of security arrangement for the departing owner. These agreements might include personal guarantees from remaining owners, mortgages or security interests in real estate, a bank standby letter of credit, or even collaterally assigned life insurance policies.

The Need for a Coordinated Team

Creating a buy-sell arrangement that fits a particular business requires expertise and experience. Expertise in areas of corporate and business law, tax law, insurance products, and the valuation of businesses are all absolute requirements. Just as important is experience in dealing with different owners and the ability to negotiate and draft an agreement that meets the needs of all parties involved.

Too often business owners make one of two key mistakes in deciding who should oversee the creation of a buy-sell arrangement:

1. Some choose a friend who is a lawyer to create the strategy and draft the document rather than an expert in the area.
2. Some do not have a coordinated team to implement the plan.

A coordinated buy-sell team would involve the following:

* An attorney who has experience creating these types of arrangements.
* A life and disability insurance professional who has worked on these issues before.
* A business appraisal firm whose expertise may be needed on an ongoing basis in the future for annual business valuations.

Consider This

As with any legal or insurance planning, the early bird is richly rewarded. Nowhere in business planning is this truer than in buy-sell agreements. The reason for this is not so much economic as political. If this planning is done before an owner is close to disability, divorce, retirement, or death, all owners are in the same position relative to each other. That makes the negotiation of a standard deal for all owners a much easier and smoother process. Planning early for a buy-sell agreement will truly benefit you, your family, and your business. In order to avoid financial disasters, consider this agreement as an essential part of your financial planning for you, your family, and your business.

Buy-sell agreements don't just protect against death. They also protect against disability, which is discussed briefly in this Key. Disability does not just impact business. A disability can devastate a family. The next chapter will explain how families can protect themselves against the disability of a breadwinner. The next chapter will also give you detailed information about disability income insurance policies that can be used for either personal or business purposes.

CHAPTER 43

Disability of a Breadwinner or Business Partner

If you are like most of our Working Affluent clients, the single greatest asset your family has is your earning power. This reality motivates most people to buy life insurance as protection against a premature death. For most people, purchasing life insurance is common sense. While most people with whom we speak are underinsured, they do have at least some protection against a premature death. However, most Average American professionals, entrepreneurs, business owners, and executives often overlook a more dangerous threat to their long-term financial stability—their own disability. What is the risk that the average individual will suffer a disability? According to marketing materials from more than one life insurance company:

> Probability of at least one long-term disability (90 days or longer) occurring before age 65 is: 44% for someone age 25; 41% for someone age 35; 36% for someone age 45; and 27% for someone age 55.
>
> Source: CIDB Disability Tables.

Inadequate disability income insurance coverage can be more costly than death, divorce, or a lawsuit. Responsible financial planning includes planning for the best possible future, while protecting against the worst possible events. No one ever plans on becoming disabled—though almost *half* of those aged 25 will have a disability of three months or longer at least once. This chapter explains not only why you need disability insurance, but also what to look for in a disability policy.

Protecting Income from Disability

For most of the Working Affluent, the most valuable asset they have is their ability to go to work and earn an income for their family. Moreover, the leading risk to this asset is long-term disability. No one ever plans on becoming disabled—though half of us will experience a long-term disability at least once in our lives. In fact, the odds hold with the two lead authors. Chris missed four months of work in 1995 when he injured his back playing basketball. It happened to one of us. It happens to half of the population. The odds are it will happen to you or your spouse. Though disability insurance may seem like a boring topic compared with some of the more exotic material in the book, this may be the single most important asset protection lesson you learn.

The Need for Disability Insurance

In our opinion, the disability of the family breadwinner can be more financially devastating to a family than premature death. In both cases, the breadwinner will be unable to provide any income for the family; however, in the case of death, the deceased earner is no longer an expense to the family. Yet, if the breadwinner suddenly becomes disabled, that individual still needs to be fed, clothed, and cared for by medical professionals or family members. In many cases, the medical care alone can cost hundreds of dollars per day. Thus, with a disability, income is reduced or eliminated *and* expenses increased. This can be a devastating turn of events and can lead to creditor problems and even bankruptcy. The Savvy Affluent are aware of this problem and have implemented adequate planning in advance to address and prevent it.

If you are older (near retirement) and have saved a large enough sum of money to immediately fund a comfortable retirement, then you probably don't need disability income protection. Of course, you may have some long-term care concerns, but that is covered in Chapter 44. On the other hand, if you are less than 50 years old, or if you are older than 50 and have several precollege-age children, you should consider *the right* disability insurance a necessity. The challenge is determining what type of disability income policy is right for you.

Employer-Provided Coverage Often Inadequate

If you are an employee of a corporation, your employer may provide long-term disability (LTD) coverage. The premiums are probably discounted from what you would pay for a private policy. We advise you to take a good look at what the employer-offered policy covers, and buy a private policy if you and the insurance professional on your advisory team decide you need it. For many people, this makes a lot of sense because employer-provided group policies are often inadequate. They may limit either the term of the coverage or the amount of benefits paid. For instance, benefits may last only a few years or benefit payments may represent only a small part of your annual compensation. Because this is most commonly an employer-paid benefit, the money received during your disability will be income taxable to you. For most, this arrangement would result in your taking home less than half of the original amount in your paycheck after taxes are paid!

Give Yourself a Checkup

Most people with employer-provided disability insurance coverage will find the benefit inadequate. To help you determine where your existing coverage may be lacking, we have provided some questions for you to ask when you are giving yourself an insurance checkup. When you are ultimately working with the insurance professional on your advisory team, you should keep some of these questions in mind as well. They will help you better compare coverage options from different companies so you can find the best policy for your specific circumstances and goals. Below is a list of some questions you should ask yourself as well as short explanations of the appropriate answers.

- How long does the disability coverage last?
- How much is the benefit? (Different plans may cap the benefits at a certain figure, for example, $5,000 per month.)
- What percentage of your income is covered? (Generally, you cannot receive more than 60 percent of income, and the benefit is capped at $7,500 or $10,000 monthly, depending on

your age). Though most group LTD plans are good for the purpose that they serve, they are only a partial cure. Because of the limitations or cap, they have a built-in discrimination against higher income employees—like you!

- Who pays the premiums? (Tip: If you pay the premiums yourself, and not as a deductible expense through your business or practice, your benefits will be tax-free.) You may be seduced by the income tax deduction of the premiums, but the extra tax burden today is much easier to swallow than the tax burden will be if you suffer a disability and have a significantly reduced income *and* increased expenses. When you and your family need the money the most, you will have more.
- Is the policy portable, or convertible, to an individual policy if you leave the group? If so, do you maintain your reduced group rate?
- If your business distributes all earnings from the corporation at year-end in the way of bonuses to all owners/partners (typical of C-corporations as a way to avoid double taxation), you should find out whether these amounts are covered by the group policy. If not, and if bonuses or commissions make up a substantial part of your income (which we have seen to be the case with many people), you'll probably need supplemental coverage.
- What is the definition of disability in the group policy? Own-occupation, any-occupation, or income-replacement? (Please see the discussion of these three terms on pages 264–265.)
- Are your overhead expenses covered if you are disabled? If you can't perform your duties at work, will the business keep paying you? If you can't generate income for the business, many of your expenses will keep on piling up, won't they? For professionals, a business overhead expense policy also covers hiring an outside professional to replace the insured during disability for up to two years.

Getting the Best Insurance Coverage for the Money

Now that you have given yourself a checkup and realize that you may need a new or supplemental insurance policy, you need to know what to look for to get the best coverage available at a reasonable price. The following questions are important for you to ask when considering a disability policy.

What is the benefit amount? Most policies are capped at benefit amounts that equal 60 percent of income. Some states and insurance companies have monthly maximums as well. You have to ask yourself how much money your family would need if you were to become disabled. Generally, you want to find companies that offer at least 60 percent of predisability after-tax income with maximums of at least $7,500 or $10,000 monthly. There are additional monthly benefits of $5,000 to $25,000 available through more specialized channels for those high earners who want more monthly income than the traditional limits.

What is the waiting period? The waiting period is the period of time that you must be disabled before the insurance company will pay you disability benefits. The longer the waiting period before benefits kick in, the less your premium will be. Essentially, the waiting period serves as a deductible relative to time; you cover your expenses for the waiting period, then the insurance company steps in from that point forward. This is not unlike the deductible you have on your car, except that auto insurance deductibles are in the form of amounts paid ($100, $250, $500, and so on), not relative to a period of time. If you have adequate sick leave, short-term disability, and an emergency fund, and can support a longer waiting period, choose a policy with a longer waiting period to save money. Although waiting periods can last as long as 730 days, a 90-day waiting period may give you the best coverage for your money.

How long will coverage last? It's a good idea to get a benefit period of coverage that lasts until age 65, at which point Social Security payments will begin. Be aware that many policies cover you for only two to five years. Unless you are 60 to 63 years old, this would be an inadequate period because most people want coverage that pays them until age 65. Unless you are so young that you haven't yet had time to qualify for Social Security, a policy that provides lifetime benefits, at costly premiums, is generally not worth the added expense.

What is the definition of disability in your policy? There are different definitions of disability within different policies at the same company and different definitions from insurance company to insurance company. The definition of disability used for a particular policy is of the utmost importance. The main categories are: own-occupation, any-occupation, and loss of income. The own-occupation policies, which pay a benefit if you can't continue your own occupation (even if you can and do work another occupation after the disability), are the most comprehensive, and of course, the most expensive. Two important elements to look for in an own-occupation policy are:

1. Are you forced to go back to work in another occupation?
2. Will you receive a partial benefit if you go back to work slowly after the disability and make less than you did before the disability?

These two benefits are of the utmost importance.

Does the policy offer partial benefits? If you are able to work only part-time instead of your previous full-time hours, will you receive benefits? Unless your policy states that you are entitled to partial benefits, you won't receive anything unless you are totally unable to work. Also, are extended partial benefits paid if you go back to work and suffer a reduction in income because you cannot keep up the same rigorous schedule you had before you were disabled? For example, this would be an important benefit for anesthesiologists, as they often work ridiculous hours in their younger years and most likely will work less after any disability.

Important note: Partial benefits may be added on as a rider in some policies and should be seriously considered as only 3 percent of all disabilities are total disabilities. Some policies even have a recovery benefit that, in the event that a business has lost clients during the disability due to the insured not being able to service them and the insured has suffered a loss of income because of this, may pay a benefit. The insured does not have to be disabled at all—there can be just loss of income due to disability-related attrition.

Is business overhead expense (BOE) covered? When you go out on your own, the last thing you think about is not being able to pay your bills. Whether you have $10,000 or $20,000 of monthly disability benefit, you likely don't have enough to cover your lost income and the costs of running the business. Though most companies have limited how much an individual can get in monthly benefit (often 60 percent of after-tax monthly income—capped at $10,000 per month), many carriers still offer up to $25,000 or more per month to cover business overhead expense. Many business owners who contact us have failed to implement this important defensive policy.

Is it noncancellable or guaranteed renewable? The difference between these two terms—noncancellable and guaranteed renewable—is very important. If a policy is noncancellable, you will pay a fixed premium throughout the contract term. Your premium will not go up for the term of the contract. If it is guaranteed renewable, it means you cannot be cancelled, but your premiums could go up. As long as noncancellable is in the description of the policy, you are in good shape.

How financially stable is the insurance company? Before buying a policy, check the financial soundness of your insurer. If your insurer goes bankrupt, you may have to shop for a policy later in life, when premiums are more expensive. Standard & Poor's top rating for financial stability is AAA. A.M. Best Co. uses A++ as its top rating for financial strength. Duff and Phelps rates companies on their ability to pay claims and uses AAA as its highest rating. Moody's uses Aa1 to rate excellent companies. There are no guarantees in life, but buying a policy from a highly rated company is the safest bet you can make and we would not recommend gambling on your disability insurance to save a few dollars.

Other issues to consider when determining if you are getting the best disability insurance coverage for your money so that you can avoid financial disasters caused by the disability of the breadwinner in your family include:

- Increased coverage
- Cost-of-living increases
- Waiver-of-premium
- Return-of-premium waiver
- Unisex pricing
- HIV rider
- Multilife pricing discounts
- Protection of future pension contributions

Disability of a Business Partner

The disability of a business partner can be just as financially crippling as the disability of the family breadwinner. There is a strong financial tie between business partners. There can be an even stronger financial dependency between business partners than there is between spouses. When a partner becomes disabled, the business will undoubtedly lose significant revenue while possibly facing increased costs in an attempt to replace the disabled partner. Absent a buy-sell agreement tied to disability income insurance with a lump sum payout to generate funds to buy out the disabled partner, the end result could be financial devastation for the remaining partner and the business.

Consider This

The likelihood of a disability is greater than the probabilities of a premature death, a lawsuit, and a bankruptcy combined. The Affluent know that disability insurance is the only way to protect future income. We cannot overstate the importance of having a comprehensive disability policy as part of any personal financial plan and a policy as a funding mechanism for a buy-sell agreement in the case of a disability of a business partner.

44

Long-Term Care Needs for Families

Some people are lucky enough to accumulate wealth because they are in the right place at the right time. Others are unfortunate and lose assets because they are in the wrong place at the wrong time. The Savvy Affluent neither rely on luck to gain wealth nor leave the preservation of their wealth to chance. The Savvy Affluent make sure that they are insured against every practical risk of loss so they can maintain and continue to build wealth. As such, they often have long-term care insurance to prevent financial disasters that may arise from long-term illness. Before we discuss long-term care insurance, let's first see how big a risk this is.

According to the Americans for Long-Term Care Security's report in August 2000 (www.ltcweb.org), more than half of all Americans will need some form of long-term care during their lifetimes. This means that next to life insurance, this is probably the insurance policy your family will need the most. The odds are high that one of your parents, one of your in-laws, and either you or your spouse will have a need for long-term care.

In the U.S., the average stay in a nursing home is between two and three years. In some areas of the country, the cost of nursing home care or quality around-the-clock in-home care may be $200 to $300 per day. This means that the average home healthcare needs cost between $150,000 and $320,000. Additionally, the U.S. Health Care Administration reports that costs are increasing 5.8 percent per year and are expected to more than triple in the next 20 years. At these projected rates, the costs may be between $500,000 and $1 million by the time you or your spouse need long-term care.

Are you sure that you, your parents, and your in-laws all have hundreds of thousands of extra dollars in your retirement and estate plans to cover this highly possible expense?

Long-term care insurance (LTCI) covers health insurance costs for those people who cannot take care of themselves. These costs may include nursing home care, in-home care, and many other expenses. This chapter will explain why and how the Savvy Affluent make long-term care planning a high priority in their planning. More specifically, this chapter will discuss the need for LTCI, why it is often overlooked, why the government won't help you, what types of coverage exist, and how they can help you.

The Need for Long-Term Care Insurance

There are two basic reasons why many Americans may need long-term care insurance. First, modern advancements in medicine, science, and technology have helped to increase the average life expectancy of people. Paradoxically, with this increased life expectancy, there is a greater chance that people may suffer a debilitating illness that may require them to seek significant long-term care. Even though medicine keeps people alive longer, there are still incurable diseases that don't kill you but will leave you requiring assistance. A neurological disorder like Alzheimer's is a perfect example. An Alzheimer's patient could need significant care for 15 or 20 years before dying. Some advances in medicine can come with a hefty price tag for some people.

The trend of increasing life expectancies, in conjunction with the increasing costs of medical expenses, means long-term care can be very expensive. The Affluent are aware that long-term care can easily wipe out retirement savings and eliminate any inheritance they might have otherwise left for children or grandchildren (or might have received from their parents or in-laws). This is why the Savvy Affluent always include LTCI planning in their comprehensive plans.

Why Most People Fail to Secure LTCI

Before we discuss the various types of LTCI policies, it is important that we address some reasons why LTCI is often not a part of people's financial plans. In this section, we will answer the following questions:

- Why won't the government cover these long-term care costs?
- Why don't most people have LTCI?

Why Won't the Government Cover these Long-Term Care Costs?

To many people's surprise, the government will not cover long-term care costs the way people would like them to. Did you know that in California an individual does not qualify for LTCI coverage unless his net worth is less than $3,000? In addition, once that individual begins receiving LTCI benefits, the state takes all but $30 a week of income from the patient. Many Average Americans and all Affluent clients would have to spend every last dollar of their savings before they could receive any health care help. Even if you have more than enough saved to pay for these types of expenses, your potential health problem could wipe out the entire inheritance that you hoped would go to your children or grandchildren.

Incidentally, many of our Affluent clients buy LTCI policies on their parents because they know they will have to take care of their parents if the need arises and they want to make sure that it does not affect their financial status. After all, such unplanned expenses could result in a major financial disaster and emotional problems. Imagine if you are getting ready to retire and suddenly one of your parents or in-laws gets sick and needs $75,000 to $150,000 per year of medical care. Unfortunately, this will most likely be paid for with after-tax dollars if you do not plan accordingly and have LTCI.

Why Don't Most People Have LTCI?

You may also be surprised to learn that many people do not have LTCI; however, many people do not want to bear the risk of self-insuring their long-term care costs. So why haven't more people purchased LTCI? In one word—ignorance. We see clients insure their lives, homes, cars, and income, but not events (like long-term care and disability) that have the next highest probability of occurring in one's lifetime (behind only death). Why? It could be an "it's not going to happen to me" mentality. It could be a false sense of security that Social Security will take care of things. It could also be frugality; some Average Americans may not want to pay LTCI insurance premiums for the next 20 to 40 years if they only have a 50 percent chance of getting a benefit from the insurance.

Types of LTCI Policies

Now that you know why you need an LTCI policy, you need to know what you should look for in an LTCI policy. There are various types of LTCI policies, which include:

Traditional LTCI policies. Traditional LTCI policies feature benefits, options, and riders that vary in availability and scope among carriers. These traditional policies do not have cash value, nor do they have a death benefit. Once a person becomes eligible for LTCI benefits (inability to perform two of six activities of daily living), the traditional policy pays a daily reimbursement for approved expenses up to the maximum daily benefit chosen by the insured. Upper and lower limits vary among carriers but are in the $20 to $300 per day range. Benefits can be received for life or for a period of time, as determined by a total insurance dollar value of the policy, often referred to as "the pool of benefits." "Facility only" or "facility and in-home care policies" are also available. Elimination periods (deductibles) apply and can range from 0 days to 90 days.

Other features, options, and riders that vary among carriers are inflation protection, bed reservations, alternative plan of care, restoration of benefits, personal care advisor, respite care, joint policy discounts, premium waver, rate classes, nonforfeiture benefits, indemnity benefits, caregiver indemnity benefits and 10-year paid-up, 20-year paid-up, and nonlevel payment options.

A major resistance to purchasing traditional LTCI is the possibility of ongoing premium payments and the chance that a person may never actually use the policy's benefits. If this is the reason that you do not have LTCI, look for a carrier that offers paid-up policies and/or nonforfeiture riders. Paid-up policies will require yearly premiums for a specified number of years, usually 10 or 20 years. After this time, premium payments stop and the insured owns the policy for life. Nonforfeiture riders allow the policy owner to name a beneficiary and, upon death, all premiums that have been paid are then paid to the named beneficiary even if benefits have been received. However, the policy must be in force at the time of death for the beneficiary to receive the paid premiums.

Universal life insurance policies. A different method of addressing long-term care needs is to purchase a universal life insurance policy with an attached rider that can accelerate all or a portion of the death benefit to be used for approved long-term care costs should the need arise. Benefits are received in much the same way as a traditional long-term care policy. This requires a single premium payment and purchase of a paid-up policy. In most cases, an existing cash value policy can be exchanged with no tax consequence (consult your tax professional regarding your particular situation). The larger the single premium paid, the larger the death benefit that can be converted to daily benefit maximums for approved long-term care costs divided over a two-year, four-year, or lifetime period at a decreasing daily maximum amount. The policy can be purchased to provide benefits for an individual or couple.

Overall, the most important feature of a good LTCI policy is a financially sound insurance carrier. Do not consider purchasing the cheapest LTCI policy that you can find. LTCI carriers must have the financial strength to sustain their ability to pay claims well into the future when the millions of baby boomers will begin needing LTC benefits. In a nutshell, don't be penny-wise and pound-foolish.

Using LTCI to Protect Your Retirement Income

Would you consider paying for your LTCI premiums if you could do so in a tax-deductible manner and do so over a finite period like five or ten years? Would you consider paying for LTCI if you knew that your heirs would receive every dollar of that premium at a later date?

Most baby boomers are saddled with the problem of having to take care of their children, themselves, and possibly their parents. The biggest financial disaster that can affect your retirement is that you, your spouse, your parents, or your in-laws suffer significant health problems and do not have a sound financial plan. The omission of an LTCI policy that covers family members who might become ill would certainly destroy your retirement and any inheritances that might exist before the illness arose.

As established earlier in this chapter, the cost of long-term care for one person can be hundreds of dollars per day. For this reason, many Affluent clients don't just purchase long-term care insurance for themselves and their spouses, they also buy long-term care insurance on their parents and in-laws. This is a growing trend we are noticing with our younger clients. They are taking out LTCI policies on their parents and in-laws as a way to take care of their parents and protect their own retirements. There are many different bells and whistles to consider and a variety of LTCI payment options, which range from single payment to 10-payment, 20-payment, and life-pay programs. Regardless of the payment option you choose, remember it is essential that you buy an LTCI policy so that you can avoid financial disasters and protect your family's assets and retirement income.

Consider This

Increasing medical costs and increasing life expectancies have led to increased spending on medical-related expenses. The reduced benefits of social security leave this increased burden to individuals and families. The impact of this expense can be devastating. Hundreds of thousands of dollars per year can be spent on long-term care. With a mental illness that could last 10 or more years, the cost to a family could be millions of dollars. For retirees on a fixed budget, this could bankrupt them. For Wealthy Families, the bulk of an estate could be unnecessarily decimated by long-term care expenses. Luckily, LTCI is available and can be purchased through a corporation to make it more tax efficient. To learn another way to make sure that you, your parents, and your in-laws don't run out of money in retirement, read the next chapter as well.

45

Running Out of Money in Retirement

The last, and one of the most important, financial disaster that we will discuss in this Key is the threat of running out of money during retirement. In this chapter, we will focus on the type of investments you can make to ensure that you avoid financial disaster and don't run out of retirement savings.

This may sound odd, but the reason this chapter is so important is because we don't know when we will die. Because you cannot predict that day you will die, you can't possibly know how much retirement savings you need or know how much retirement income you can afford to take out each year. A very common mistake many retirees make is that they fear running out of retirement assets so much, they never touch principal. This leads to a lower quality of life in retirement and to unnecessary estate taxes at death.

One of two things will certainly happen. You will either be like many retirees and die with money left over for your heirs (and for the government via estate taxes), or be like the others and live longer than expected (or spend too much) and run out of money in retirement. If you die with money left over, we assume you would rather leave it to your heirs than to the federal government (this is where this chapter overlaps with estate planning—the Sixth Key). We also assume that you don't want to have to rely on your children, your children's spouses, or your grandchildren to support you.

In this chapter, we will explain how to get the most out of your retirement plan assets without risking running out of money in retirement. The Savvy Affluent get the most out of all of their assets. The Savvy Affluent also make sure that they will not experience financial and emotional disasters like running out of money in retirement and be forced to ask children or grandchildren to support them. A very valuable tool to help avoid this financial catastrophe is the life annuity.

Life Annuities

Retirement is a time for you to worry less, not more. You have already worked for 30 or more years, raised children, dealt with weddings (and maybe divorces), and handled thousands of day-to-day crises with your kids, among many other troubles. The last thing you want to do in retirement is worry about how you're going to support yourself and still leave something for your children, grandchildren, or your favorite charity. The annuity and insurance strategy that the Affluent use eliminates the risk, guarantees an adequate income in retirement, and leaves as much money as possible for heirs and/or charities. In our best case scenario, we can do all of this while reducing, if not eliminating, income and estate taxes in the process. The first part of this strategy includes a life annuity.

The life annuity (not to be confused with the variable annuity) is designed by actuaries to pay interest and principal back to you over your lifetime. The amount the insurance company pays you is fixed and will not decrease if the stock market crashes or if interest rates fall. Moreover, if you outlive your life expectancy, the insurance company continues to pay you or your spouse for as long as you are alive. This is a good way to remove the investment risk of your retirement plan assets and lock in a fixed income in retirement.

You may be wondering how much income one can expect from a life annuity policy. To answer this question, simply look at Table 45.1, which shows some numbers for clients of ours (some individuals, some couples) at varying ages. Of course, these numbers are only examples and may differ based on a variety of economic and medical factors. However, once a life annuity is purchased, the monthly or annual income amount cannot change (unless you purchase a cost of living rider that increases the annual payout 1 percent to 3 percent annually).

Table 45.1   Client's Income from Life Annuity*

Client	Cost of Life Annuity	Monthly Income for Life
Dr. B—age 82	$433,000	$6,243
Dr. F—age 65	$1,000,000	$7,900
Dr. and Mrs. G—ages 67 & 63	$1,500,000	$9,200*

*Pays this amount as long as either Dr. or Mrs. G is alive.

If you are afraid of running out of money or are just uncomfortable with investment risk and how it may impact your retirement, you may want to consider what the Savvy Affluent have used for years—life annuities. Your multidisciplinary planning team can help you integrate life annuities into your planning to minimize risk, maximize after-tax retirement income, and maximize your estate. How life annuities can be part of an estate plan will be discussed next.

Using a Life Annuity to Leave Money for Heirs

Life annuity policies also are a valuable tool to help you leave left-over retirement funds to your children and grandchildren, without enduring financial burdens. In most cases, the life annuity policy pays you more than you need to cover your cost of living. We recommend you gift the excess to an irrevocable life insurance trust (you'll find more in the Sixth Key, which focuses on estate planning) and buy life insurance to replace the value of the pension assets. Because pension assets are only worth 30 percent to your heirs after income and estate taxes (also discussed in the estate planning Key), this solution almost always gives more to the heirs, reduces income taxes paid on withdrawals, and provides a fixed income stream in retirement. If you're not sure how this solution would work in your situation, please feel free to call us and we'll run an illustration for you.

The Exclusion Ratio Can Save Taxes

Interestingly, there is a way to get tax-free income with a life annuity. If you purchase a life annuity with nonretirement plan assets, you will receive a significant tax benefit. The Affluent know this and consequently include a life annuity policy in their financial plans so that they can save even more in retirement and avoid financial disasters.

Each life annuity of this type has what is called an "exclusion ratio." This is the amount of the monthly or annual payment that is not income taxable. The older you are, the greater the tax-free percentage of the life annuity payment. For an 80-year-old retiree, 70 percent of the annuity payment may be tax-free. As an example, if you received annual annuity payments of $100,000 that were 70 percent tax-free, you would pay tax on only $30,000 of that payment per year. Assuming a cumulative tax rate of 25 percent, you would pay only $7,500 in taxes on $100,000 of income. For this reason, many retirees like to purchase life annuities rather than live off the interest of their savings and subject themselves to the risk of outliving their funds.

In the context of retirement plans, should you decide against utilizing the life annuity and take your chances with the stock market, it is possible that you could end up with a sizeable retirement plan balance at the time of your death. While you might think this is desirable because it will benefit your children or grandchildren, you would be gravely mistaken. Many of your retirement plans will be subject to taxes of 80 percent when you die. Avoiding this hidden tax trap is a concern that warrants its own chapter within the Sixth Key.

Consider This

Life insurance can protect a family and a business from financial disaster resulting from a premature death. Disability income insurance can protect a family and business partners from an injury that reduces a breadwinner's, or partner's, ability to earn a living. Long-term care insurance can protect a retiree from losing retirement funds and can help protect a family's estate. Various annuities can help protect a retiree from running out of money. The next section, the Eighth Key—Invest Wisely—will explain important investment philosophies. The Ninth Key—Use the Secret Investments of the Affluent—will share the two investment secrets of the Affluent. If you want to accumulate wealth, as well as protect it, these two Keys are essential.

THE EIGHTH KEY

INVEST WISELY

Investing wisely may seem like a simple concept, but the application of investing wisely is much more complicated than you would think. One reason is that wisdom and luck are very different but are often hard to differentiate. Many unwise investments have performed well . . . at least for some period of time. Remember, Enron was the investment community's darling at one time. To measure the wisdom of an investment strategy, one does not measure performance over a short period of time. It is the process and application that should be analyzed over a complete market cycle defined as a bull high to a bear low and back again or vice versa.

Let's look at this another way: If you applied the modified Machiavellian concept of "the ends justify the means" to an investment scoring philosophy, you would say that the person who purchased a lottery ticket and won $25 million was a smart investor and the millions who spent the same $1 on losing lottery tickets were failures. As such, you should instead look and compare the probabilities of success with the risks, complexity of the investment, and interaction with the other elements of the plan to determine the wisdom of the investment philosophy. Doing this, you might come to the more reasoned conclusion that none of the investments in lottery tickets were wise, one was simply lucky. Picking individual high-risk equities in hopes of finding one that hits it big is another example of a lottery mentality with similar appeal to the unwise. Like the lottery, this strategy has a very low probability of success.

The applications of the numerous principals discussed throughout this book are the keys (pun intended) to successful investing. The Fourth Key on asset protection showed you how to protect your investments from lawsuits. The Fifth Key on tax planning showed you how to reduce taxes on your income. The Sixth Key on estate planning showed you how to pass your wealth onto your heirs with as little tax and complication as possible.

This Key is going to tell you the secret of how to invest wisely. It will help you avoid the most common investment mistakes by teaching you some important investment fundamentals, explaining how these may or may not apply to the Affluent, and explaining some common, and some not-so-common, investment alternatives. More specifically, this Key will explain the limitations of a Nobel Prize–winning investment theory that most investment firms follow, the real costs of taxes and inflation, the pitfalls of mutual funds for the Affluent, and discuss alternative investment strategies that address these concerns. The next part, the Ninth Key, will discuss two investment secrets of the Affluent—real estate and life insurance—which address all of these concerns, making them the investment keys to building and maintaining family fortunes.

CHAPTER 46

A Nobel Prize Is Not Enough

Many investment advisors may boast that their strategy is based on a Nobel Prize–winning theory. Though this is impressive, it has two faults:

1. Nearly everyone's strategy is based on that same theory.
2. The theory has a number of limitations that were acknowledged by the Nobel Laureates themselves.

The purpose of this chapter is threefold. First, we will give you a very basic understanding of the aforementioned Nobel Prize–winning investment theory. Second, we will point out the limitations of the theory. Third, we will suggest how to make the theory work for your particular comprehensive financial plan.

The Modern Portfolio Theory and the Capital Asset Pricing Model

In 1990, the Nobel Prize in Economics was awarded to Harry Markowitz, Merton Miller, and William Sharpe for their Modern Portfolio Theory (MPT) and Capital Asset Pricing Model (CAPM). With apologies to Messrs. Markowitz, Miller, and Sharpe, we would like to offer simplistic summaries of the Capital Asset Pricing Model and Modern Portfolio Theory. There are three concepts you must be able to grasp before putting them together to form the CAPM and MPT. Those are:

1. Types of risk
2. Risk vs. reward
3. Diversification of investments

Types of Risk

CAPM divides the risk of any investment into two types of risk: specific risk and market (or systematic) risk. Specific risk is unique to an individual investment, while systematic risk affects all investments in the market and is also known as "market risk." Let's look at examples of each.

> **Specific risk.** Do you remember the Tylenol scare about 25 years ago? Someone tainted a number of bottles of Tylenol with cyanide. This obviously affected the stock price of Johnson & Johnson, the maker of Tylenol. The risk of this type of occurrence is an example of specific risk because it didn't have an effect on all makers of analgesics in the market, just Johnson & Johnson.
>
> **Market or systematic risk.** Do you recall the stock market crash of 1929? That incident affected all investments in the market. The risk of a crash is certainly the most extreme example of market risk. A more current example is what the market pundits call a market correction or a 10 percent decline from a recent high.

When you make an investment, that investment is subject to both market and specific risk. In a portfolio of investments, you are subject to market risk, which affects the whole portfolio, and a combination of specific risks that affect each individual investment distinctly.

Risk vs. Reward

Over an extended period of time, rewards are generally higher for those who take more risk. Individuals who start their own businesses and are ultimately successful will probably make considerably more money than those individuals who took the less risky route and went to work for someone else. The entrepreneur risked his time and money. If successful, he will be rewarded handsomely for the risk he took.

Doctors and lawyers bypass the opportunity to make money right out of college. Instead, they spend more money going to medical school or law school and delay their income-producing careers by another three to seven years. For this risk of time and money, they are generally rewarded with higher income opportunities than other college graduates. Within the medical field, for example, some doctors pursue even more education and defer income even further to become surgeons. Still further, there are plastic, neurological, orthopedic, and dermatologic surgeons who undergo additional training. Within those fields, there is additional training as orthopedic surgeons may become spine specialists or dermatology surgeons may go on to learn Mohs (a specialty technique for removing cancer cells) to better handle cancer cell extraction. Usually, an increased investment in time and money (risk) leads to greater income potential (reward).

Diversification of Investments

Diversification is a business school term for "not putting all of your eggs in one basket." When applied to investments, it has two meanings. First, it means diversifying among asset classes. This is more popularly known as asset allocation. Asset allocation involves investing in a combination of stocks, bonds, real estate, cash, and other investment classes. Diversification also applies to the individual investments made within each asset class—not investing in just a few stocks, just a few bonds, or in one or two parcels of real estate. As an example, most investment managers recommend a portfolio of at least 30 securities to achieve a minimally acceptable level of diversification.

Earlier, we explained the idea that an investment portfolio is subject to (1) market risk and (2) the specific risks of each of the assets in the portfolio. One interesting finding of the CAPM and MPT is that in a well-diversified portfolio, all specific risks cancel each other out. In other words, specific risk can be diversified away. Investors can reduce the overall risk in their portfolios by spreading their risk across and within different asset classes. At face value, this makes perfect intuitive sense. However, the mathematical proof for this statement and the subsequent model for creating the most efficient set of portfolios were worthy of a Nobel Prize.

How Do the CAPM and MPT Work for You?

The Capital Asset Pricing Model and Modern Portfolio Theory provide a mathematical model for minimizing systematic risk in any investment portfolio. Once an investor determines the level of risk he is comfortable with (risk tolerance), he can follow the mathematical model to construct a portfolio that will optimize the risk-reward balance. In other words, by following this theory, the investor can maximize his expected returns for any level of risk. All such maximized portfolios exist on what the financial people call the "efficient frontier."

Certainly, we are not going to contend that the findings of three Nobel Laureates are incorrect. Rather, we are going to point out the acknowledged limitations in their theory and offer additional insights that might help you.

As acknowledged by the laureates, the CAPM and MPT are designed to work in a simplified world where:

- There are no taxes or transaction costs.
- All investors have identical investment horizons.
- All investors have identical perceptions regarding the expected returns, volatilities, and correlations of available risky investments.

As there is no such thing as a simple world, these three components actually present the limitations of the CAPM and MPT as financial tools that provide wise investment advice. Below we discuss these problems and suggest ways that the Affluent overcome them in an effort to invest wisely.

Problem #1: All Investors Pay Different Taxes and Transaction Costs

The first limitation of the theory involves taxes and transaction costs. Obviously, we consider tax to be a significant concern of the Affluent. If we didn't, we wouldn't have devoted an entire part of the book exclusively to this topic. If all of your stock investments are in a nontaxable account, like an IRA, you don't have to worry about taxes until you begin taking distributions. You could look to maximize the pretax returns on your portfolio for a given amount of risk because taxes have no impact until you take withdrawals.

A common situation is to have a portion of the total stock portfolio in a retirement account and a portion in a taxable environment. If this is true for you, you will need to determine which investments will be made in the tax-favored accounts and which investments will be made in taxable accounts. If you are in prime earning years and are in the 35 percent-plus federal income tax brackets, the following rules should suit you well.

1. Hold all interest-bearing and dividend-producing assets within a tax-favored account. Otherwise, as much as 44 percent of the earnings will go to paying income taxes each year. You are better off deferring the tax and earning money on the government's dime.

2. Hold all long-term growth assets in your taxable accounts. If you don't intend to sell these assets for at least one year, you will only pay 15 to 24 percent capital gains taxes when you sell. You can control the deferral of taxes by controlling recognition of gains. If you hold these assets in a pension account, you would be taxed at 35 percent federal (plus state) when you make withdrawals. Why pay the government twice?

These are just basic strategies to supplement the CAPM and MPT when taxes are an issue. There is much more to be learned about taxes in the chapters within the Fifth Key.

Problem #2: All Investors Do Not Have Identical Investment Horizons

Another obvious problem with the CAPM and MPT is that all investors do not have identical investment horizons. Some investors need their money in 30 days and some don't need it for 30 years. The investor who needs his money in less than a month would be well served by a CD or money market account. Investors that don't need their money for 30 years should have nearly 100 percent of their investments in equities (stocks) and other long-term investments.

If you have assets that you do not need for five years, you can afford to take some risks with those assets and should seriously consider investing in the stock market. If you need the money in less than a year, cash equivalents are your best option. For the assets that need to be accessed in one to five years, some combination thereof may work well.

Problem #3: All Investors Have Very Different Perceptions of Risk and Expected Returns

The environment where the CAPM and MPT work best is one where everyone has the same knowledge of all assets and the same access to purchasing assets. Yet, investors have very different perceptions of expected returns, volatilities, and correlations of available risky investments. For stocks and bonds, where there is more research available than you could possibly read, perceptions of the risk of any given stock are broad. People can't even agree on the value or the risk of certain stocks.

As far as availability, there is also a very wide gap. If you are only investing $100,000, you may be restricted to mutual funds that can have very high transaction costs and taxes (see problem 1 on page 285). If you have more than $500,000 to invest, you have access to unique products and your transaction costs are considerably lower relative to the smaller investor. If you have $5 million or more, you can access products that others can only dream of buying. These may include small businesses and initial public offerings, to name a couple.

For those of you who have experimented with, or are experts in, real estate investing, you know the gap in knowledge between buyer and seller is a key competitive factor for the investor. Many professional real estate investors have admitted that over 50 percent of their profits are a direct result of a buyer not understanding the real estate market. The CAPM and MPT call for a percentage of your portfolio to be invested in real estate assets. However, for the real estate expert who understands this market better than most, we would deviate from the strategy and recommend he stick with what he knows best and profit from his advantage in this arena.

For the investor with little knowledge of real estate, we would suggest he avoid investing in real estate (other than a home) for two reasons. First, the time necessary to manage the property or the costs to pay someone else to do so will decimate the earnings the property generates. Second, there is no reason to jump into a market where you have a distinct disadvantage. This adds risk to your portfolio instead of reducing it as you had hoped to do by utilizing the CAPM and MPT.

The Affluent know what they know. The Savvy Affluent know what they don't know. By understanding the investment landscape (if not the investments themselves), the Savvy Affluent can avoid unnecessary risk in an investment portfolio. In the next chapter, you will learn how to avoid decimation of wealth by taxes and inflation.

Consider This

The Capital Asset Pricing Model and Modern Portfolio Theory have contributed greatly to the field of portfolio selection. In fact, these theories are the basis for a significant percentage of institutional investors and mutual fund managers. They have also played a large role in the field of financial risk management. However, as you saw in this chapter, there are problems with the practical application of these theories. You should work with an experienced financial planner and investment advisor who can help you apply these theories to your particular situation while integrating them into your comprehensive financial plan by working with the other members of your advisory team. As you will learn from the remainder of the book, you may wish to invest in a vehicle that offers you other benefits in addition to capital appreciation such as asset protection, tax deferral, or protection against a premature death. These are the types of investments the remainder of this Key and the Ninth Key will address.

CHAPTER 47

Taxes, Inflation, and Your Investments

In Chapters 3 and 4, you learned that most printed material and consulting firms focused their efforts on Average Americans. The Savvy Affluent understand that this has never been more true than in the world of finance. Though most of the money in the world is owned by a very small percentage of the people, almost all of the advertising is directed at the Average American. As such, it can be very misleading and detrimental to the uninformed Affluent. Consider the following.

"XYZ fund returned 18.6 percent last year." "My money manager has beaten the S&P consistently for five years." "In this magazine, we'll profile the best returning mutual funds." As financial professionals, we read and hear these types of statements on a daily basis. Why? Because everyone looks at the investment returns as the currency of investing, as a way of comparing money managers, mutual funds, CDs, bonds, and so on. What most people fail to consider is the impact that taxes and inflation have on those investments as well as the risk involved in each investment. When you consider that all investments and financial professionals report their pre-inflation/pretax returns, it is easy to see why some people realize no additional purchasing power from their investments; they simply don't understand what they are really getting.

Uncle Sam Back for Another Helping: Taxes

The last chapter discussed how taxes were not considered in Markowitz and Sharpe's Nobel Prize–winning Capital Asset Pricing Model of investments. A new development in the mutual fund arena is that mutual funds may have to report after-tax gains, not pretax gains. How much will that change the numbers? A lot! Consider what Lipper, a mutual fund tracking firm, concluded:

"Over the past 20 years, the average investor in a taxable stock mutual fund gave up the equivalent of 17 percent to 44 percent of their returns to taxes."[*]

Without boring you with the math, this number means that some mutual funds sell most of the stocks they have purchased within one year. This is also called turnover for portfolio turnover. This means you get much more short-term capital gains tax treatment (28 to 35 percent) on your appreciation than you do long-term capital gains tax treatment (15 to 24 percent). For example, if your mutual fund appreciated by 11 percent last year, it probably cost you close to 4 percent in taxes. Which number is more important to you, the 11 percent or the 7 percent?

Mutual funds are not the only tax problem. How many of you have CDs, money market accounts, or bonds? All of the income from these vehicles is taxed as ordinary income. This will likely be taxed at rates between 27 percent and 35 percent, not to mention up to 10 percent of state income tax. For this reason, 5 percent to 6 percent in dividend or interest income may only be worth 2.5 percent to 4.0 percent after taxes. While this is depressing, it isn't the end of your problems.

Inflation: When a Dollar Is only Worth 50 Cents

You would always rather have a dollar today than a dollar tomorrow, right? There is an area of finance and economics that deals with this simple concept. They call it the "time value of money." It allows us to compare the value of a dollar today to the value of a dollar in the future. When determining the present value of future dollars, many people want to know what a dollar in the future will buy them; for example, what is it worth in today's dollars? What they are really talking about is inflation.

---

[*]CNN/Money.com 4/17/07.

Obviously, things become more expensive as we get older. We have all heard our parents talk about a Coke costing a nickel or a movie costing a quarter. The fact that a movie costs close to $10 today is because of inflation (though many might call it highway robbery given the quality, or lack thereof, of the films today). The average annual inflation rate over the past 70 years has been approximately 3.1 percent. This means that approximately every 22 years, things cost twice as much.

Calculating the Impact of Inflation

The after-tax return that an investment achieves is called the "nominal return." This does not take inflation into account. When you divide the nominal return of an investment over time by the rate of inflation over that same period of time, you get the real rate of return, or inflation-adjusted rate of return.

Think back to the mutual fund mentioned earlier where an 11 percent pretax return meant a take-home 7 percent after taxes. That 7 percent return is actually more like a 3.8 percent real return (1.07 divided by 1.031 equals 1.038), after inflation is factored into the results.

Invest Wisely while Planning for Inflation

If they want to reduce taxes, most Savvy Affluent investors invest in the stock market through tax-managed investment accounts, variable annuities, various types of life insurance policies (variable universal life, equity-indexed universal life, or private placement life insurance), or managed accounts if the funds are inside of tax-deferred retirement plans.

However, if you want the most accurate hedge against inflation, then real estate would be the ideal investment—as real estate values almost always move directly with inflation. Because real estate investing applies to so many of the lessons in this book, it makes up half of the Ninth Key. When you finish reading this Key, be sure to make your way to the Ninth Key—Use the Secret Investments of the Affluent—to learn more.

Consider This

When it comes to investing, there is no surefire method for avoiding taxes or inflation. However, there are a number of tools that are discussed in this Key and in the Fifth Key. The more you know about your options, the easier it will be for you to understand what you are really getting from your investments. Of course, there is no substitute for having a strong team of advisors that includes an investment specialist who understands tax management and other advisors who are tax savvy to help you meet all of your needs. One way to avoid unnecessary taxes on investments is to avoid mutual funds. This is explained in the next chapter.

48

Outgrowing Mutual Funds

If you are reading this chapter, it is probably because you have more than $100,000 in cash or mutual funds. These may be inside or outside of your tax-deferred retirement plans. In Chapter 47, we discussed alternatives to taxable mutual fund accounts that may be ideal for your nonretirement plan accounts. Some of these alternatives offer asset protection, tax-deferral, and death protection. In this chapter, we will discuss an alternative to mutual funds both inside and outside of retirement plans. Before we compare mutual funds and individually managed accounts, we must first explain what they are.

Mutual funds and individually managed accounts (IMAs) represent two of the most popular investment programs used by individuals to create wealth. On the surface, at least, one could argue that they are not all that dissimilar. Both offer investors a professionally managed portfolio of securities generally composed of stocks, bonds, or a combination of the two. They are both tailored to provide ample diversification.

When looking beneath the surface, however, two distinctly different approaches emerge. Each offers particular advantages depending upon one's needs. Which is the more prudent choice? Which will help you make wise investments like the Savvy Affluent? This is a question properly answered only by the individual investor. The information that follows is designed to help you make a wise investment decision, one with which you are comfortable and which, we hope, will prove over time to be the right choice.

Mutual Funds

A mutual fund is a company that invests in stocks, bonds, and other securities on behalf of individual investors with similar financial goals. A no-load mutual fund is one that is sold directly to investors without an initial sales charge or "load."

Many financial advisors now provide access to no-load funds as part of a comprehensive range of services. However, the charge for the advisor's assistance tends to offset the lack of an initial sales charge, effectively minimizing any cost differences between load and no-load funds. Of course, you get the assistance of an advisor whom you would otherwise have to pay anyway. For purposes of this discussion, therefore, no-load funds will refer to funds purchased directly from the company without the help of an advisor.

Both load and no-load mutual funds are essentially cooperatives of investors who pool their money for a common purpose. Investors contribute to the pool by buying shares in the fund. Each share represents an equal percentage of ownership in the fund's assets.

The fund draws from the pool not only to make investments but also to pay for the services of a fund manager (who decides when and if to buy and sell securities for the fund based on its stated objective), marketing and distribution costs, custodian fees, and transaction costs. Mutual funds are not limited but generally hold 100 or more different securities. No matter how many shares of the fund the investor holds, you cannot control the buying and selling of these securities inside the fund. You can only buy or sell the basket of securities the fund has by buying or selling your shares of the fund.

Individually Managed Accounts

Perhaps obviously, an IMA is an account that is individually managed by a professional investment manager who decides when to buy and sell securities based on your stated investment strategy or goal.

Unlike mutual fund investors, managed account investors do not pool their money. Rather, they own the securities in their accounts directly. They may have many similar holdings with a number of their clients but each portfolio is separate. The investor can direct the manager to buy only certain types of stocks or to avoid certain stocks (perhaps no tobacco stocks for moral reasons or no health care stocks because you work as a physician and enough of your income is tied to health care). This obviously gives you greater flexibility and control than you would have with a mutual fund.

There is no doubt that mutual funds are easy. Their forms are easy. Their marketing materials are readily available. The companies are household names with all the advertising they do. The marketing and advertising efforts would have you believe that the mutual funds offer better returns with lower fees. Let's see if this is true.

Are Managed Accounts Worth the Money?

One of the most common problems we see with clients is that they are obsessed with the fee associated with any type of planning. If you took this approach to everything you bought, you'd only eat 99 cent Big Macs at every meal. There is truth to the saying "you get what you pay for." You should not be quick to dismiss the advantages of one investment strategy over another based purely on price. The recent popularity of no-load mutual funds is proof that many Affluent investors, particularly those who like a no-frills approach to investing, are doing just that.

You paid for this book in hopes that it would help you. That's $30 well spent, right? You are considering asset protection, insurance, estate planning, and retirement strategies that undoubtedly will cost you something. Why? Because the strategies will offer you something valuable in return. A prudent investor considers differences in:

- The quality of service provided in return for the fee.
- How the accounts treat capital gains and losses relative to your situation.
- The effect that other investors may have on an investment manager's decisions.
- The methods used to report information.
- The way in which fees are handled.

These are very important factors to consider when comparing investment options because the fee is not important. What you earn net of the fee and taxes is what is really important.

Is Your Tax Situation a Consideration?

With IMAs, you pay taxes only on the capital gains you actually realize. Because you own the securities in your account directly, you can work with your tax advisor to implement planning strategies that mutual fund investors may not be able to duplicate. There are actually IMA firms that will call you to ask you how you want to end the year (more gains, more losses, balanced to $0 tax).

With mutual funds, investors pay taxes on their pro rata share of capital gains experienced by the fund, whether or not they benefited from the sale of the security. The following hypothetical example serves to illustrate this point.

Assume that a fund purchases stock at the beginning of the year for $25 per share. Over the next few months, the stock's price rises to $50 per share. Coincidentally, an investor buys shares in the fund just as the stock's price reaches this peak.

Later in the year, the stock's price falls to $40 per share, and the fund sells its position. At the end of the year, the investor is allocated a pro rata share of the fund's gain on the stock (the difference between the purchase price of $25 and the sale price of $40), even though the investor did not fully benefit from the gain; in fact, the stock actually declined in value after the investor purchased shares in the fund at $50.

Over time, IMA investors and mutual fund investors who hold their investments for the same period and whose portfolio managers follow identical strategies will report little, if any, difference in capital gains taxes—at least on those particular investments. For the mutual fund investor, however, the point at which the gains are realized may be moved forward and that can affect the investor's tax planning strategy (see Table 48.1).

The Cost of IMAs

So, what do IMAs really cost?

Investors who open IMAs usually do so with a minimum investment of at least $100,000. Some firms have minimums that can be as high as $10 million. Depending on the client's particular situation, most firms will make exceptions. As an example, our firm invests through our registered investment advisor subsidiary, The O'Dell Group (TOG). TOG has a published account minimum of $500,000. However, we will aggregate family accounts (all IRAs, 401(k)s, and other assets of parents and children) to get there. We will also take a smaller account of an investor who is earning a lot of money and who is likely to get to that minimum in a few years.

Table 48.1 Comparing Individually Managed Accounts and Mutual Funds

	Individually Managed Account	Load Mutual Fund	No-Load Mutual Fund
Investment Portfolio	Tailored to meet investor's particular needs.	Two-way communication, including in-person discussions with financial advisor. Can also call toll-free number.	One-way communication: Call toll-free phone number and talk to sales representative.
Establishing Investor's Goals	Investor benefits from financial advisor's help.	Investor benefits from financial advisor's help.	Investors determine on their own.
Investment Manager Selection	Chosen by investor with financial advisor's help.	Chosen by mutual fund.	Chosen by mutual fund.
Investment Manager Evaluation	Screened and evaluated by investor and financial advisor.	Screened and evaluated by investor and financial advisor.	Investors must screen and evaluate on their own.
Performance Monitoring	Financial advisor monitors on investor's behalf.	Financial advisor monitors on investor's behalf.	Investors must monitor on their own.
Tax Planning	Investors have some control over the timing of capital gains.	Investors have little control over the timing of capital gains.	Investors have little control over the timing of capital gains.

Redemption Requests	Investors are not affected by the actions of others who use the same manager.	Manager may be forced to sell securities at undesirable prices to raise cash to meet redemption requests.	Manager may be forced to sell securities at undesirable prices to raise cash to meet redemption requests.
Reporting	Detailed monthly or quarterly statements, monthly letters, quarterly newsletters, periodic investment literature from manager.	General quarterly statements, semiannual investment reports, possibly periodic newsletters.	General quarterly statements, semiannual investment reports, possibly periodic newsletters.
Up-Front Costs	$0	Up to 6% of investment or an additional 1% per year added to the annual cost.	$0
Annual Costs	On average for a stock-based portfolio, between 2.5% and 3% of total investment.	On average for a stock-based portfolio, between 2% and 3% of total investment.	On average for a stock-based portfolio, between 1.5% and 2% of total investment.

Fees for IMAs can vary greatly. A common estimate in the industry is about 1 percent of assets, 0.25 percent paid quarterly. Now, a smaller account may have higher fees and a larger account always pays lower fees. Some special private placements, private equity, and hedge funds can have significantly higher fees. All fees will be disclosed either in the firm ADV (for registered investment advisory firms), a prospectus (for a registered security) or a private placement memorandum (for private placements). You should never invest in anything before receiving an ADV and/or a prospectus.

Subsequent transaction costs are paid either by paying commissions on individual trades or by paying an asset-based fee on a quarterly basis. In addition to covering transactions, these fees encompass reporting, custody, and the services of a financial advisor as well. For a stock-based portfolio, on average, total fees range annually from 1.3 percent to 3 percent of the assets under management. There are no additional charges.

Mutual funds have lower minimum investment requirements, often $1,000 or less. With a no-load mutual fund bought directly from the company, the entire investment is placed in the fund at the time of initial purchase. With a front-end load fund, on the other hand, the investor's money is placed in the fund only after deducting a sales charge. In the case of a 3.5 percent load fund, the fund would invest $965 of the investor's initial $1,000.

Beyond the initial sales charge or lack thereof, the difference in fee structure between load and no-load mutual funds virtually disappears. Management fees, transaction costs, custody fees, and distribution and marketing costs (known as 12b-1 fees) are deducted automatically from the fund's assets. These fees are usually not seen directly by investors but instead are specified in the fund's prospectus and statements of additional information. Mutual fund expenses for stock-based portfolios typically range from 1.5 percent to 2 percent per year for no-load funds and from 2 percent to 3 percent per year for load funds.

According to Morningstar, a third-party research publication that follows open-end mutual funds, the average diversified domestic equities fund incurs about 1.63 percent in annual costs, including a 1.32 percent expense ratio and 0.31 percent in transaction costs. Tack on an additional 0.94 percent annual sales charge on average for load funds or an estimated 1 percent annual charge for no-load funds purchased through a financial advisor, and that annual cost figure rises to approximately 2.6 percent.

Investors should note that transaction costs tend to vary depending on the type of securities in the fund. Trading foreign securities, for instance, can cost almost twice as much as trading domestic securities.

The Savvy Affluent want to make sure that their comprehensive plan is integrated and managed so they do not pay unnecessary taxes or become exposed to risk that is not appropriate for their overall portfolio. The Savvy Affluent know that off-the-rack mutual funds are not likely to fit as well as a custom-tailored individually managed account.

Consider This

While you may appear to be building your fortune by purchasing no-load funds, such savings may not be enough to offset the loss of the value-added services that normally include investment planning, monitoring, and communication that only a financial advisor can provide. Beyond perceived cost differences, mutual funds limit investors' tax planning choices and offer individual investors no control over securities in the fund.

The Savvy Affluent use individually managed accounts to build their fortunes and protect their assets because of the tax benefits and the additional added benefits. They avoid mutual funds trap of losing 17 to 44 percent of their returns to taxes. Another benefit of individually managed accounts is that they afford the ability to add alternative investments to the portfolio. The explanation of these investments and the benefits the Savvy Affluent look for from these investments are explained in the next chapter.

CHAPTER

49

Alternative Investment Strategies

In the last chapter, you learned that individually managed accounts help the Affluent invest wisely, build their fortunes, and protect their assets better than mutual funds because of their flexibility. This flexibility offers tax management benefits and customization to better fit the investor's situation. Traditionally, most individually managed accounts purchase stocks and bonds that are readily available to anyone (publicly traded securities). However, the Savvy Affluent realize that the investment world does end with stocks and bonds. There are additional classes of investments that cannot be made available to the public because of their complexity or level of risk. These investments can offer greater levels of diversification, inflation hedging, and potentially higher returns.

In this chapter, we will discuss who can legally access these alternative strategies, why investors may wish to purchase them, and the inherent risks. Then, we discuss a few favorite alternative investment strategies of the Savvy Affluent. Many of the Savvy Affluent can credit the knowledge and utilization of the material in this chapter and in the Ninth Key as the secret for their significant increase in net worth.

Accredited Investors

Alternative investment strategies can be offered to Savvy Affluent investors who have the financial means to survive the significant losses that can accompany riskier transaction. These investments are only available to a class of investors known as *accredited investors*. One definition of this term can be found on the TIAA-CREF web site:

To qualify as an accredited investor, an investor must either be: a financial institution; an affiliate of the issuer; or an individual with a net worth of at least $1 million or an annual income of at least $200,000, and the investment must not account for more than 20% of the investor's worth.

Why Invest in Alternative Investments

In Chapter 46, we discussed that greater risk is generally accompanied by a potential for greater return in financial markets, which consequently helps one build his fortune and protect his assets. Alternative investments, by definition, are riskier than traditional investments. As an asset class, the alternative investments traditionally have to offer a significant risk premium (added expected return) to investors to convince them to invest. Many investors in these investments are just looking for higher returns. Since the Super Affluent have the financial means to wait out down markets and they can survive lost investments, they are ideal candidates for these investments. There are other structural or legal reasons these investments are not available to the Average American investor. This leaves only the wealthy or accredited investors as the target investors.

In addition to the expected returns, there are other reasons to consider alternative investments. A partial list includes:

- Increased diversification of holdings by expanding portfolio to include items not within the traditional portfolio.
- Decreased volatility by investing in strategies not correlated to the stock or bond markets.
- Preserved capital can also be managed through an alternative allocation.
- Increased access alternative investments are sometimes called an access class for the reasons mentioned above about accredited investors.

The Risks of Alternative Investments

We mentioned that alternative investments have a higher risk than traditional investments. What are those risks? A partial list includes:

- **Lack of regulation.** While not required to be registered with the SEC, many hedge fund managers choose to do so to gain access to institutional investors that require it. Many do not register these securities. This is the old-fashioned caveat emptor, or buyer (investor) beware situation.

- **Lack of transparency.** Assets held by hedge funds may not have a price quoted each day. Think of your personal residence or car as an example. This also means there is less liquidity.
- **Excessive leverage.** Some managers borrow money on borrowed money increasing risk by an exponential amount.
- **Fraud.** There are people who are not qualified to manage your money but are able to build trust and confidence.
- **Manager selection risk.** Not all managers are equal. In fact, there is evidence that the difference in manager performance is greater than the benefit of using alternative investments.

The Savvy Affluent do not just accept these risks. They work with their investment team to analyze investment alternatives to find investments that fit into the strategy they have developed for their portfolio.

Alternative Investment Strategies

Behind the press reports of big payouts, high returns, and bankruptcies, there are sound investment strategies that are grouped together under a category called hedge funds. One broad brush term is typically used to paint the picture for more than two dozen investment strategies. Instead of using the term hedge fund, we recommend you view these funds as alternative investment strategies or access class funds. There are literally hundreds of ways to invest outside of the traditional channels. We will break this down to make it easier to follow. We will begin by giving a categorical list of investments that traditional managers are often prohibited from offering to clients who are accredited investors.

- **Short-selling securities.** This is selling someone else's shares in return for the promise to replace them later at what you believe will be a lower price. This is a way for an investor who speculates that a stock value will depreciate to benefit from the devaluation of the stock. The risk of short selling is unlimited because every dollar increase to a shorted stock is a dollar the investor loses, and there is no theoretical limit to a stock's appreciation. For long investors who buy and hold a stock, they can only lose the original investment because the stock price can't fall below zero.

- **Buying on margin.** This is buying shares with borrowed money. This is a way for someone to leverage someone else's money. If the stock appreciates by more than the interest on the loan, there is a chance to earn money. If the stock price decreases, you may face a margin call requiring you to invest more or your stock will be sold to cover your debt.
- **Option trading.** These are individual options to buy or sell 1,000 shares of a stock at a particular price. There are options to buy or sell the security at that price and the investor can buy or sell the option.
- **Investing in any unregistered security.** This includes private placements and other worldwide investments that were not registered within the United States.

We have compiled a list of alternative investment strategies that are available to accredited investors. There is not enough space in this book to review them all. If you are interested in learning more about any of them, feel free to contact the authors.

Partial List of Alternative Investment Strategies

- Absolute return strategies are designed to achieve a steady rate of return in up or down markets thereby minimizing volatility. Categories include:
  - Equity Market Neutral
  - Convertible Arbitrage
  - Fixed-Income Arbitrage
  - Statistical Arbitrage
  - Risk Arbitrage
  - Multistrategy
  - Merger Arbitrage
  - Credit Arbitrage
- Opportunistic equity strategies seeks to achieve above-market returns by anticipating market inefficiencies before they occur. Categories include:
  - Long/Short Equity
  - Global Macro
  - Short Only

- ◆ Long/Short Specialty
- ◆ Long/Short International
- Enhanced fixed income strategies seek to return income above the market rate of return for a given risk profile. Categories include:
  - ◆ Capital Structure Arbitrage
  - ◆ Distressed Securities
  - ◆ Global/Emerging Market Debt
- Energy and natural resource investment strategies direct the purchase of oil, coal, timber, and other natural resources. These may have tax benefits as well.
- Real estate strategies include direct or leveraged purchase of commercial real estate properties. This is discussed in the Ninth Key.
- Private equity includes the purchase of stocks not registered with the Securities and Exchange Commission. This is also called a private placement.

You Have to Be Able to Stand the Heat to Stay in the Kitchen

It is important to point out that not all strategies are successful all the time and not all investors in alternative investments achieve their goals. But there is a formula that has worked over the years. Ironically, large endowment funds of some of America's premier universities turned to these strategies due to the shortcomings of traditional investing and successfully reduced their risk exposure while preserving the endowment capital in perpetuity. An endowment is expected to provide a certain level of income, usually at an increasing amount, each year, every year. Down years and performance under the required income level will wipe out the corpus of the endowment. Managers of these funds didn't really care what the stock market did. They had to ensure the endowment grew each year. They turned to alternative investments and have not looked back. This is an excellent example of wealth management as opposed to wealth building or accumulation strategies. For the individual investor, using the endowment model of multiple alternative strategies would be used for the portion of your portfolio sometimes called the "stay rich pocket" as opposed to the "get rich pocket."

When the Savvy Affluent are hiring an asset manager to manage an investment portfolio, their secret is to find an investment advisor who can also help find, review, and possibly purchase other investment classes to round out the total portfolio. There are countless hedge funds, private placements, options, and currency- and commodity-based investments. To expand your options, you may want to make sure your investment advisor is accustomed to helping Affluent clients with their unique needs. Another way to look at the overall investment portfolio is to review it for leverage and efficiency. This is discussed in the next chapter.

Consider This

So far, you have made it through eight Keys to Fortune Building and Asset Protection. Within these keys, there are dozens of practical lessons. It may seem very overwhelming to manage all of this within a financial plan. It is overwhelming! This is why you need two things to successfully manage your financial planning:

1. Leverage
2. Efficiency

As you learned in the Second Key, you need to leverage your team. Otherwise, there will be no efficiency of time because there are only 24 hours per day and 7 days per week. You can't do it all alone. You need to leverage your investments to achieve Super Affluence.

You also need efficiencies to make this work. The best way to do this within your planning is to try to kill two birds with one stone. By hiring advisors who are experts in multiple areas, you will get some benefit. More important, focusing on planning tools and strategies that solve multiple planning problems and are flexible enough to be used in different ways is a great way to gain leverage and efficiency.

When it comes to investing, the Savvy Affluent have used two "secrets" more than any others to achieve leverage and efficiency. Strangely, these two investments are not common with Average Americans and one of them is widely considered as a bad investment for Average Americans. These two very important investments are discussed in detail in the next part, the Ninth Key—Use the Secret Investments of the Affluent.

THE NINTH KEY

USE THE SECRET INVESTMENTS OF THE AFFLUENT

If you have read the entire book so far, you have learned eight very important philosophical keys to fortune building and asset protection, and over fifty practical applications of these lessons. Many of these keys to success have been used by the Savvy Affluent throughout time. The two keys we revisited at the end of the last chapter were leverage and efficiency.

The reason these two concepts are so important to the Affluent is that there are only 24 hours in a day and everyone wants to work less and earn more. As stated in the Second Key, leverage and efficiency are the keys to accomplishing this. In this chapter, we will discuss two investments that combine leverage and efficiency better than any others. These investments are real estate and life insurance. Why do we call these very popular investments "secrets" when everyone in America has heard of, or even purchased, both of them? The reason is that many Average Americans don't think of real estate and life insurance as investments. Rather, they perceive real estate and life insurance as very costly necessities. Further, most financial advisors discourage the use of these investments (especially life insurance) when the Super Affluent maximize their use.

In this Key, we discuss why life insurance and real estate are a secret investment of the Affluent. We will also explain why each of these assets is so important to the creation and maintenance of affluence. After we explain each investment secret, we will separately discuss the basics of real estate and life insurance and explain how both tools achieve leverage as very efficient and flexible financial planning tools. At the request of many of the readers of previous books, we have included Chapter 57, which shows a comparison of life insurance to mutual funds as an investment. Then, we end the Key by discussing creative applications of insurance and explaining the secret of leveraging the ultimate leverage tool.

CHAPTER 50

Investment Efficiency

The concept of investment efficiency is not one you will find in most finance textbooks. In the First Key, you learned that the Savvy Affluent embrace their affluence. As part of this acceptance, they also recognize that general information in books, newspapers, articles, online, or on television is likely to be inappropriate for them because it is geared toward Average American's financial planning needs. If you can adopt a similar philosophy, you can easily expand your planning opportunities to include two investments that can give your family greater flexibility, leverage, and efficiency. These two investments are real estate and life insurance.

The concept of investment efficiency is extremely important in the context of an overall financial plan. In this context, an efficient investment is one that:

1. Addresses two or more planning goals at the same time.
2. Helps a client reach a planning goal with less effort or with a smaller investment of time or money than other investments.
3. Is flexible enough that it can be modified to address different planning needs as the client's personal circumstances change.

The Need for Efficient Investments

There are many reasons why efficient investments are such an important key to acquiring and maintaining affluence. First, efficient investments address multiple planning goals simultaneously.

As we will see in this Key, the efficient investments described here can build wealth while reducing taxes, provide asset protection, allow for college funding access, and provide estate planning benefits. These investments become cornerstones of the flexible, multi-disciplinary financial plan.

Second, efficient investments have less tax friction than other investments. As we have discussed repeatedly in this book, the Affluent consider tax ramifications in making their daily choices and investment decisions. Real estate and cash value life insurance have tremendous tax benefits that are unmatched by other investment classes.

Third, efficient investments utilize leverage. The Second Key explained how leverage is necessary for all wealth accumulation. Efficient investments may allow you to meet a planning need by spending $5,000 instead of having to spend $25,000 or $50,000. By using leverage with efficient investments, you will have more money left over for necessary expenses or inefficient investments. Because we all want to achieve our own desired levels of affluence as quickly and safely as possible, it only makes sense to consider using leverage whenever possible. Without the use of efficient investments to achieve leverage, you are just like the landscaper who only has so many hours of daylight when he can work. You will never get ahead.

Fourth, efficient investments are your safety net. Perhaps you have heard the phrases "Life is Plan B" or "Life Happens." We speak to thousands of Affluent clients and Wealthy Families every year at our seminars and in our consulting practice. As our specialty is planning and implementation, we have designed and helped execute hundreds of financial plans for clients. Through all of our experiences, we can tell clients one thing with certainty. The plan we help them create will never go as planned. We know that life will throw them a series of curveballs. We just don't know what those curveballs will be. So, we have to plan with an expectation that we will have to make changes. By using flexible investments that can serve different purposes, we create plans that are more likely to fit the clients' future needs with fewer modifications (and costs) than if we had used inefficient investments.

Consider This

The Second Key discussed the importance of leverage in accumulating wealth. The goal of leverage is to create efficiency. In wealth accumulation, this means earning more with less effort. The same leverage concept can be applied to the implementation of planning solutions. If you utilize a tool that offers numerous benefits, you add efficiency to your planning. The two investments that offer the widest range of benefits are real estate and life insurance. Let's start by discussing real estate in the next chapter.

CHAPTER 51

Real Estate Basics

The Merriam-Webster's online dictionary defines real estate as "property in buildings or land." For the Affluent, real estate comprises primary and secondary residences, investment real estate, rental properties, commercial real estate, and real estate investment trusts. In our experience, there has been no investment class with greater growth in the last five to ten years than real estate.

An illustration of Americans' increased interest in real estate is the growth in popularity of channels like HGTV and television shows like "Flip this House" and "Designed to Sell." If you watch these shows, you will see Average Americans throwing caution to wind, buying properties, and trying to sell them within 8 to 12 weeks. Though this phenomenon slowed in 2007, it doesn't change the fact that there was certainly a big wave of buying and selling property.

There are a number of reasons for the massive growth in the United States real estate market (similar growth took place in England and other countries as well). To better understand how real estate works and some of the pros and cons of investing in real estate, it is important to understand how the market has developed recently.

Money Needs a Place to Live, Too

After the dot-com craze ended with a loud crash, there was a search for the next big thing. Affluent people needed a new investment while investment dollars needed a new place to land. Though real estate had always been popular with the Super Affluent, it was the surge of investment dollars into the real estate market by the Average American investor and Affluent investors that caused the residential housing markets to skyrocket. A big reason for this wave was the Second Key to Affluence, leverage, which will be discussed with respect to real estate in Chapter 52.

As the institutional investors, builders, and developers realized that there were many new buyers in the real estate market, they ramped up their investment and production in real assets. In any financial market, if there are new buyers, or more available money for the buyers to spend, prices will appreciate. With real estate, there is only so much land and so many existing homes to buy. People are living in most of them so the inventory of available units can never be a very large percentage of the homes. New properties take time to build. To simplify the situation, there was limited supply and increasing demand. There was no place for prices to go but up. One simple example that we witnessed with a family member may illustrate this point. Jonathan purchased a one-bedroom loft condominium in a suburban Rhode Island town for $55,000 in 2002. In 2005, he sold it for $289,000. This is just one of thousands of stories we could tell.

Dollar Plummeting: Helping the Market and Real Estate Soar

It may not be obvious to everyone, but we live in a global market. What happens in Japan influences trading in London. What happens on the London exchange has a serious impact on Wall Street. In addition, corporate and individual investors scour the globe for the best investments they can find. Savvy investors pay as much, if not more, attention to currency exchange rates as they do to interest rates. Savvy investors often focus more on the terms (interest rates) and currency of the deal than they do on the price.

From 2001 to 2007, economic policy choices in Washington, D.C., devastated the U.S. dollar. As of August 2007, the dollar reached an all-time low against the Euro. Consider the data in Table 51.1.

As evidenced by Table 51.1, if a U.S. investor had sold his dollars in 2001, purchased pounds, and put them under his bed, he would have realized a 6.4 percent return per year just by holding the pounds. If he had done the same thing with Euros, he would have realized an 8.24 percent return per year. Of course, the investor could have still

Table 51.1　The Fall of the U.S. Dollar*

	1 British Pound Was Worth	1 Euro Was Worth
June 2001	$1.402	$0.853
July 2007	$2.035	$1.372
Depreciation of US $	31%	38%
Appreciation of foreign currency vs. US$/year	6.4% per year	8.24% per year

*These are average monthly exchange rates as reported by www.gocurrency.com.

invested those pounds or Euros in anything and received additional returns. However, the purpose of this example is to show that currency can have a significant impact on an investment. This is what happened with real estate in the U.S. during the first part of this decade.

In 2001, a British investor with 100,000 pounds could have bought a house in the United States that cost $140,200. In 2007, a British investor with the same 100,000 pounds could have bought a house in the United States that cost $203,500. In other words, British investors could get a lot more for their money if they invested in real estate in the United States.

More dramatically, in 2001, a European investor with 100,000 Euros could have bought a house in the United States that cost $85,300. In 2007, a European investor with the same 100,000 Euros, could have bought a house in the United States that cost $137,200. Since U.S. goods were so cheap, many foreigners and foreign corporations increased their investment in the United States real estate market. This had something to do with the rising values as well.

Some Savvy Affluent and some lucky investors saw this trend well in advance. As a result, a great deal of wealth was created in United States real estate markets in the last decade. For these investors, the key is to get the most out of these investments and to maintain their new wealth. This will be covered in the subsequent chapters in this Key.

Consider This

Since the dot-com bust, the U.S. economy has been on shaky ground. This is evidenced by the series of interest rate cuts that were made over the last decade to stimulate investment in the market and in real estate. A reduction in each market can lead to serious economic depression. An indicator that the economy is not strong is the value of the dollar vs. other currencies.

To stimulate investment in businesses or real estate, money has to be kept cheap. The price of money is another name for interest rates. Between 2002 and 2006, interest rates in the United States were the lowest in history. When money is cheap, leverage increases. As an extreme example, a 15 percent interest rate loan costs $15,000 per year per $100,000 borrowed. A 3 percent interest rate loan costs $3,000 per year per $100,000 borrowed. So, the difference between environments with 3 percent and 15 percent interest rates is that the 3 percent loan option allows investors to borrow five times the money with the same monthly payment. This allows for a 400 percent increase in investment in the economy—and a 400 percent increase in leverage on the original down payment. This concept will be explored in detail in the next chapter.

As you can see, real estate in the United States has become more popular as an investment class over the last seven years for a variety of reasons. The economic factors (like currency exchange rates) can be positive or negative influences on the value of a real estate portfolio. Lately, currency exchange rates have been a very positive influence on the U.S. real estate market. The Savvy Affluent understand the risks of the real estate market and accept this risk because of the other benefits real estate offers. These will be discussed in the next two chapters.

CHAPTER

52

Real Estate Leverage

Almost every purchase of real estate is made with leverage—in the form of debt. Most people don't think of it as leverage when they take out a home loan and borrow money from the bank to pay for a piece of real estate. In fact, the Average American family doesn't like having debt. There are thousands of companies offering services to help people get out of credit card debt, pay down auto financing, consolidate student loans, and refinance home mortgages. The Savvy Affluent do not need to reduce debt—they want to increase the amount of debt they have!

The Savvy Affluent understand that real estate leverage in the form of debt and home loans is the key to building wealth. To illustrate this point, let's consider the case study of Cletus.

Case Study: A Home Pays for Itself . . . and More

Cletus purchased a home for $400,000. He put $100,000 down and financed $300,000 at an interest rate of 6 percent. Five years later, he took advantage of a very hot real estate market and sold the house for $550,000. His interest-only mortgage cost Cletus $90,000 in interest payments. His total property taxes during the five years totaled $20,000. After he factored in the tax deduction for the taxes and mortgage interest, the after-tax cost of living in the house for five years was only $71,500 (assuming a marginal 35 percent combined federal and state tax rate). Because he used the home as a primary residence, the first $250,000 of appreciation was tax free. After paying off the loan, he had $150,000 profit. When you subtract the $71,500 in after-tax costs of interest and property tax from the $150,000 profit, you see that Cletus actually made $78,500 while living in the home. In other words, you could say that Cletus was paid $78,500 to live in a house for five years. That is a 78.5 percent return over five years (or 12.3 percent per year) plus a free place to live for five years. That is a great return on the initial investment.

The fact that Cletus had such a positive experience in real estate is not that unique. The financial benefits he realized resulted from two types of real estate leverage:

1. Leveraging the bank's money.
2. Leveraging tax benefits.

Since the bank was willing to loan Cletus $300,000 of the $400,000 purchase price, the total out-of-pocket expenses to live in the house were only a $100,000 down payment plus $71,500 combined after-tax property taxes and interest for a total of $171,500. When he sold the home for $550,000, he was able to pay off the bank, recoup the $71,000 of expenses and still put $78,500 in his pocket.

Without leverage what would have happened? First, he would have had to come up with $400,000 to buy the house. Then, he would have had to pay $20,000 in property taxes ($13,000 after the tax deduction of 35 percent). At the time of sale, he would have only netted $550,000 minus $413,000 for a total of $137,000. That is a 33.2 percent return over five years, or 5.9 percent per year. That is less than half of the return from the leveraged purchase.

What if you didn't have tax benefits from the purchase of a primary residence? What would have happened to the original transaction? The $100,000 down payment would have been followed by $90,000 of interest and $20,000 of property tax payments. The total out-of-pocket expense would have been $210,000. Then, the $150,000 sale would have resulted in capital gains taxes of 15 percent or $22,500—not to mention any state capital gains taxes. You would have put up $210,000 in the beginning. When you sold for $550,000, you would have to pay back the $300,000 debt and pay $22,500 in taxes. That would leave $227,500. That is a measly 8 percent return over five years, or 1.6 percent per year.

The Affluent know that real estate leverage in the form of debt and home loans are the key to building wealth and protecting assets. Perhaps you should use this secret of the Affluent in order to accumulate wealth.

Consider This

Real estate has been a very popular investment class (or secret) over the last 10 years for various reasons. In the example we offered, you can see that Cletus benefited greatly from:

1. The leverage of using someone else's money.
2. The leverage of the tax incentives that accompany a certain type of real estate investment.

There are also tax benefits for commercial purchases of real estate. Many of these benefits are discussed in the next chapter.

53

Flexibility and Efficiency of Real Estate

For over a century, Average Americans have purchased real estate because they needed a place to live and didn't want to rent. Some upper middle class Americans purchased a second property to use as a place of business or to rent and generate extra income. Others may have been fortunate and frugal enough to be able to afford a second property as a place for family (aging parents or college-age children) to live. Still others were able to afford small vacation properties. When Average Americans purchase real estate, they generally strive to limit their amount of debt.

The Savvy Affluent know that real estate is a flexible and efficient investment that helps them build their fortunes and protect their assets. Affluent Americans purchase real estate for different reasons and have the opposite view of debt. Savvy investors never look at gross investment returns. They look at net returns; that is, the total after-tax benefit to the family. What types of benefits might real estate investors offer to the Savvy Affluent?

Real estate can offer various benefits to investors. These may include:

- A hedge against inflation
- Asset protection
- Retirement income
- Tax benefits

Hedge against Inflation

One efficient and flexible benefit that real estate may offer to investors is a hedge against inflation. All investments offer some potential type of return. The absolute return an investment yields is called the nominal rate of return. If you invest $100 one year and sell the investment for $110 one year later, the nominal return on that investment is 10 percent.

During the time when an investment is held, there will generally be some level of inflation. Inflation is the measure of how much more expensive things become over a period of time. Those things that are measured to determine the inflation rate include food and beverages, housing, apparel, transportation, medical care, recreation, education, and communication and other goods and services. If you go to the Bureau of Labor Statistics' web page at www.bls.gov, you can get all the data you want on how inflation and the consumer price index is calculated and what inflation rates have been over any time period.

This concept is important for making efficient and flexible investments because, if over the period of time when the investor above turned $100 into $110, inflation rose at 4 percent, the investor didn't really earn $10 of purchasing power. If you divide the nominal return of the $100 ($100) by the inflation-adjusted investment ($100 x 104% = $104), you would get 1.0577 or a 5.77 percent increase in purchasing power. This is called the inflation-adjusted return or the real rate of return. This measures how much you actually improved your situation. (See Table 53.1.)

Table 53.1   Historical U.S. Inflation

Time Period	Total Inflation	Average Annual Inflation
July 1937 to July 2007	1,336.54%	3.88%
July 1947 to July 2007	838.28%	3.80%
July 1957 to July 2007	636.04%	4.07%
July 1967 to July 2007	523.65%	4.68%
July 1977 to July 2007	241.47%	4.18%
July 1987 to July 2007	83.04%	3.07%
July 1997 to July 2007	29.78%	2.64%

There are some very complicated discussions about how real estate hedges inflation. The simplistic version is that homes are collections of things (plumbing, lumber, appliances, and so forth). As the cost of these things go up, so should the cost of homes. Another simplistic point is that the cost of housing is included in the calculation of inflation and housing is a very significant expense. Therefore, it is highly unlikely that inflation would move very much in a different direction from real estate. For these reasons and others, real estate is generally (correctly) considered to be a hedge against inflation.

Asset Protection

Real estate also offers the investor the benefit of asset protection or a place to invest and protect against creditors. If you are trying to achieve a certain level of affluence, you want to limit all financial risks that could set you back in your quest. For many Wealthy Families, maintaining wealth is even more important than building wealth because they already have so much. In either case, asset protection is a very important reason for doing anything (as was discussed in the Fourth Key).

In certain states, like Florida and Texas, the primary residence is completely exempt from creditors, with a few restrictions (timing of the creditor claim, size of homestead, and location of homestead). Families who are worried about lawsuits can put a significant portion of their net worth into homes that are protected under state homestead laws. Someone in Florida or Texas could own a $10 million home, be sued, file bankruptcy, discharge the creditor, and still keep the $10 million home. The former commissioner of baseball, Bowie Kuhn, had a set of circumstances that looked a little like this. Feel free to look that up in your free time if you want to see the details.

For real estate that is not protected under homestead laws, there are other ways to protect the investment from creditors and still enjoy the upside potential of the assets. Basically, the use of debt and limited liability companies can be a very powerful combination to protect real estate. This is covered in the Fourth Key— Protect Assets. The point that we are trying to make in this chapter is that many investors like investing in real estate because they can protect this asset.

Retirement Income

We don't usually think of real estate as a retirement vehicle, but the Savvy Affluent see it that way. Commercial real estate, residential real estate and real estate investment trusts (REITs) can all be used for this purpose. Many savvy investors who purchase real estate because of the leverage opportunity hold the real estate for tax reasons. Once these investors reach retirement, they realize that they have a portfolio that can generate income without requiring too much time managing the investments. For properties that do require significant attention, a management company can be hired to handle those issues. Income without a lot of personal effort makes for an ideal income producing asset in retirement.

Because real estate can be purchased with a fraction of the total value (e.g., a small down payment), it offers a lot of leverage. Because real estate can be a good tax-deferred wealth accumulation vehicle and a source of income, it is also a very flexible investment. Since real estate can solve many planning problems, it is a very efficient investment. By increasing leverage and offering efficiency to the investor, real estate helps investors spend less time on their planning and be better prepared for the challenges that will undoubtedly arise.

Tax Benefits

As you have read over and over in *Wealth Secrets*, the Savvy Affluent always consider taxes when making efficient and flexible investments and all other financial decisions. It shouldn't surprise you that the investment secrets of the Affluent offer significant tax benefits. When it comes to real estate, there are a number of tax benefits that may attract investors. A short list of the many tax benefits that real estate can offer to investors in different situations includes:

> **Up to $500,000 tax-free gains on home.** The sale of a primary residence allows homeowners a capital gains exemption of $250,000. If the owners of the home are married, they can each use the $250,000 exemption on the same property. This means that a couple who owned the residence in both of their names and lived in it for two of the five years before the sale are exempt from capital gains taxes on up to $500,000 of gain. At the time of this writing, federal capital

gains tax rates are 15 percent for most taxpayers. In addition, state capital gains taxes will be exempt. This could mean between $75,000 and $120,000 of tax savings.

Tax deferral on unrealized gains. Investments that offer the investor a dividend, interest payment, or rental income result in tax liabilities every year. When real estate is purchased as an investment, taxes are only triggered when rental income is received or the asset is sold.

Tax deferral on realized gains. When real assets are sold, the seller can take advantage of a 1031 exchange. Under the rules of Internal Revenue Code section 1031, sellers can reinvest the proceeds of a real estate sale into another real estate project of the same value or greater than the one they sold and no taxes will be due. This allows clients to postpone the tax and take advantage of leverage on the larger investment (which hasn't been reduced because of taxes).

Caution: Tax deferral is not always a good idea. Just because a deferral method exists, doesn't mean you should use it. At the time of the writing of this book (late 2007), the federal long-term capital gains tax rate was only 15 percent. It is very possible, and highly likely, that long-term capital gains tax rates could increase in the future. In the recent past, these tax rates were as high as 28 percent. If an investor defers gains from one project to the next then to the next, the total gain will be due at some point. If the rate is higher at the time of the eventual sale, the investor is stuck paying that amount of tax. That is the chance the investor takes when choosing a 1031 exchange. We have seen many Savvy Affluent clients choose to pay long capital gains taxes on sales of real estate when rates are low.

Tax deductions. There is not a straightforward tax deduction for investing in real estate like there is for a qualified plan contribution or charitable donation (assuming they haven't been phased out for very high-income taxpayers). The deduction comes in the way of depreciation. Investments made in real estate for business purposes can be depreciated. Depreciation offsets income on the tax return. Some investors purposely purchase real estate so that they can offset income with the depreciation, thus saving ordinary income taxes.

Sometimes, the benefits of the asset in question are the primary reasons for the investment. This is a classic tail wagging the dog scenario. One of the biggest investment mistakes we see is an investment in real estate primarily for the benefits discussed above. The primary reason for any investment should be that it will offer a higher combined after-tax benefit when compared with other investment alternatives with the same level of risk. Considering investment risk, tax risk, and creditor risk should go into that calculation.

Consider This

As you learned in the Fifth Key, the Savvy Affluent always consider taxes. In this chapter, you learned that real estate can help reduce or eliminate ordinary income taxes and capital gains taxes. These are benefits the Savvy Affluent cannot ignore.

Real estate can offer great benefits, flexibility, and an opportunity for extremely powerful leverage. Another tool that is even more flexible with similar leverage opportunity is life insurance, which is discussed in Chapters 54 through 59.

CHAPTER 54

Life Insurance Basics

Life insurance is a contract between you and an insurance company. The most common term of the contract is that the insurance company will pay your named beneficiaries the face amount or death benefit of the policy when you die. Some life insurance policies accumulate cash over time (permanent policies) and some do not (term policies). For the purpose of the Ninth Key, we will be focusing on all types of life insurance *except* term insurance. To help you better understand some of the types of insurance, we have put together a brief description of the different categories of life insurance and then discuss the pros and cons of each type. The different categories we will discuss include:

- Term Life Insurance
- Whole Life Insurance (WL)
- Universal Life Insurance
- Variable Life Insurance (VL)
- Variable Universal Life Insurance (VULI)
- A hybrid: Equity-Indexed Universal Life Insurance (EIUL)
- Private Placement Variable Universal Life Insurance (PPVUL)

Term Life Insurance

Given its affordability, term life insurance is the most common type of life insurance policy. However, because it does not have a cash value (wealth accumulation) component, term insurance can only play a very limited role in your financial plan. It can provide temporary death protection for your family or for business partners as part of a buy-sell agreement.

The premium on a term policy is low compared with other types of life insurance policies because it carries no cash value and provides protection for a limited period of time (referred to as a term). This limited time frame is usually 10 to 20 years, though some companies offer a 30-year term product. A term life insurance policy pays a specific lump sum to your designated beneficiary upon your death. The policy protects your family by providing money they can invest to replace your salary and to cover immediate expenses incurred as a result of your death. Term life insurance is best for young, growing families, when the need for death protection of the breadwinner is high and excess cash flow is especially low.

> **Pros:** Affordable coverage that pays only a death benefit. Term life insurance initially tends to cost less than other insurance policies because it has no cash value.
>
> **Cons:** Term life insurance premiums increase with age because the risk of death increases as people get older. Some term premiums may rise each year, or after 10, 20, or 30 years. Over the age of 65, the cost of a new term insurance policy becomes very expensive, often unaffordable. Term insurance is not available beyond a certain age. It is a terrible tool for estate planning because the coverage cannot be continued at a reasonable price as you approach life expectancy.

Whole Life Insurance

Whole life insurance pays a death benefit to the beneficiary you name and offers you a cash value account with tax-deferred cash accumulation. The policy remains in force during your entire lifetime and provides permanent protection for your dependents while building a cash value account. The insurance company manages your policy's cash accounts.

> **Pros:** Whole life insurance has a savings element (cash value), which is tax-deferred. You can borrow from this account free of income tax or cash-in the policy during your lifetime. It has a fixed premium that can't increase during your lifetime

(as long as you pay the planned amount) and your premium is invested for you long-term. Because it has the cash accumulation component, whole life insurance can play a role in tax reduction, wealth accumulation, asset protection, estate planning, and even reduction of the retirement plan tax trap.

Cons: Whole life insurance does not allow you to invest in separate accounts (i.e. money market, stock, and bond funds). Thus, your policy's returns will be tied to the insurance company's ability to invest its capital. It also does not allow you to split your money among different accounts or to move your money between accounts and does not allow premium flexibility or face amount flexibility.

Universal Life Insurance

Universal life (UL) insurance is a variation of whole life insurance. The insurance part of the policy is separated from the investment portion of the policy. The investment portion is invested by the insurance company—generally, in bonds, mortgages, and money market funds. This investment portion grows and is tax deferred. The cost of the death benefit is paid for out of the investment fund. A guaranteed minimum interest rate applied to the policy ensures that a certain minimum return on the cash portion of the policy will be paid no matter how badly the investments perform. If the insurance company does well with its investments, the interest return on the cash portion will increase.

Pros: The product is similar to whole life insurance yet has more flexible premiums. It may be attractive to younger buyers who may have fluctuations in their ability to pay premiums. Because it is so flexible, universal life insurance can play a role in tax reduction, wealth accumulation, asset protection, estate planning, and even reduction of the retirement plan tax trap.

Cons: If the insurance company does poorly with its investments, the interest return on the cash portion of the policy will decrease. In this case, less money would be available to pay the cost of the death benefit portion of the policy and future premiums may be necessary in addition to the premiums originally illustrated.

Variable Life Insurance

Variable life insurance provides permanent protection to your beneficiary upon your death. The term "variable life" is derived from the fact that you can allocate your dollars to various types of investment accounts (within your insurance company's portfolio), such as an equity fund, a money market fund, a bond fund, or some combination thereof. Hence, the value of the death benefit is variable, and the cash value may fluctuate up or down, depending on the performance of the investment portion of the policy.

Although most variable life insurance policies guarantee that the death benefit will not fall below a specified minimum, a minimum cash value is typically not guaranteed. Variable life insurance is a form of whole life insurance and because of investment risks it is also considered a securities contract and is regulated as a security under the Federal Securities Laws and must be sold with a prospectus.

> **Pros:** Variable life allows you to participate in various types of investment options without being taxed on your earnings (until you surrender the policy). You can apply interest earned on these investments toward the premiums, potentially lowering the amount you pay. Because of the ability to invest in more aggressive assets such as mutual funds, variable life insurance is an ideal tool for wealth accumulation and retirement planning, especially if you are looking for growth over a longer term.
>
> **Cons:** You assume the investment risks. When the investment funds perform poorly, less money is available to pay the premiums, meaning that you may have to pay more than you can afford to keep the policy in force. Poor fund performance also means that the cash and/or death benefit may decline, although never below a defined level if the policy so provides. Also, you cannot withdraw from the cash value during your lifetime.

Variable Universal Life Insurance

Variable universal life (VUL) insurance pays your beneficiary a death benefit. The amount of the benefit is dependent on the success of your investments. If the investments fail, there is a guaranteed minimum death benefit paid to your beneficiary upon your death. Variable universal gives you more control of the cash value account portion of your policy than any other insurance type. A form of whole life insurance, it has elements of both life insurance and a securities contract. Because the policy owner assumes investment risks, variable universal products are regulated as securities under the Federal Securities Laws and must be sold with a prospectus.

Pros: Variable universal life enables you to make withdrawals or borrow from the policy during your lifetime, and it offers separate accounts in which to invest. Because it combines the flexibility of universal life with the ability to invest in mutual funds of the variable policy, universal variable can be the ideal tool for tax reduction and retirement wealth accumulation over a long time horizon. It also affords one another opportunity to invest in the equities markets on a tax-deferred basis.

Cons: It requires the policyholder to devote time in managing the policy's accounts. The policy's success is dependent on the investments you make. Premiums must be high enough to cover your insurance and your accounts.

A Hybrid: Equity-Indexed Universal Life Insurance

Equity-indexed universal life insurance (EIUL) pays your beneficiary a death benefit. The amount of the benefit is dependent on the success of the investments of the insurance company. If the investments fail, there is a guaranteed minimum death benefit paid to your beneficiary upon your death. EIUL gives you more upside than a traditional UL policy because the insurance company contractually agrees to credit the policy's cash value with the same return the S&P 500 Index (excluding dividends) realizes over the same period of time (subject to a cap). Because of the cap on the upside (two carriers we researched cap the investment returns at 12 percent per annum and 14 percent per annum). In return for taking away a piece of your upside, they offer a minimum annual return of 1 percent or 2 percent annually.

Pros: EIUL enables you to make withdrawals or borrow from the policy during your lifetime and it offers the investor the upside of the market (with a cap). Unlike variable life and variable universal life, EIUL offers the investor downside protection so the cash value will always see a positive crediting rate—even in a bad market.

Cons: EIUL policies vary from carrier to carrier. Some only allow for 50 percent or 75 percent participation (others offer 100 percent) of the rate of return from the S&P. This means that if the S&P 500 returns 10 percent, you may only get 5 percent or 7.5 percent. The policyholder must pay particular attention to the carrier's contractual obligations. Also, the minimum guaranteed returns are typically 1 percent to 2 percent, which is much lower than most traditional insurance products that offer minimum crediting rates of 3 percent to 4 percent. EIUL is another case where you have to give up something to get something. Like all insurance policies, you need to understand what you are getting before you can make a smart decision.

Private Placement Variable Universal Life Insurance (PPVUL or PPLI)

Private placement variable universal life (PPVUL) insurance is often referred to Private Placement Life Insurance (PPLI). PPVUL (or PPLI) shares most of the characteristics of the VUL discussed earlier. However, the PPVUL differs from the VUL in a few ways. Some of these differences make it very attractive for the Super Affluent. These differences are:

1. The PPVUL is only available to accredited investors.
2. PPVUL does not have materials available to the public. They must be requested by a bona fide accredited investor.
3. PPVUL has higher minimum premium requirements (differ by company and minimum premiums generally range from $500,000 to $5 million in the first five years).
4. PPVUL has lower fees than traditional insurance products.
5. PPVUL offers more investment flexibility. Policy owners typically choose among hedge funds or can suggest their own investment management firm to manage the funds within the PPVUL if premiums are large enough.

Pros: PPVUL allows the client to choose hedge funds or, if the premiums will total $5 million over five years, suggest their own independent financial advisor to manage the funds within the insurance contract. Commissions tend to be much lower than traditional insurance policies. PPVUL enables you to make withdrawals or borrow from the policy during your lifetime, and it offers separate accounts in which to invest. Because it combines the flexibility of variable universal life with lower fees, more investment flexibility, and investment gains within the subaccounts are not taxed, PPVUL is the ideal tool for tax reduction and retirement wealth accumulation over a long time horizon for clients who are in high marginal tax brackets. It also affords another opportunity to invest in the equities markets on a tax-deferred basis.

Cons: Very high minimum premium requirements. Limited to accredited investors only. Because this is a private placement, there is very little written marketing material to review. Very few insurance companies do enough of this type of work to be considered efficient. Most insurance agents don't or won't sell it. The policy owner bears all the risk of the investments within the investment subaccounts.

There is an emerging class of insurance policies that offers the lower costs of the PPVUL but does not have the same accredited investor requirements and sizable minimum investments. Contact our firm for more on this developing market trend.

Consider This

There are many different types of life insurance policies. All of them have their place in the planning for the Affluent. What is important to realize is that all policies offer wealth accumulation benefits and tax-free death benefits. The leverage opportunities of life insurance are discussed in the next chapter.

CHAPTER 55

Life Insurance Leverage

The basic concept of life insurance is built on the shifting and sharing of risk. The benefits of insurance have always revolved around its leverage. In this chapter, we will break life insurance leverage into basic leverage and advanced leverage. You can think of the basic leverage as ways to turn small dollars into big dollars. Advanced leverage is turning a small amount of someone else's small dollars into your big dollars. Because of this significant leverage, life insurance is seen as the most efficient way to transfer wealth and protect a family or business. Let's look at some applications of life insurance leverage, including:

- Part 1: Death Benefit
- Part 2: Estate Planning
- Part 3: Free Tax Accumulation

Part 1: Death Benefit

The Seventh Key to Affluence is avoiding financial disasters. The Sixth Key to Affluence is preserving your estate. The most efficient tool to address both of these keys is life insurance. By paying small amounts to an insurance company, you can protect your family from lost income and estate taxes. To illustrate this point, let us consider the story of Rob Whelan, a hard-working, 35-year-old who has just started a family.

Rob has a wife Ronelle and two young children, Nigel and Dikembe. Rob is a hard-working guy who holds two jobs to help his family get ahead. He works in finance during the week and is a professional dancer who makes extra money during the weekends, while Ronelle is a singer. He owns a house and has just started saving for the children's education. He knows that his family relies on his income and that the music would stop altogether for his family if he died. He recently asked us to help him find a life insurance policy that would help to protect his family's financial future. With the $1,000 per month he was saving from his dancing, we were able to secure a $1.6 million life insurance policy on Rob. Because Rob doesn't know how long he can dance, he only wanted to look at policy illustrations that assumed payments of 10 years. He pays $12,000 per year for 10 years to pay for the death benefit and accumulates cash values to pay for future premiums (after the 10 years). If Rob were to die, the death benefit would adequately cover his mortgage, his children's college funds, and leave Ronelle with enough money to raise the children. Now that Rob has insurance, the beat can go on for his family even if it doesn't for him.

What happens if Rob doesn't die? Some people would say that Rob has wasted a lot of money protecting his family when he could have just bought term insurance. However, that couldn't be further from the truth. If Rob's insurance policy earns 8 percent before fees and expenses (this particular policy offers an investment return that is tied to 100 percent of the S&P index) for 20 years, Rob will have more than $124,000 of cash value at the end of 10 years. In other words, at the end of 10 years, it may look like a Christmas club at the bank: $120,000 paid in, $124,000 left, plus he had $1.6 million of protection for his family. Not a bad deal.

If Rob keeps his coverage for another 10 years, but does not pay another dollar of premium, he could expect the cash values to grow to approximately $230,000 and still maintain the financial protection for his family. That is a 6.5 percent after-tax return (from a pretax, prefee return of 8 percent within an equity indexed life insurance policy) between years 10 and 20 while offering protection. If Rob had invested that $124,000 in stocks and bonds at 8 percent instead of keeping the insurance policy, he would have paid at least 15 percent federal tax on gains and up to 9 percent of the gain to state taxes. In Rob's state, state income taxes are 7 percent. This means 22 percent of the 8 percent gain would have gone to taxes, giving him a 6.24 percent gain on his investment. The insurance actually outperformed the market and it protected his family.

Let's assume Rob leaves the policy in place for another 10 years until he is ready to retire. At the end of 30 years, the policy cash value would be approximately $431,000. That equates to a 6.34 percent compounded rate of return on an insurance policy with underlying investments yielding 8 percent gross returns. Another way to say this is that the internal costs of administration, fees, and management of the policy are 1.66 percent. When taxes are 1.76 percent for Rob, you realize that insurance is actually giving his family a better return on cash than the same index funds held outside of insurance policies, and he is getting protection for his family.

Part 2: Estate Planning

Let's assume that Rob wins $1 million on the reality show *So You Think You Can Dance* or Ronelle's singing career finally hits the big time and they are making more money than they need to support their lifestyle. Because they love their children and want to give them every opportunity they didn't have, they want to put money aside for them. Rob and Ronelle meet with their advisory team, who explain a number of options. One of the techniques they chose to implement is the creation of an irrevocable life insurance trust (ILIT). Under the ILIT, Rob and Ronelle will make $24,000 annual gifts to the trust to remove the funds from their estate. Then, the $24,000 would be used to purchase a second-to-die life insurance policy on Rob and Ronelle. When they finally pass away, their children will receive $10 million tax free. Even if Rob and Ronelle were to die next year, the children would get $10 million.

The ILIT is flexible, too. Rob and Ronelle can direct the attorney to draft the language of the ILIT in a way that allows the children to get access to cash values of the policies for certain expenses that Rob and Ronelle find important. If the children need money for college or a wedding or dance lessons, the trust can be drafted to allow the children to access the insurance policy's substantial cash value to do so. For example, one ILIT policy we reviewed had cash values in excess of $600,000 in year 20, more than $1.3 million in year 30, and in excess of $2.5 million in year 40. The family could protect itself from the premature death of both spouses, build an estate for future generations, and provide a fund to help pay for college, weddings, first homes, and much more if Rob and Ronelle live. Because life insurance withdrawals, policy loans, and death benefits can all be income tax free, this life insurance investment offers amazing leverage and unmatched flexibility.

Part 3: Tax-Free Accumulation

As established in the beginning of this Key, most people don't think of life insurance policies as investments. However, large companies have been purchasing life insurance policies in great numbers over the last five years in order to protect their assets and accumulate more wealth. In addition, the Super Affluent have used these tax-efficient investment tools for years. We have a number of clients who invest more than one million dollars per year into life insurance contracts. We also have many clients who invest hundreds of thousands every year into life insurance policies. These clients have some interest in the death benefit, but they are primarily interested in the wealth accumulation benefits of life insurance.

Let's look at a healthy 35-year-old male, like Rob in the earlier example. He may look at his equity-indexed universal life insurance policy as his unlimited after-tax pension. The big differences between the insurance policy cash values and his pension are that he can take all (or none) of the money from the insurance policy before he is 59½ without penalty, he doesn't have to take it out at 70½, he doesn't have to contribute for employees, and the insurance policy appreciates at the time of his death instead of depreciating in value by 70 percent like his pension does when he dies and leaves it to his children. We will further develop this concept later in this Key.

The economics of investing into a life insurance policy look like this:

- Beginning at age 35, Rob invests $1,000 per month for 30 years.
- The policy grows at 8 percent per year (before expenses and fees).
- Cash values in year 30, when Rob retires, are approximately $1.1 million.
- He takes tax-free policy withdrawals and policy loans of over $110,000 every year from age 65 until age 90! That is

$360,000 of investments yielding more than $2.75 million of tax-free retirement income while offering death protection to the family as well.

By leveraging the tax-free accumulation and death benefit features of equity-indexed universal life insurance, Rob is able to protect his family from his premature death and provide a very tax-efficient investment return for himself at the same time. He can solve two planning challenges with one investment. That sounds pretty efficient!

Consider This

Life insurance offers more leverage than any other investment tool—even real estate. First, a very small premium payment can protect a family from a premature death, protect a business in a buy-sell arrangement, accumulate wealth without taxes, or efficiently transfer the wealth from one generation to another. Second, life insurance offers tax leverage as both a wealth accumulator and as a tax-free death benefit for a family. For more detail on the flexibility and efficiency of life insurance, you should proceed to the next chapter. To see a much more detailed analysis that compares this investment with low-cost index funds, be sure you read Chapter 57.

56

Flexibility and Efficiency of Life Insurance

Would you be surprised to read that life insurance is the most important tool in the financial plans of the Savvy Affluent? If you simply follow the common sense advice of the Average American-focused mass media, you certainly would. On the other hand, if you have been reading the last six chapters, you wouldn't. No other financial, tax, insurance, or legal tool can play as many roles in a financial plan as life insurance.

In this chapter, we will discuss the key characteristics of cash value life insurance; that is, permanent (not term) insurance policies whose excess premium is invested in a tax-efficient manner with a cash value account for the benefit of the policy owner. In subsequent chapters, we will share applications that allow you to leverage these characteristics.

Key Characteristics Making Life Insurance So Valuable

Life insurance has many characteristics and offers various benefits. The Savvy Affluent take advantage of life insurance as an investment because it is a flexible planning tool that will help them address so many planning challenges in an efficient way. The following attributes that make life insurance a valuable investment apply to permanent (cash value) life insurance and capture the interest of the Savvy Affluent:

1. **Amounts in life insurance policies grow tax-deferred.** While investments outside of retirement plans and life insurance policies are taxed on income and realized capital gains, funds growing within a cash value life insurance policy grow completely tax free. This is why life insurance is so attractive as a wealth accumulation and tax reduction vehicle. It is seen as the unlimited after-tax retirement plan by the Super Affluent.

2. **Account balance values in life insurance policies can be accessed tax free at any time.** When you take funds out of a retirement plan (pension or IRA), these withdrawals are always subject to income tax and may be subject to a penalty if withdrawn before age 59½. With a cash value life insurance policy, you can take tax-free loans against the cash value at any time. There is never a tax penalty and there is no tax on the loan as long as you keep the policy in force and the policy is not a modified endowment contract (MEC).

3. **Life insurance is asset-protected.** All 50 states give some measure of asset protection to cash value life insurance policies. Thus, this asset can play a role in your asset protection plan. Working with your advisor team, you can determine how best to leverage the rules in your state.

4. **Life insurance has beneficial tax valuation.** In dealing with the 70 percent-plus tax trap facing pensions and IRAs, life insurance can play a very valuable role. The essence of this rule is that life insurance enables the plan owner, who would otherwise lose 70 percent of his plan holdings to estate and income taxes, to instead pass 100 percent of those dollars and more to heirs. Revisit the Fifth Key for more information on this important benefit.

As you can see, life insurance can offer many benefits to the policy owners. It can grow tax free, provide a tax-advantaged death benefit, and is protected from lawsuit creditors. This flexibility is what allows the Savvy Affluent to use life insurance to meet their planning challenges more efficiently.

Consider This

The most important characteristic of life insurance is that it is flexible. You don't have to decide exactly what you want to use the life insurance for before you buy it. You can add more premium later, gift the policy to a person or entity, sell the policy, save it for the death benefit, use the cash values for lifetime needs, return the money you took out or not return the money you took out. The biggest misunderstanding about life insurance is that most people don't see it as an investment tool. The next chapter illustrates how a cash value life insurance policy outperforms mutual funds.

CHAPTER 57

Proof that Life Insurance Outperforms Mutual Funds

If you Google the phrase "buy term and invest the difference" you get 20,500 results. This is not an unfamiliar phrase for most Americans. What this common sense adage means is that, when considering buying cash value life insurance, you will be better off buying the cheaper term life insurance product and investing the difference into the market. The difference is determined by subtracting the term insurance premium from the cash value insurance premium. Though not explicitly stated, this generally means that you should invest the difference in mutual funds.

In this chapter, we will prove that life insurance is a wiser investment for building wealth and protecting assets than buying term and investing the difference. In order to do so, we will provide two examples that illustrate our argument.

The Debate: Life Insurance vs. Buying Term and Investing the Difference

Both authors have MBAs in finance from UCLA. Chris has a degree in applied mathematics and used to work as an actuary. David is a practicing attorney. What this means to you is that we are good with numbers, we don't always believe what we hear, we like to see the proof of something on paper before we will believe it, and we can be pretty skeptical at times. How does this apply to you and this chapter? We decided to do a very detailed analysis of insurance policies and mutual funds to get to bottom of the life insurance versus

340

mutual funds investment debate. This is offered for your benefit in case you need to see the proof as well.

If you think back to the First Key, you may remember our explanation of why the popular press focuses on issues of the Average American. The "life insurance versus buying term and investing the difference" commentary is another example of the financial media perpetuating common sense for common people. These are people who generally do not have significant tax and asset protection concerns because they don't earn much, don't pay very high taxes, and aren't able to acquire very much wealth to protect. The Affluent are concerned with after-tax investment returns (i.e., what you take home from the investment after all taxes are paid) and asset protection of those investments. If you want to learn these lessons, you must read this chapter. What you will learn may surprise you— unless, of course, you are already a member of the Savvy Affluent.

Basic Assumptions for the Comparison

To accurately compare two investments, you have to develop and use similar assumptions. This is often referred to as "normalizing" the data. In all examples, we will assume a 35-year-old healthy male makes investments of $1,000 per month for 30 years and then maximizes his withdrawals for 25 years in retirement. This will cause him to run out of money at 90 years of age. This is well beyond his life expectancy. In both the mutual fund and cash value life insurance policy, there are an infinite number of potential combinations of premium payments and withdrawals. So, we chose a reasonable set of assumptions and applied the same constraints to both the mutual fund and cash value life insurance examples so we would have a fair comparison.

The Comparative Analysis = Stack the Deck in Favor of Mutual Funds

In this first comparative analysis, we will offer unrealistic assumptions that will give the mutual funds every opportunity to make a case for being the better investment choice. The purpose of this set of unreasonable comparisons is to emphasize that cash value life insurance is a much better investment than mutual funds. After we complete this analysis, we will offer a similar analysis with realistic expectations.

In the Mutual Fund Corner . . .

- We are going to compare an investment in a theoretical no-load mutual fund that has no annual costs or expenses of any kind.
- The theoretical mutual fund has an annual return of 8 percent per year (of course, you could assume a fund with 10.6 percent gross returns and 2.6 percent fees and come to the same conclusion).
- We are going to assume the S&P 500 index (excluding dividends) has an annual return of 8 percent per year for the next 55 years.
- We will assume that every investor lives in a state with no state income tax, even though only Alaska, Florida, Nevada, New Hampshire, South Dakota, Tennessee, Texas, Washington, and Wyoming do not have state income taxes. Note: You could remove New Hampshire and Tennessee from this list because they do collect tax dividend and interest income.
- We will assume that the tax on all gains will be at the lowest possible capital gains tax rate of 15 percent for the next 55 years, even though we believe rates will increase significantly at some time (and, as you have seen in past chapters, 15 percent is lower than the tax rate has been on such gains for much of the last 80 years).
- We are going to assume that the cost of the "buy term" portion of "buying term and investing the difference" is $0. In other words, we will completely disregard the buy term portion and just compare mutual funds to life insurance without any accounting for the friction of the term insurance.

In short, these unreasonable assumptions will yield projections that are not reasonable for actual mutual funds investors who will be paying management fees every year and are likely to have to pay state taxes and certainly will have to pay something for their term insurance.

In the Life Insurance Policy Corner . . .

- We are going to use an insurance policy from one of the nation's top insurance companies. This company has an A+ rating from the rating firm A.M. Best Company (this is the second highest of 15 ratings offered by this rating organization). This insurance company is also rated by Comdex (another ratings firm) as being in the top 8 percent of U.S. insurance companies, in terms of financial stability.

- To prove that this was not an anomaly, we found a second insurance policy from another A.M. Best A+ rated company that was rated by Comdex to be in the top 12 percent in terms of financial stability among insurance companies in the country. The ultimate income results of this secondary policy were within 3.96 percent of the first one.

- We are going to attempt to compare investments of equal risk by choosing an equity-indexed universal life insurance product that is readily available to the public in most states. This policy's performance is tied to the S&P 500 index. Unlike the mutual fund investment, however, the insurance product has a minimum annual investment return of 1 percent per year. That is, even if the S&P has a return one year that is less than 1 percent, the insurance company will still credit the policy as if the S&P returned 1 percent. This actually reduces the risk for the insurance policy vs. the index fund, but we will assume they are the same.

- We will assume the same 8 percent long-term gross return of the S&P 500 index over 55 years.

- We will assume a fully commissionable insurance policy that has no term insurance blending to reduce commissions and increase cash values.

In this set of assumptions, we are giving a realistic projection of the S&P 500 equity indexed universal life insurance policy. In both this analysis and the subsequent more realistic comparison, the projection for the equity indexed universal life insurance policy will be the same.

The Comparative Analysis with the Deck Stacked for Mutual Funds

Let's examine how the no-fee, lowest possible tax, mutual fund portfolio and a cash value life insurance policy should perform with 30 years of investments at $1,000 per month, followed by 25 years of withdrawals by referring to Table 57.1.

Table 57.1 No-Fee Funds with No-State-Tax-Paying Investors vs. Cash Value Life Insurance

		Investment in No-Fee, Low-Tax Funds				Investment in Life Insurance			
Year	Age	Annual Mutual Fund Investment	6.8% After-Tax Growth	Retirement Withdrawal	Year End Balance	Annual Insurance Premium	Withdrawals and Loans	Value at Death	Improvement over Funds at Death
1	35	$12,000	$408		$12,408	$12,000	$0	$290,236	$277,828
10	44	$12,000	$10,431		$169,824	$12,000	$0	$458,195	$288,371
15	49	$12,000	$19,167		$307,040	$12,000	$0	$736,828	$429,788
20	54	$12,000	$31,307		$497,700	$12,000	$0	$1,060,400	$562,700
25	59	$12,000	$48,174		$762,622	$12,000	$0	$1,453,765	$691,143
30	64	$12,000	$71,612		$1,130,728	$12,000	$0	$1,950,735	$820,007
31	65		$70,823	$89,220	$1,112,331		$110,000	$1,850,343	$738,012
35	69		$65,285	$89,220	$1,025,352		$110,000	$1,707,042	$681,690
40	74		$55,962	$89,220	$878,933		$110,000	$1,585,889	$706,956
45	79		$43,008	$89,220	$675,485		$110,000	$1,472,044	$796,559
50	84		$25,009	$89,220	$392,795		$110,000	$1,399,308	$1,006,513
55	89		$0	$89,220	$0		$110,000	$1,415,004	$1,415,004
Total		$360,000		$2,230,493		$360,000	$2,750,000	$1,415,004	

Increase in Retirement Income: $519,507

% Increase over Mutual Funds: 23.30%

To save space, we compressed Table 57.1 to show a sample of the 55 years of data. Even with the deck stacked against the insurance policy, by considering an index fund with no fees, an investor with no state income taxes, and with no costs of term life insurance, the insurance policy still outperformed the index mutual fund investment. The mutual fund investment of $12,000 per year in a no-fee, low tax environment yields annual after-tax income of $89,220. The investment in the equity indexed life insurance policy offers tax-free withdrawals and policy loans of $110,000 per year. The investment income from the investment insurance policy was more than 23 percent greater than that of the too-good-to-be-true mutual fund. In addition, the family of the investor who purchased the insurance policy also has death benefit protection. The benefit in the last column is in addition to the increase in retirement income. In short, the investment in a life insurance policy significantly outperforms the investment in mutual funds even with ridiculously skewed assumptions.

The Comparative Analysis with Realistic Assumptions

Now, that we have determined that this type of cash value life insurance policy outperforms a too-good-to-be-true exaggerated mutual fund, let's conduct a second comparative analysis with realistic assumptions. The differences between this analysis and the previous one are threefold. First, we assume that the mutual fund has a total of 0.50 percent in annual expenses. This is quite low for most mutual funds and quite reasonable for index funds. Second, we assume that the investors live in a state with 5 percent state income taxes. This is also a very reasonable assumption because 33 states have marginal income tax brackets greater than 5 percent. Twenty-four of those states have marginal income tax brackets greater than 6 percent and some have rates as high as 9 percent. Third, we assume that the term insurance costs would be approximately $500 per year. This is a rough estimate, but it reflects a slight reduction in the investment funds for the "buy term and invest the difference" scenario.

Let's look at how these more reasonable assumptions affect the projections. Table 57.2 compares how a low-fee, moderate tax, mutual fund portfolio and a cash value life insurance policy should

Table 57.2 Low-Fee Funds for Low-State-Tax-Paying Investors vs. Cash Value Life Insurance

		Investment in Low-Fee, Moderate-Tax Index Funds				Investment in Life Insurance			
Year	Age	Annual Mutual Fund Investment	6% After-Tax Growth	Retirement Withdrawal	Value at Death	Annual Insurance Premium	Withdrawals and Loans	Value at Death	Improvement over Funds at Death
1	35	$11,500	$345		$290,236	$12,000	$0	$290,236	$0
10	44	$11,500	$8,512		$458,195	$12,000	$0	$458,195	$0
15	49	$11,500	$15,280		$736,828	$12,000	$0	$736,828	$0
20	54	$11,500	$24,338		$1,060,400	$12,000	$0	$1,060,400	$0
25	59	$11,500	$36,460		$1,453,765	$12,000	$0	$1,453,765	$0
30	64	$11,500	$52,681		$1,950,735	$12,000	$0	$1,950,735	$0
31	65		$52,040	$69,108	$1,850,343		$110,000	$1,850,343	$0
35	69		$47,560	$69,108	$1,707,042		$110,000	$1,707,042	$0
40	74		$40,272	$69,108	$1,585,889		$110,000	$1,585,889	$0
45	79		$30,519	$69,108	$1,472,044		$110,000	$1,472,044	$0
50	84		$17,467	$69,108	$1,399,308		$110,000	$1,399,308	$0
55	89		$0	$69,108	$1,415,004		$110,000	$1,415,004	$0
Total		$345,000		$1,727,711		$360,000	$2,750,000		
		$15,000	Term Insurance Premium				$1,022,289	Increase in Retirement Income	
		$360,000	Total Term + Investment				59.20%	% Increase over Mutual Funds	

perform with 30 years of investments at $1,000 per month, followed by 25 years of withdrawals.

With realistic expectations, the annual after-tax retirement income of the mutual fund investment is $69,108 per year. The insurance policy offers tax-free withdrawals and policy loans of $110,000 per year. That is a 59 percent improvement in income over the mutual fund investing. The death benefit is the same with the purchase of the term insurance, but the income suffers dramatically. The reason the insurance policy outperforms the index funds is that the actual expenses and the taxes of the funds, combined with the term life insurance costs are significantly higher than the supposedly high internal costs of the cash value life insurance policy. This is one of the most misunderstood comparisons in financial planning.

Possible Explanation

We hope it is clear to you that the adage "cash value life insurance is a poor investment" is generally inaccurate. Before we wrote this book, we believed that the taxes were the biggest factor in the success of cash value life insurance policies as wealth accumulation vehicles. Certainly, for Americans in the higher combined marginal tax brackets, this is absolutely true. Yet, with the analyses above, we saw that the insurance policy was still a better investment for investors who only pay taxes of 15 percent on their investment gains. This was surprising, as it indicated to us that the taxes couldn't be the primary reason for the insurance policy's superior performance. It must be the type of insurance policy itself.

Before equity indexed universal life insurance policies were invented, the only practical life insurance investment choices were whole life, universal life, and variable universal life policies. Whole life insurance policies are very inflexible. Further, whole life and universal life policies typically have returned 4 percent to 7 percent over the last 10 years. Though this return is respectable, it did not keep pace with the appreciation of the S&P 500 index (excluding dividends) over the same period. In a strong market, the mutual funds could possibly outperform those policies in states with low taxes. If the people who did the original comparison of buying term and investing the difference used whole life policies, those results would perpetuate the aforementioned myth.

The variable universal life policies that offer mutual fund choices within the insurance contract could theoretically keep pace with a strong market because their underlying investments are mutual funds. However, these policies have always had the highest internal fees of all insurance products. If you have a variable-type policy with high fees being purchased by an investor in a state that has no state income tax on investment gains, the mutual fund investment may outperform the variable universal life policy. This would also further the common sense myth.

With equity-indexed universal life (EIUL) policies, one has access to both the tax benefit and lower costs of certain types of policies and the access to the upside potential of the S&P 500 index. When you combine these benefits with the results from the direct comparison above, you can see why the Savvy Affluent prefer EIUL policies to index-based mutual funds.

Consider This

The misconception that "buying term and investing the difference" outperforms the investment in life insurance is common. If you continue to seek financial advice through Average American media channels, you may continue to get this kind of inaccurate and inappropriate information. This chapter gave examples of how cash value life insurance policies significantly outperformed realistic funds. Even when we compared the insurance policy to an unrealistic (and unavailable) mutual fund with no expenses and sold it to a taxpayer in a state with no income taxes and gave that investor the term insurance for free, the cash value insurance policy still outperformed it.

Throughout this book, you have learned that life insurance will protect against a premature death, serve as a source of liquidity for estate planning, and provide asset protection for your investment dollars. Now, you know that the investment in life insurance can be significantly more attractive than an investment in mutual funds. The Savvy Affluent maximize their investments in life insurance as a way to accumulate more wealth and protect assets. This is likely to be a significant key to your achieving and maintaining your desired level of affluence.

CHAPTER 58

Creative Applications of Insurance

After reading the chapters within this Key, you should now understand that life insurance is a wise investment alternative. In addition, you should have also learned that life insurance offers asset protection and tax and estate planning benefits. With all of these benefits and the unmatched flexibility of life insurance policies, you can see why insurance is the cornerstone of financial planning for the Affluent. In this chapter, we will show you how you can use life insurance as a wise investment tool. The Savvy Affluent know these creative applications of insurance:

- Unlimited after-tax retirement plans.
- Insured college savings fund for children or grandchildren.

In using one or both of these approaches, you can efficiently accomplish more than one goal with a single investment tool and create even more efficiency in your financial plan—the way the Savvy Affluent do.

The Unlimited After-Tax Retirement Plan

In Chapter 26, we explained how the Savvy Affluent maximize their use of retirement plans. This is desirable because the Affluent want to take advantage of three key elements of a qualified retirement plan:

1. Tax deduction for plan contributions.
2. Tax-free growth of plan assets.
3. The highest level of available asset protection for plan assets.

The Savvy Affluent combine the benefits of using retirement plans described in Chapter 26 with the philosophy of leverage discussed in the Second Key by involving family members in their businesses so that they can make additional contributions to retirement plans for family members as well. There are, however, limits to how much leverage Wealthy Families can achieve through retirement plans.

To increase the amount of retirement-plan-like benefits their families can enjoy, the Savvy Affluent look to investment vehicles that offer similar benefits to retirement plans. Life insurance is the investment vehicle that has the characteristics that are most like retirement plans. Cash value life insurance offers tax-free accumulation and asset protection. Though life insurance premiums are not tax deductible, the funds come out of the policy through policy loans and withdrawals without tax. For those of you who are familiar with Roth IRAs, cash value life insurance can be seen as an unlimited Roth IRA that also offers death benefit protection.

The Roth IRA is a type of individual retirement account in which contributions are made with after-tax (nondeductible) dollars. If certain requirements are met, earnings accumulate within the Roth IRA tax free and no federal income tax is levied when qualifying distributions are taken from the Roth IRA. The major restrictions of the Roth IRA are that only $2,000 per year can be invested in a Roth IRA and funds cannot be accessed before age 59½. When compared with a Roth IRA, the benefits of life insurance are that the annual premiums are practically unlimited and the funds can be accessed before age 59½. These benefits make cash value life insurance a very attractive alternative or complement to retirement plans.

The Ultimate College Savings Tool

When we have children, most of us want to give them every opportunity to succeed and protect them from unnecessary pain. The Seventh Key showed us how to financially protect our families from our premature death, yet protecting children from our death is not enough to ensure their financial success. In Chapter 7, we discussed the leverage of effort and education. Obviously, the more education we receive, the greater opportunity we have to succeed.

For this reason, a common dream of American parents is to send their children to college to take advantage of this opportunity. The Savvy Affluent stress the importance of law school, medical school, and business school. Their children do not need to go to work right after college to support themselves, so they have an advantage over students who can't afford to continue their education.

To take a lesson from the Savvy Affluent, we want to help our children pay for college and any additional education we can afford. We can make investments to save for college, but that doesn't ensure that there will be enough to pay for college if we pass away. For that reason, we have to buy life insurance if we want to give our children every opportunity to succeed.

The Savvy Affluent understand that they have to invest for their children's educational expenses and they have to buy life insurance to guarantee the funds will be there even if they aren't alive to see the child off to college. The Savvy Affluent also understand the analysis in the last chapter that explained how life insurance outperforms mutual funds after you factor in tax costs. For this reason, the Savvy Affluent make investments in life insurance to protect their children from the financial devastation a premature death of the breadwinner can bring and to provide a tax-efficient investment alternative for savings for college. This one tool can handle educational expenses whether you live to see your children off to college or not.

Consider This

You have already learned that life insurance is flexible and efficient. It can offer income protection, asset protection, tax-efficient wealth accumulation, and liquidity benefits. The applications of the life insurance can range from the traditional buy-sell, estate planning, and income replacement options to more creative applications like retirement enhancing and college savings funding. There is even a way to leverage the ultimate leverage tool—life insurance. This concept is the topic of the next chapter.

59

Leveraging the Ultimate Leverage Tool

As does real estate, life insurance can offer a variety of benefits such as reduced taxes, asset protection, and wealth accumulation. Also like real estate, life insurance can be supercharged by using the financial leverage of other people's money (OPM). In real estate transactions, it is extremely common to use OPM—in the form of home loans and mortgages. Using OPM is much less common for the purchase of cash value life insurance, although the concept maintains the same rationale as it does for real estate. Thus far, only the Super Affluent have taken advantage of what is called "premium financing"—using other people's money to buy life insurance.

In this chapter, we will show you how to benefit in the same way that banks have benefited for years—by borrowing and leveraging other people's money. All you need is a home, some real estate, a business, accounts receivable, a brokerage account, or a letter of credit from a bank and you can do your estate planning with someone else's money!

Advanced Leverage: Using Other People's Money to Buy Insurance

How do you think banks make money? The answer is simple: They borrow money from people through deposits, certificates of deposit, checking and savings accounts, and so on. They then lend money to people to buy homes or cars or to start businesses. Because they may only pay you 1 to 2% percent for the money they borrow from you and they lend money at rates of 6 to 9 percent, they are making money . . . with someone else's money! This method has proved successful for centuries in all different parts of the world.

The process of using other people's money to buy life insurance is quite simple. First, you borrow money from a bank. Ideally, you want to borrow money at a favorable, and possibly tax-deductible, rate. Then, you use the loan proceeds to purchase a life insurance policy. Of course, the loan you take out has interest payments (that may or may not be tax deductible). You may pay the interest payments or let them accrue. You also have to eventually pay back the loan principal. With insurance, you have dividends, cash accumulation, and a death benefit. If the cash accumulation (which may be tax deferred or even tax free) in the insurance policy is large enough to pay off the loan, you can use tax-free loans from the policy to pay off the loan. The remaining death benefit in the insurance policy would then be yours!

An alternative method, after securing the loan and purchasing the insurance policy, is to use the dividends to pay the interest on the loan. If you borrowed $100,000 to buy a $500,000 life insurance policy and the dividends are large enough to pay the interest payments, you can agree to pay off the $100,000 loan with a portion of the death benefit from the insurance. In this case, your family still has $400,000 left. That's $400,000 that cost you $0 out of pocket. Here's an example to illustrate the point.

In 2003, we had one client secure an interest-only home equity loan for as low as 2 percent. We had many clients take out home equity loans at rates of 5 to 7 percent. If you assume a 30 percent to 44 percent income tax bracket, these clients received tax deductions that reduced their after-tax loan rates to between 2.5 percent and 5.0 percent. At the same time, a AAA-rated insurance company credited 5.5 percent (tax free) to its universal life policies and more than 7 percent to its whole life policies. An equity-indexed universal life insurance policy credited more than 8 percent that year. The point is that you can ultimately use the accumulated difference between the crediting rate and the loan rate to pay down the loan principal, too. This will leave the entire death benefit to your family.

Loan, Annuity, and Insurance

Another option that is becoming popular is the Loan, Annuity, and Life Insurance Triple Play. The strategy goes something like this.

1. You mortgage your real estate and borrow as much equity as possible (let's assume $500,000). This maneuver provides asset protection for the real estate.
2. You use the loan proceeds to buy a life annuity with an interest rate payout higher than your mortgage rate.
3. For the next 10 years, the annuity payout will be partially tax free (as return of basis) while you may be able to deduct the interest portion of your loan payment.
4. You will then use the annuity payment to fund a life insurance policy of say $1 million.

Under the right circumstances, there are cases where the annuity payment net of income taxes will be sufficient to make the premium payments on the life insurance policy and the mortgage payment on the loan—you may even have a little left over! At death, the life insurance policy pays the balance of the loan, and there will still be more than $500,000 in death benefit for your family, which cost you . . . nothing.

Things to Look Out For

Interest is not deductible if the money is borrowed for the explicit use of buying life insurance. Furthermore, borrowing money always increases your risk of loss of principal. If you borrow money and the investment you choose declines in value, you are still on the hook for the repayment. Always be conservative with the investments you choose when you are already leveraged. We typically recommend very strongly that investors not fall into the trap of investing in a variable insurance product with financed money as we believe the financial risk is too great.

Of course, there are risks to every strategy. A variable interest rate on the loan could increase above the annuity payment. The life insurance policy could perform poorly (i.e., if you choose a variable policy and the market turns sour). As such, using other people's money to purchase life insurance is a complex strategy you should discuss with your multidisciplinary advisory team.

Overall, leveraging the ultimate leverage tool—life insurance—is a secret of the Affluent that has helped them achieve outstanding leverage and efficiency. Consequently, this has helped them maintain their fortunes and protect their assets. Using life insurance as an investment tool is a growing trend with many Wealthy Families and businesses, because they don't want to write checks for tens or hundreds of thousands of dollars to buy life insurance. They like the idea of using someone else's money. They may have a lot of wealth, but not a lot of available money to pay premiums—especially if the money is tied up in a business or other investment. By using someone else's money, they can achieve even greater affluence without having to come up with the money to do so. This is the most efficient way to use leverage to achieve affluence.

Consider This

Life insurance has various applications and can offer numerous benefits. This is why the Savvy Affluent have maximized the use of this tool for decades. In this Key, we discussed numerous applications such as using insurance as a retirement plan and as a college savings vehicle. We even discussed how to use other people's money so you don't have to pay for the insurance with your own money. There are countless other applications of insurance policies that can be valuable when liquidity and tax-efficient growth are desired. Work with your team of advisors to see how this tool may help you. The last Key of the book—Plan for Success—will help you take the next steps so you can start realizing the benefits that can be achieved from implementing the strategies of *Wealth Secrets* and the secrets of the Affluent.

THE TENTH KEY

PLAN FOR SUCCESS

Everyone wants to be rich, but fewer than 5 percent of Americans will achieve a significant level of wealth. Why is this? There are countless ways to fail, but only one way to achieve financial success; you must efficiently leverage your assets, effort, and time while avoiding financial catastrophes. In this book, we sought to explain the Wealth Secrets of the Affluent, share the steps to success, explain how to work with the advisors, and point out how to address most financial planning needs. Despite this guidance, most readers still won't follow our advice. Try hard not to be one of them.

Every year, many Affluent Americans spend hard-earned money and valuable time attending our seminars, hoping to learn important financial and legal lessons. More than 90 percent of the response forms we receive from attendees acknowledge that the information is valuable and that they plan to take immediate action to improve their financial situations. However, when we check in with attendees months or years later, we find out that fewer than 10 percent actually make a serious improvement.

We'll assume that you will be a member of the 10 percent who will actually take the necessary actions to reach your financial goals. Because you want to achieve affluence and we want to help you do so, we would like to show you what you have to do to get started and successfully continue the process throughout your life. If you follow these steps, you can be sure you will build your fortune and protect your assets. Here are the steps:

Step 1: Accept that you have a problem you can't handle alone.

Step 2: Hire the right team.

Step 3: Pay advisors to help you develop the plan.

Step 4: Implement the plan.

Step 5: Monitor the plan.

Step 6: Review the plan at least annually.

Step 7: Question advisors and planning decisions.

Step 8: Be willing to make changes to the plan or the advisory team.

There is an old saying, "Plan to succeed or prepare to fail." We can't stress this strongly enough. If you follow these eight steps, you will be on your way to building a fortune and protecting assets just like the Savvy Affluent do.

Step #1: Accept That You Have a Problem You Can't Handle Alone

With apologies to all 12-step participants, we can't think of a better way to make this point without borrowing a familiar philosophy. The building of wealth and protection of assets is a complicated process that requires expertise in the areas of:

- Accounting
- Asset protection
- Benefits planning
- Business structuring
- Estate planning
- Insurance planning
- Investments
- Tax planning
- And others

You can't continue to be an expert in your career and become an expert in all the areas in which you need financial planning assistance. To expect to do all of this alone is akin to expecting a pediatrician to become in expert in other fields of medicine as a patient ages and develops new medical concerns. This leads to the next step.

Step #2: Hire the Right Team

Once you realize that you need help with your financial planning, you have to find the professionals who have the expertise and experience to help you. Don't let the brevity of the description of this step fool you. This is a very important step in your quest for affluence. The choice of members for your team of advisors is as important to your long-term financial success as the choice of a spouse is to your emotional security. Some people might say the advisory team is even more important because many financial mistakes are irreversible.

Step #3: Pay Advisors to Help You Develop the Plan

A scalpel in the hands of a physician is a tool that can save a life. The same scalpel in the hands of a mugger can take a life. How you use your advisors can be the difference between the life and death of your affluence and assets. Once you have the right team of advisors to help you, you have to make sure you utilize their skills and talents properly. The best way to get the most out of your relationship with your advisors is to pay them to give you their unbiased analysis and recommendations.

Even if your advisors also provide other services or can be paid from the sale of products, they can still be valuable members of your team. By offering to pay them what their time is worth to work with you, they will be able to give you honest advice without an ulterior motive to sell you anything. The Savvy Affluent pay advisors to create a plan, and they pay these advisors to meet as a group at least once each year to review the situation and provide additional recommendations.

Step #4: Implement the Plan

Noting the need to implement the financial plan may seem like a silly step, but you would be surprised how many people pay for plans to be created only to put them on the shelf and let them collect dust. Like an X-ray, MRI, or any diagnostic medical tool, the financial plan is a tool that analyzes the current state of affairs. Like a doctor's diagnosis and treatment plan, the financial plan also serves as a series of recommendations and action items. It seems foolish to go through the work and cost of creating a plan, only to ignore the analysis and recommendations. Yet, we see this lack of implementation from numerous clients each year.

Another common mistake in implementing the financial plan is something we call the unanimous position dilemma. Some clients won't implement a piece of the plan until they run it by every member of the team and get 100 percent agreement. Other clients need more buy in, including approval from family, friends, the guy at the health club, the butcher, and whoever else will listen. The Savvy Affluent hire the right team to work together for them. If there is a disagreement among the team on a certain element of the plan, they educate themselves as much as possible and attempt to evaluate the merits of each side. The client may choose to move forward on that element or not, but he doesn't ask nonexpert friends and family for their input, especially when these friends are in completely different financial situations. Also, the Savvy Affluent do not let disagreement among team members on one action item prevent them from implementing other items. Typically, there will be at least 5 to 10 action items within the financial plan, so a stalemate on one item shouldn't cause a slowdown with the other elements of the plan.

Step #5: Monitor the Plan

Step 5 could also be called "communication and monitoring of the plan." Just as the client's active involvement is important in the initial plan creation and implementation, so, too, is it for the plan monitoring. The crucial role here for the client is communication, especially with the advisor firm that is acting as the quarterback and typically drafted the plan in the first place.

The advisors on your team can't do their jobs if they don't know what everyone else is doing. Yet the Savvy Affluent also realize that they are too busy to keep everyone abreast of each nuance of the plan. If advisors have to track down data from you or from the other advisors, there is going to be a significant cost for all of this duplication of effort. That is why the quarterback advisor is so helpful in monitoring the plan. The quarterback can coordinate the other advisors and get them the information they need to properly play their roles.

Technology Can Help

Modern software products can be helpful as well. Two years ago, in fact, a new client of ours showed us an online tool that tracked all investments daily, kept secure online-accessible scanned copies of every legal document and insurance policy statement, and had tools for the advisors to use to run scenarios for the client under different circumstances, which they could leave online for every advisor to see. It was such an impressive tool that we went out and bought a license to use it ourselves. Every client who we have worked with using this service always has the same question after it has been in place for a few months: "How did we ever manage without this?" We call this the ATM or cell phone response!

Step #6: Review the Plan

The Savvy Affluent and Super Affluent have at least one full-day meeting or multiple-day retreat with their advisors each year. During these meetings they review the plan. The reason for the meetings is to force the advisors to be in the same room without the distractions of their offices. If you pay the advisors to be there for you, they will focus solely on your needs and concerns and have time to brainstorm with you on future planning. This is a benefit you would never get from any number of conference calls.

Although you may not be able to afford multiday retreats to Hawaii or fly fishing in Wyoming as some clients do, you can certainly afford a three- to four-hour meeting with all of your advisors each year. This meeting should be distraction free and should be guided by an agenda developed in advance by the quarterback advisor and you.

Step #7: Question Advisors and Planning Suggestions

The Savvy Affluent understand that they can trust their advisors and still ask questions about the existing and suggested planning. Most advisors who work with affluent clients respect the intelligence of their clients and want their input. This is not a universal feeling, but we prefer working with clients who take the time to try to understand as much of the planning as possible. You should also encourage your other advisors to question the other members of the group. You don't want a fight over every issue, but you do want your team to discuss pros and cons of every possible alternative in an effort to find the best decisions for you. This is especially important on elements of the plan where there are significant arguments on both sides of the proposed action step.

> To review the authors' firm's planning process, visit www.ojmgroup.com.

Step #8: Don't Be Afraid to Make Changes to the Plan or the Advisory Team

Over time, a family's circumstances change. Often these changes can be very significant. These changing circumstances may dictate significant changes to the plan and its implementation. Of course, if there is an open line of communication between the client and quarterback advisor and the team of advisors participates in periodic plan reviews, these changes will not take anyone by surprise. Nonetheless, it is important to be flexible enough to reexamine the plan assumptions when there are significant changes (divorce, closing of a business, or others) and be open to making changes to the implementation strategy as well.

As for the advisors on your team, they are not lifetime appointees. Earlier in the book, we emphasized the importance of getting second opinions. This is particularly important when you have been with certain advisors for a long time and haven't looked for additional input from outside experts. We also explained why the "if it ain't broke, don't fix it" mentality can be very costly to your planning.

Sometimes, your team requires advisors with different fields of expertise. Other times, the interactions among group members are hurt by certain persons or personalities. In these instances, it may be best for you to ask an advisor to leave the team. Because it is your money, you can think of it as firing the advisor, because you don't need the advisor to agree with your decision. The fact that someone has worked with you for a while is not a good enough reason to keep that advisor on your team if you are not getting good advice or if you might be better served by a new advisor whose expertise or personality may be a better fit under your new circumstances.

Next Steps

We admit to making the planning process seem fairly easy in the last few pages. Practically, there will always be roadblocks. The biggest one you will face is time. There will never seem to be enough hours in the day to do what you want to do and there will always be other things that appear to need to be done right away. The only way that you will ever overcome this roadblock will be to make the planning process a priority for you, your family, your business partners, and your advisors. Once you make your planning a priority, you can start to approach the eight steps to implement the proper planning.

Of course, planning for your long-term, sustained financial success requires a great deal of effort in addition to a commitment of your time. This process will cost you money. This process will not be without a certain amount of frustration and aggravation. This is normal. You are trying to change the way you have done things for years. As such, the most important key to achieving affluence is remembering that everything worth having is worth the effort.

Once you find the right team, get the team up and running, and work through the initial bugs in developing your team process, your financial life will get easier every year. This is another little secret of the Savvy Affluent that has helped them maintain their wealth and protect their assets through multiple generations.

Consider This—Final Words of Encouragement

Changing your philosophy and planning to incorporate Wealth Secrets of the Affluent may seem overwhelming. There are many different steps to be taken within each of the 10 Keys to success. On top of that, this book includes only a partial list of the potential strategies that you could utilize to achieve your desired level of affluence. Practically speaking, there is no way one person could handle the challenge of planning alone. There is no way to do all of this planning without the help of a team of advisors. This is why the most important thing you can do is find the right team to work with you.

Once you hire the team, you have to make the time and effort to work through the steps in this chapter. If it seems like a lot to do, you should understand that every Super Affluent family began as an

Average American family until one person saw greater opportunities to leverage the family's wealth. If you dedicate yourself to the process in this Key, you can be that person for your family.

We wish you the success and affluence you desire. If you are having a tough time getting started or need a little help bringing your plan to the next level, please feel free to contact us at jarvis@ojmgroup.com or mandell@ojmgroup.com or via phone at (800) 554-7233. You can also sign up for our free e-newsletter at www.ojmgroup.com to receive updates and to hear about upcoming seminars. We always enjoy hearing from our readers, and we would be honored to help you achieve your goal of affluence, wealth, fortune, and asset protection.

Index